링구아포럼
TOEFL iBT b
- Grammar -

Part B

4판 3쇄	2008. 4. 3			
지은이	링구아포럼 리서치센터	발행인 김성수	발행처 링구아포럼(주)	전화 교재구입 02) 395-0249 / 대표전화 02) 395-1468
등록번호	제1-2680호	등록일자 2000. 5. 17	ISBN 978-89-5563-152-4 (54740)	가격 **8,500**원

Copyright © 2006-2008 by LinguaForum, Inc.

No unauthorized photocopying.

All rights reserved. No part of this book may be reproduced or transmitted in any form or by any means, electronic or mechanical, including photocopying, recording, or any other information storage and retrieval system without the written permission of the publisher.

TOEFL® is a registered trademark of Educational Testing Service. This book has been neither reviewed nor endorsed by ETS.

이 책은 링구아포럼이 독창적으로 개발하였습니다.

이 책의 내용, 사진 등 일부 혹은 전체 내용을 어떠한 방법으로도 무단 복사, 복제, 전재하는 것은 저작권법에 의해 금지되어 있습니다.

Printed in the Republic of Korea

R/N (CRbTFGMSPB): 01060630KL/01150640KL/01240640KL/03250640KL/07180640KL/03150750KL/11120750KL/04030850KL

Part B

링구아포럼™

a preface

링구아포럼의 TOEFL *i*BT b-Grammar는 초·중급(Low Intermediate) 수준의 영어 학습자를 위해 개발된 문법 교재이다. 토플은 이미 전세계로부터 공신력을 인정받은 시험으로서, 비영어권의 학습자에게 올바른 영어 학습 방향을 제시해 왔다. 차세대 토플(*i*BT TOEFL)에서는 문법만을 위한 독립적인 영역이 없어졌지만, 그럼에도 불구하고 Reading, Listening, Writing, Speaking을 위한 문법 학습은 여전히 중요하다.

본 교재는 문법의 내용을 보다 쉽게 이해할 수 있도록 새로운 접근 방식과 내용 분류를 시도하였으며, 기본 원리에 대한 설명을 한층 강화하였다. 또한 네 단계(Check Up / Grammar Review / Grammar Up / Grammar in Context)에 걸친 충분한 연습 문제를 제공함으로써 문법 내용에 대한 이해를 돕고 다른 영역과 통합된 측면에서의 학습 효율을 높일 수 있도록 구성되었다. 특히, Grammar in Context에서는 실전 *i*BT TOEFL 에서의 적응력을 높이기 위해 장문의 독해 지문을 이용한 연습 문제를 제시하여 문법 지식과 독해 능력이 자연스럽게 이어질 수 있도록 구성하였다.

마지막으로 본 교재는 Writing, Speaking과 밀접하게 관련된 문법 내용을 본문과 연습 문제 곳곳에 반영하였다. 이러한 부분을 효과적으로 활용한다면 문법과 Writing, 문법과 Speaking의 연결고리를 형성해갈 수 있을 것이다. 차세대 토플에서 문법 영역이 없어졌으니 이제 더 이상의 문법 공부는 필요 없다는 섣부른 판단을 내리기 이전에, 다른 영역과의 연계 속에서 진정한 문법을 위한 문법 학습에 눈을 뜨게 되기를 진심으로 바란다.

LinguaForum Research Center
Grammar Project Team

CONTENTS
PART B

Chapter 11
어순의 기본과 도치
Word Order and Inversion　　　171

11-1　꼬리에 꼬리를 무는 어순과 Speaking　　　172
11-2　어순의 도치　　　176
11-3　동사–목적어의 어순　　　180

Chapter 12
시제
Tenses　　　187

12-1　기본 시제: 현재, 과거, 미래　　　188
12-2　완료 시제　　　193
12-3　진행 시제　　　196
12-4　시제의 일치　　　198

Chapter 13
조동사
Modal Verbs　　　203

13-1　조동사의 개념, 역할 및 종류　　　204
13-2　Degrees of Certainty　　　206
13-3　필요, 조언, 의무, 책임　　　208
13-4　능력, 허가, 부탁, 제안　　　211

Chapter 14
법과 가정법
Mood and Subjunctive Mood　　　219

14-1　법과 명령법　　　220
14-2　가정법의 기본　　　222
14-3　가정법의 다양한 표현법　　　226
14-4　주의해야 할 조건절　　　230

Chapter 15
수동태
Passives　　　235

15-1　효과적인 수동태 문장의 사용　　　236
15-2　주의해야 할 수동태　　　239
15-3　수동태와 기타 사항　　　243

Chapter 16
명사절, 부사절
Noun Clauses and Adverb Clauses   **251**

16-1 명사절 (1): 의문사절과 whether / if절   **252**
16-2 명사절 (2): that절   **255**
16-3 부사절 (1): 시간, 조건   **258**
16-4 부사절 (2): 이유, 대조, 목적, 결과   **261**

Chapter 17
형용사절
Adjective Clauses   **267**

17-1 관계대명사절의 형태와 역할   **268**
17-2 관계대명사 what   **272**
17-3 관계부사절   **274**
17-4 쉼표와 관계사절   **277**
17-5 형용사절, 명사절, 부사절 비교   **278**

Chapter 18
전치사구
Prepositional Phrases   **283**

18-1 전치사와 끊어 읽기, 이어 읽기   **284**
18-2 주요 전치사: in, on, at   **287**
18-3 기타 전치사   **291**
18-4 주의해야 할 전치사 표현   **297**

Chapter 19
구와 절
Phrases and Clauses   **301**

19-1 구와 절 형태 종합   **302**
19-2 절의 축약 (1): 생략   **304**
19-3 절의 축약 (2): 분사구   **306**
19-4 절의 축약 (3): 전치사구와 부정사구   **310**

Chapter 20
일치, 삽입, 생략, 강조
Agreement, Parenthesis, Ellipsis, and Emphasis   **317**

20-1 일치   **318**
20-2 삽입   **322**
20-3 생략   **323**
20-4 강조   **325**

Appendix   **331**

목차

CONTENTS
PART A

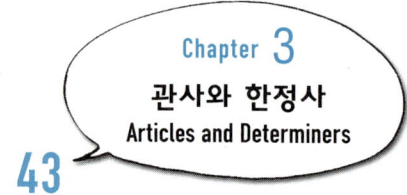

Chapter 3
관사와 한정사
Articles and Determiners
43

Chapter 1
문장의 구조
Sentence Structures
11

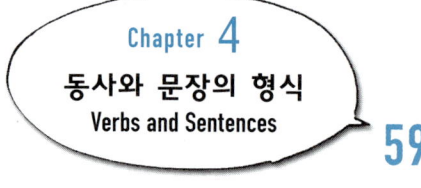

Chapter 4
동사와 문장의 형식
Verbs and Sentences
59

Chapter 2
명사
Nouns
27

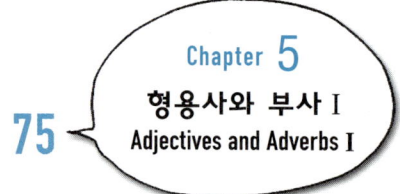

Chapter 5
형용사와 부사 I
Adjectives and Adverbs I
75

Chapter 8 123
준동사구 I
Verbal Phrases I

Chapter 6 91
형용사와 부사 II
Adjectives and Adverbs II

Chapter 9 139
준동사구 II
Verbal Phrases II

Chapter 7 107
대명사
Pronouns

Chapter 10 155
접속사와 병렬
Conjunctions and Parallelism

목차

CHAPTER 11

어순의 기본과 도치
_Word Order and Inversion

11-1 꼬리에 꼬리를 무는 어순과 Speaking

일상 생활에서 영어의 사용이 거의 불가능한 한국의 교육 환경에서는 영어를 자연스럽게 학습하려는 시도보다는 영어를 인위적으로 학습하되 자연스러운 습득이 가능한 방법을 찾는 것이 올바른 접근법이다. 영어와 한국어의 차이점을 정확하게 이해하고 이를 효과적으로 활용하는 것은 자연스러운 영어 학습을 가능하게 하는 매우 중요한 방향을 제시한다. 그 차이점 중에서도 어순의 비교는 가장 기본적인 학습 내용이다.

1 한국어와 영어의 어순 [Word Order] 비교

- '한국어는 끝까지 들어봐야 한다' 라는 말이 있듯이, 한국어에서는 문장의 마지막에 나오는 술어를 들은 후에야 비로소 행위자(주어)의 생각이나 행동을 알 수 있다.

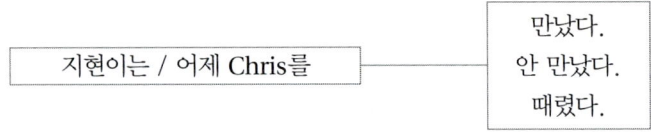

- 영어에서는 행위자(주어)가 무엇을 하려는 지에 대한 생각 및 행동(술어)의 결론을 먼저 내리고, 그 행동과 관련된 대상(목적어)과 행동의 시기, 방법, 이유, 결과 등이 따라 나온다.

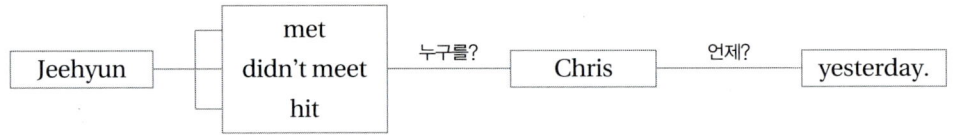

2 꼬리에 꼬리는 무는 어순 [Chain of Thought]

- 영어의 문장은 술어(Predicate*)의 의미가 정해지면 그 술어의 의미와 관련된 내용들이 중요도에 따라 순차적으로 전개되므로, 술어 뒤에 전개될 내용을 자연스럽게 예측할 수 있다.

He **sent** / a letter / to his grandma / in England / to say how much he loved her.

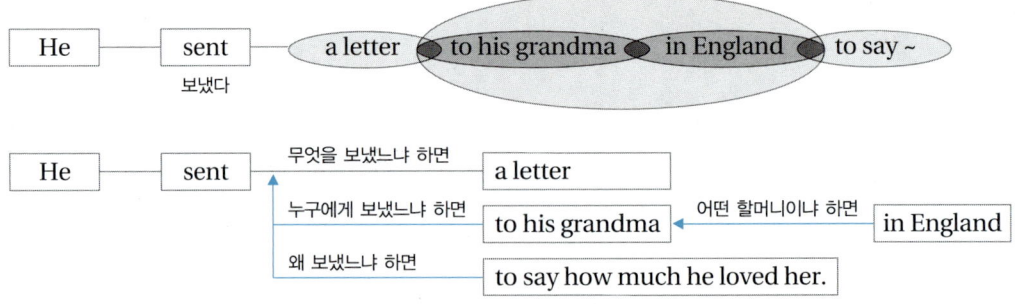

▶ 위의 도형에서 a letter, to his grandma, to say how much he loved her는 모두 동사 sent와 의미적으로 연결되어 있으며, 중요도의 순서대로 나열되어 있음을 알 수 있다. 한편, in England는 명사 his grandma와 의미적으로 연결된다.

> **Pop Quiz 1** 주어+동사 다음에 이어질 내용을 논리적 흐름에 맞게 예상해 보시오.
>
> (1) Lucy offered ~   (권하다)
> (2) The baby-sitter* put ~   (놓다)
> (3) This rug* is made ~   (만들어지다)
> (4) A smell in the yellow room makes ~   (~이/가 ~상태가 되게 하다)

3 명사 다음에는 형용사어구

- 명사가 나오면 그 다음에는 명사를 수식하는 형용사(구 또는 절)가 나올 수 있음을 늘 예측해 보도록 한다.

> **Pop Quiz 2** 다음 볼드체 명사 뒤에 나올 수 있는 수식어를 예상해 보시오. (한국어를 사용해도 됨)
>
> (1) There are **many reasons** _____
> (2) They put up **a wall** _____
> (3) The company will make **an announcement** _____
> (4) **A person** _____ studies better.

4 어순 학습과 Speaking 연습

- 술어는 행동의 결론을 표현하고, 목적어 및 수식어는 그 행동과 관련된 세부 내용을 표현한다.
- 따라서, 주어와 술어를 먼저 말하고 나머지를 생각한다. 즉, Speaking의 기본 훈련에서 가장 중요한 학습 방법은 말하고자 하는 내용 전체를 한꺼번에 영어로 말하려 하지 말고, 주어와 술어만을 말한 후에 나머지(목적어 및 수식어 등)를 천천히 생각하며 말하는 연습을 하는 것이다.

친구를 급히 만날 수는 있지만, 급하게 친구를 만들 수는 없다.
You can meet (a friend in a hurry),
but you can't make (a friend in a hurry).

Check Up

1 🔊 **Speak-out** 다음 우리말을 영어로 ①1번에서 6번까지 각각 주어와 술어만을 말한 다음에, ②문장 전체를 큰 소리로 다섯 번씩 말하시오.

(1) 큰 도시에서 사는 것은 작은 마을에서 사는 것보다 더 편리하다.
⇨ _____ _____ / _____

(2) 나는 작은 마을에서 살고 싶다.
⇨ _____ _____ / _____

(3) 내가 작은 마을에서 살고 싶은 이유가 두 가지 있다.
⇨ _____ _____ / _____

(4) 가장 큰 이유는 작은 마을은 큰 도시의 교통 체증으로부터 자유롭기 때문이다.
⇨ _____ _____ / _____

(5) 두 번째 이유는 아침의 상쾌한 공기, 가을의 파란 하늘, 밤의 빛나는 별들을 즐길 수 있기 때문이다.
⇨ _____ _____ / _____

(6) 나는 큰 도시를 떠나 작은 마을로 이사하기를 원한다.
⇨ _____ _____ / _____

2 다음 문장을 논리적 흐름에 따라 앞에서부터 이해해 보시오.

(1) Ms. Stuart never complains / about her husband / to other people.
⇨ Stuart 부인은 전혀 불평을 하지 않는다 [무엇을?] _____
   [누구에게 불평을 하지 않느냐 하면] _____

(2) I received / a collect phone call* / from my brother / in Hawaii.
⇨ _____ _____ _____ _____

(3) The chili is / so harsh* and unpleasant / that we can't have it / any more.
⇨ _____ _____ _____ _____

(4) We are excited / to go to the Philippines / for summer holiday.
⇨ _____ _____ _____

(5) You should remember / to bring an apron / to protect your clothes.
⇨ _____ _____ _____

3 다음 문장을 의미 단위로 나누고, 연결 관계에 유의하여 도형을 완성하시오. (← 표는 '수식한다'는 의미임)

(1) Maria doesn't like washing dishes very much.

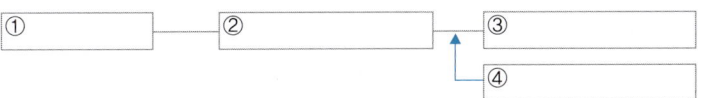

(2) When he was in prison, he learned a lot of things from books.

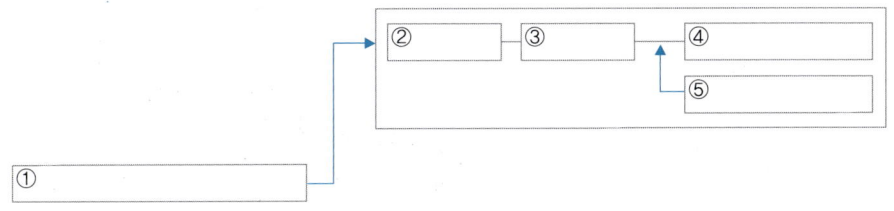

(3) You can send him an email with a click of your mouse.

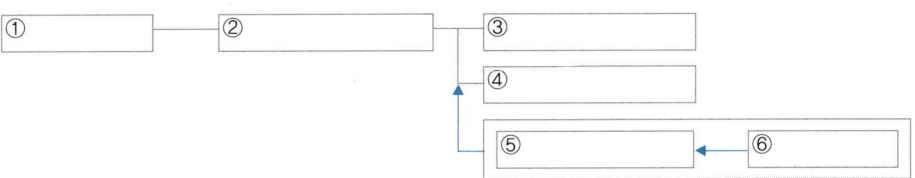

(4) Bill checked his answers with the key after he did all exercises.

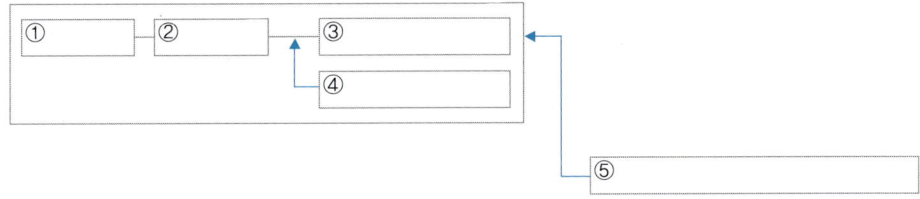

- **predicate** [prédikət] n. 술부(Full Predicates), 술어(Simple Predicates) -adj. 술부(술어)의 -v. [prédəkèit] 단언(단정)하다, 진술(서술)하다, 내포하다, 함축하다/Predicate은 predict(v. 예측하다)의 파생어이다. 즉, 술부란 실행자(주어)의 행동(동사)만 정해지면 그 뒤에 이어질 내용들의 예측이 가능하다는 뜻에서 붙여진 이름이다.
- **baby-sitter** 보모, 부모 대신 아기를 돌보는 사람
- **rug** [rʌg] n. 양탄자, 융단
- **collect (phone) call** 수신자 부담 전화
- **harsh** [hɑːrʃ] adj. 쓴, 불쾌한, 거슬리는

11-2 어순의 도치

'So am I.' 또는 'Neither do I.'와 같이 단순한 경우가 아니면 도치된 문장이 Speaking에서 사용되는 경우는 드물다. (영화의 대사에서는 극중 인물이 권위를 나타내려고 도치 문장을 자주 쓰는 경우가 있기는 하다.) 그러나 독해에서는 도치된 문장을 쉽게 발견할 수 있는데 이를 정확하게 해석하기란 쉽지 않다. 따라서, 도치가 이루어지는 원리를 학습하여 도치가 일어나기 이전의 문장 구조를 파악함으로써 문장을 보다 쉽고 정확하게 이해할 수 있도록 한다.

1 도치란?

- 술어(동사)와 연결되어 있는 보어, 목적어, 부사(구)가 표현의 다양성 및 강조를 위해 문장 앞으로 이동하면 주어와 술어의 어순에 변화가 생기는데, 이를 도치(Inversion; Inverting the normal word order)라고 한다. 즉, 도치란 '주어+술어+목적어'와 같은 기본 어순을 파괴함으로써 앞으로 이동된 어구를 더욱 강조하는 표현법이다.
- 술어의 어순 변화(동사 또는 조동사가 주어 앞으로 이동)가 학습의 핵심이다.
- 도치는 주로 장소에 관한 전치사구 및 부정어구가 술어를 수식하는 문장에서 발생한다.

2 도치의 기본 원칙

- 수식을 받는 술어가 수식어(부사)와 함께 이동한다.
- (1, 2군)조동사*의 쓰임에 유의한다.

Type 1. 술어(전체)가 주어 앞으로 이동

술어(전체)에 1군 조동사가 없고, 술어(전체)와 연결되는 수식어구가 하나인 경우

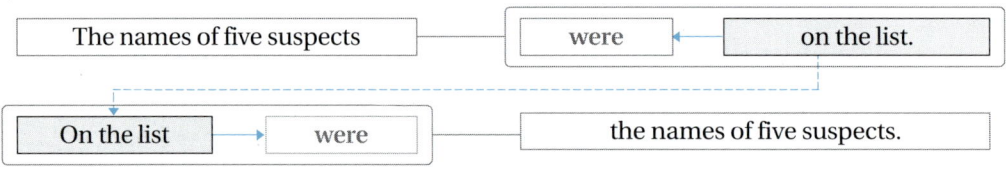

▶ On the list를 강조하기 위해 문장 앞으로 이동시키면, 수식 받는 요소(were)도 함께 이동한다.

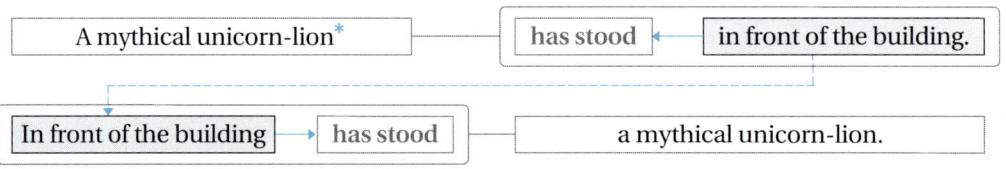

▶ 2군 조동사가 포함된 has stood가 함께 이동한다.

Type 2. 조동사와 동사의 분리: 조동사의 첨가(do) 및 어순 변화

① 1군 조동사가 포함되어 있거나, ② 술어와 연결된 문장 성분이 두 개 이상(ex. 목적어와 전치사구) 있거나, ③ 부정의 의미를 갖는 수식어를 도치하는 경우

① 1군 조동사가 포함된 경우

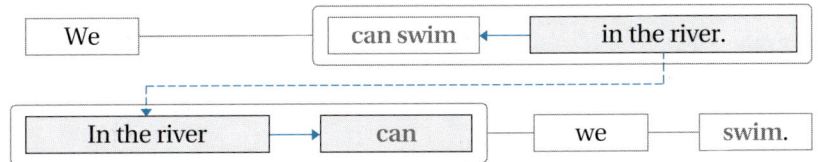

②, ③ 부정의 의미를 갖는 수식어 또는 술어와 연결된 문장 성분이 두 개 이상 포함된 경우

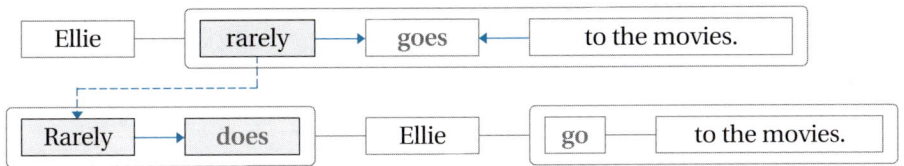

He **hit** me at the back of the school.

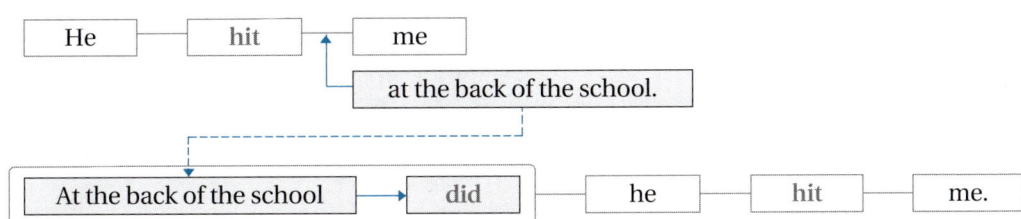

Pop Quiz   밑줄 친 부분을 강조하는 도치 문장을 만들고, 큰 소리로 세 번씩 말하시오.

[Type 1]

(1) A strange man **came** along the street.
(2) The swimmer **splashed** into the water.
(3) A rabbit and a turtle **were lying** under the tree.

[Type 2]

(4) We **should be** quiet in the library.
(5) You **should use** the exit only in an emergency.

(6) It <u>rarely</u> **rains**.
(7) It <u>rarely</u> **rains** in Egypt.
(8) They **said** <u>nothing</u> about my hairdo.
(9) She <u>hardly</u> ever **breaks** a promise, as far as I know.
(10) They **would** <u>seldom</u> **visit** their family.
(11) I **have** <u>never</u> <u>seen</u> such a beautiful sunset.
(12) He **can make** an excuse for telling a lie <u>under no circumstances</u>.

3 Fronting vs. Inversion

■ Fronting에서는 주어(+조동사)+술어의 기본 어순이 유지되는 반면, Inversion에서는 기본 어순이 파괴된다.

ⓐ A strange man **came** <u>along the street</u> with her.   Basic Sentence
ⓑ <u>Along the street</u> a strange man **came** with her.   Fronting
ⓒ <u>Along the street</u> **did** a strange man **come** with her.   Inversion, but **unusual**
ⓓ <u>Along the street</u> **came** a strange man.   Inversion

▸ ⓐ 주어+술어+수식어
ⓑ 수식어+주어+술어 / Fronting을 통해 along the street을 강조
ⓒ 수식어+조동사+주어+술어 / 형태적으로는 Inversion이 가능하지만 두 개 이상의 전치사구가 술어(동사)를 수식할 때에는 어느 전치사구를 활용해서라도 도치 구문을 만들지 않고 Fronting을 활용하는 것이 좋다.
ⓓ 수식어+술어+주어 / Inversion을 통해 along the street을 강조(Fronting 보다 강조하는 의미가 강함)

■ 대명사가 문장의 마지막에 위치하게 되면 발음상 매우 어색해지므로 주어가 대명사일 때에는 도치를 사용하지 않는다.

Where are my keys? — They are <u>here</u>.   Basic Sentence
<u>Here</u> they are.   Fronting
<u>Here</u> are they.   Inversion, but **awkward**
<u>Here</u> are <u>your keys</u>.   Inversion

4 Information Questions와 간접의문문

1) Yes-No Questions의 간접의문문

A: Do you <u>know</u> **when** Joe will leave for Barcelona?   Normal Word Order
B: No, I have no idea.

2) Information Questions의 간접의문문

A: **When** do you **think** Joe will leave for Barcelona? Fronting / Not Inversion
B: I guess October.

▶ **Information Questions** Yes/No로 대답할 수 없고 구체적인 정보를 묻는 의문문은 의문사로 시작해야 한다. 주로 believe, imagine, say, suppose, think, wish 등이 주절의 동사로 사용되는 간접의문문에서 발생한다.

Check Up

1 🔵 Speak-out 다음을 도치가 일어나기 전의 기본 어순으로 바꾸어 쓰고 해석하시오. 그리고, 도치된 문장의 의미를 느끼며 큰 소리로 세 번씩 말하시오.

(1) Along the walls sit the Asian leaders.
   ⇨ _____

(2) Under the Christmas tree was a pile of small boxes.
   ⇨ _____

(3) Never had ten minutes gone by so slowly.
   ⇨ _____

(4) No sooner had he left Korea than he missed kimchi.
   ⇨ _____

(5) Rarely could Joel write a letter because he was so busy.
   ⇨ _____

2 🔵 Speak-out 다음 우리말을 영어로 세 번씩 말하시오.

(1) 제 나이가 얼마나 되어 보이나요?
(2) Mark가 무엇을 하고 있다고 상상하나요?
(3) 왜 그들이 그녀를 백설공주라고 부른다고 생각하나요?
(4) 당신은 죽으면(pass away*) 어디로 간다고 믿나요?

❏ **(1, 2군) 조동사** 조동사(Modals)는 문장에서의 역할에 따라 1군 조동사(will, can, may, must, should 등)와 2군 조동사(be, have, do)로 나누어진다. (Ch.13-1 참고)
❏ **a mythical unicorn-lion** 해태(시비나 선악을 판단할 줄 안다는 상상의 동물로서, 사자와 비슷하게 생겼지만 머리 가운데 뿔이 달려 있다. 중국 고서에는 "성품이 충직하여 사람이 싸우는 것을 보면 바르지 못한 사람을 뿔로 받는다"라고 설명하고 있다. 한국에서는 화재나 재앙을 물리치는 능력을 가진 신적인 동물이라고 여겨 궁궐, 절 등에 장식되기도 했다.) / mythical [míθikəl] *adj.* 신화의, 상상의, 허구의
❏ **pass away** 일반적으로 die와 동일한 의미를 갖는다. 그러나 pass away는 '개인'의 죽음에 대한 '공손한' 표현이기 때문에 '여러 사람들'의 죽음을 '사실'로 전달할 때에는 die를 써야한다. ex. One million people **died** in the war. (pass away는 안 됨)

11-3 동사-목적어의 어순

일반동사 다음에는 대부분 목적어, 부사, 또는 전치사가 따라 나온다. ①동사에 뒤따르는 부사 및 전치사의 구별 학습은 Listening과 Speaking에, 그리고 ② '주다(수여)'의 의미가 담긴 동사를 몇 형식의 구조로 사용하는 것이 좋은지에 대한 학습은 Speaking과 Writing에 매우 중요한 기초가 된다.

1 Two-word Verbs*와 목적어

1) Phrasal Verbs

- '자동사+부사' or '타동사+부사+목적어/타동사+목적어+부사'

  She would **climb up** / the tree / in front of her house.
  Be careful / not to **wake** him **up**.
  Jake hasn't **paid back** / all that money / he borrowed / yet.

  ▶ 부사 뒤에 대명사가 오면 발음하기가 불편하므로 대명사는 부사 앞에 위치한다.
  ex. Be careful not to **wake up** him. (×)

2) Prepositional Verbs

- '자동사+전치사+전치사의 목적어'

  We're **laughing** / **at** a story.
  Water **consists** / **of** hydrogen / and oxygen.
  How long it will take / **depends** / **on** you.   (~ depends you on. ×)

2 끊어 읽기와 Two-word Verbs

- 정확한 끊어 읽기와 이어 읽기 학습은 Listening과 Speaking에서 매우 중요하다.
  Mr. Peterson **gave up** / his job / because of a lack of interest.
  She is eager / to **comment** / **on** the current social issues.

- Phrasal Verbs는 동사와 부사를 이어(붙여) 읽고, Prepositional Verbs는 동사와 전치사 사이를 끊어 읽는다.

- 일반적으로 부사는 강세 발음되며, 전치사는 약세 발음된다.

3 '주다(수여)'의 의미가 담긴 동사들

1) 4형식 구조? 3형식 구조?

- 4형식 구조를 사용하는 것이 기본이다.
  Robbie made her a chocolate cake.   간접목적어 ≠ 직접목적어

- 간접목적어를 강조하기 위하여 3형식 구조로 전환하기도 한다.
  Robbie made a chocolate cake for his girlfriend.

- 직접목적어가 대명사일 때에는 (자연스러운 발음을 위해) 3형식 구조를 사용한다.
  Robbie made it for his girlfriend.
  Robbie made it for her.

2) 4형식으로 사용할 수 없는 3형식 동사 (p.62 참고)

Ms. Rachel explains how to make apple butter to them.
Let me introduce you to a nice group of his friends.
announce, describe, donate, explain, introduce, recommend, report, suggest 등

4 3형식 구조로 전환될 수 없는 4형식 동사들 (p.62 참고)

- charge, cost, envy 등*
- 4형식으로 쓰이는 동사들은 주로 '수여'의 의미를 나타내지만, 모두가 그렇지는 않다. 또한, 4형식 구조라 해서 '~에게 ~을'로만 해석되는 것도 아니다.
- 주로 '수여'의 의미가 없고 '~에게 ~을'로 해석되지 않는 동사가 4형식 구조로 사용된다.

They charged Peter two dollars for being late.　　(Peter에게 2달러 벌금을 부과했다)
I envy Marie her nice boyfriend.　　(Marie가 멋진 남자친구를 갖고 있는 것이 부럽다)
▶ 4형식 구조: '명사(간접목적어) ≠ 명사(직접목적어)' / 5형식 구조: '명사(목적어)=명사(목적격 보어)'

We wish you a merry Christmas!　　(당신이 즐거운 성탄절을 보내기를 바란다)
▶ We wish a merry Christmas to you. (문법적으로 틀린 것은 아니지만 4형식 구조가 더 좋다.)

Check Up

1 알맞은 표현을 고르고, 큰 소리로 세 번씩 말하시오.

(1) Don't throw (away it, it away) until we've finished cooking.
(2) I'm sure that a lot of people will object (to it, it to).
(3) If you give me your cup, I'll fill (up it, it up) for you.
(4) You couldn't succeed if you didn't believe (in him, him in).
(5) Because I've not seen the report, I can hardly comment (on it, it on).
(6) After due* consideration, we decided to turn (down it, it down).

2 🔊 Speak-out 밑줄 친 표현이 부사이면 *adv.*를 쓰고, 전치사이면 *prep.*를 쓰시오. 그리고, 끊어 읽기와 이어 읽기에 유의하여 큰 소리로 세 번씩 말하시오.

_____ (1) Helen thanked me for fixing up her old bike.
_____ (2) She will never succeed in keeping the peace between her pet dogs.
_____ (3) Bill is trying on the clothing and shoes which his girlfriend gave him.
_____ (4) Did her parents approve of her decision to marry a foreigner who came from Canada?
_____ (5) The company consists of more than 50 researchers who are all smart and competent.

3 🔊 Speak-out 알맞은 문장을 고르고, 큰 소리로 세 번씩 말하시오.

(1) _____ ⓐ My father used to sing a song us to sleep at night.
　　　　　 ⓑ My father used to sing us a song to sleep at night.
(2) _____ ⓐ Ms. Anderson made for her husband a sweater.
　　　　　 ⓑ Ms. Anderson made a sweater for her husband.
(3) _____ ⓐ The book cost us 20 dollars.
　　　　　 ⓑ The book cost 20 dollars to us.
(4) _____ ⓐ He envies your high score to you.
　　　　　 ⓑ He envies you your high score.

4 🔊 Speak-out 다음 우리말을 영어로 옮길 때 ① 주어와 술어만을 먼저 말하고, 다시 ② 문장 전체를 큰 소리로 다섯 번씩 말하시오.

(1) 은하수(the Galaxy)는 수많은 별들로 구성된다(consist of).
　　_____ _____ / _____

(2) Grant 부부는 그들의 아기를 돌보느라(look after) 바쁘다.
　　_____ _____ / _____

(3) Neil[ni:l]은 그의 여자친구를 나에게 말해주었다(describe).
　　_____ _____ / _____

❏ **Two-word Verbs** 동사와 부사(Phrasal Verbs) 또는 동사와 전치사(Prepositional Verbs)가 결합하여 하나의 동사처럼 사용되는 경우를 말한다. 동사와 결합하는 부사, 혹은 전치사의 예는 다음과 같다: away, back 등(항상 부사) / at, for, from, into, of, with 등(항상 전치사) / about, along, down, in, off, on, over, round, through, up 등(부사/전치사)

🐟 **comments** 🐻

❏ **charge, cost, envy 등** 4형식 구조에서 3형식 구조로 변환할 수 없지만, 3형식 문장을 이끌지 못하는 것은 아니다.
　ex. The tickets for adults **cost** ten dollars each.
　　　I **envy** Marie's nice boyfriend.
　　　My friends **envy** the fact I have two girlfriends.
❏ **due** [dju:] *adj.* 적당한, 충분한

Grammar Review

1 다음 문장이 바르게 쓰였으면 ○표를 하고, 잘못 쓰였으면 ×표를 하시오.

_____ (1) We've decided to set up a base camp at the border.
_____ (2) Charlie may hate her, but his survival depends her on.
_____ (3) Nowhere it was more dramatic than at sea.
_____ (4) Do you think what he is trying to do with them?
_____ (5) Pip loves taking pictures of nature and has made a plan to travel widely in New Zealand.
_____ (6) She recommended me a doctor who is good with children.

2 주어진 표현을 어순에 맞게 배열하여 큰 소리로 세 번씩 말하시오.

(1) us / for every transaction / Some banks / a fixed fee / charge / .
➡ _____

(2) Never / see / again / the little girl / did / the wolf / .
➡ _____

(3) do / between Kate and Daniel / imagine / What / happens / after the book ends / you / ?
➡ _____

3 다음 글을 읽고, 빈 칸에 들어갈 알맞은 표현을 고르시오.

(1) _____ anything stranger appeared in the village! Through the
    Ⓐ Never had   Ⓑ Had never

marketplace walked a man carrying a door on his back! "Why are you carrying that door?" a vendor asked him. "(2) _____ my home from thieves!"
                                         Ⓐ Protecting   Ⓑ To protect

the man said. "Is it to replace one you had at home?" asked the vendor. "No!" came the reply. "This is the door I have at home!" The vendor asked, "How does it protect your home if you carry it on your back?" The man explained

(3) _____, "To enter my home, a thief must open the door! If I carry the
    Ⓐ to the vendor   Ⓑ the vendor

door with me, a thief cannot open it! Then he cannot get in, and my home is safe!" Truly logical (4) _____ ... but also wrong!
    Ⓐ he was   Ⓑ was he

Grammar Up

Time Limit: 6 min, _____ / 18

어법상 빈 칸에 들어갈 알맞은 표현을 고르시오.

1 _____ surrounding the house is made of wood.

(A) Its
(B) The fence
(C) For the fence
(D) The fence is

2 Drinking _____ of developing liver cancer.

(A) increases
(B) increases and
(C) increases the risk
(D) the risk increases

3 All living things contain _____ called carbon 14.

(A) a substance
(B) is a substance
(C) a substance is
(D) that a substance

4 _____ blown off than children laughed at his bald head.

(A) The man's hat had sooner
(B) The man's hat no had sooner
(C) No sooner had the man's hat
(D) No sooner the man's hat had

5 _____ usually very cold in the Antarctic, even in August.

(A) Its
(B) They are
(C) The weather
(D) It is

6 She always wears a red apron when she _____.

(A) in the kitchen works
(B) in kitchen the works
(C) works in the kitchen
(D) the kitchen works in

7 Not a word _____ while she is studying.
   (A) does she usually say
   (B) says usually that she
   (C) which she usually says
   (D) she says usually

어법상 잘못된 부분을 고르시오.

8 He describes us the tango as a very sexy dance.
                    (A)   (B)(C)   (D)

9 Little I did dream you would become a doctor!
           (A) (B)   (C)   (D)

10 Sounds can be measured to find out how loud are they.
       (A)   (B)   (C)   (D)

11 The man hasn't succeeded it in despite his efforts for the last ten years.
                                (A)   (B)   (C)   (D)

12 I wonder which of the rooms is her ghost said to haunt.
         (A)   (B)   (C)   (D)

13 In some parts in the world, there is not enough to eat food.
       (A)   (B)   (C)   (D)

14 Do you think where the man standing next to the table is from?
                    (A)   (B)   (C)   (D)

15 Near the fireplace lying was a pair of worn-out boots.
       (A)   (B)   (C)   (D)

16 I'm not sure where is he going to live the rest of his life after retiring.
                   (A)   (B)   (C)   (D)

17 Not until January I will have a holiday.
       (A)   (B) (C) (D)

18 Planning things such as a picnic, concert, and party makes happy people.
       (A)   (B)   (C)   (D)

Grammar in Context

The Courteous Magpie

In Korea is told a fable about a pheasant, a pigeon, and a magpie. One winter, there was little food. Never before had the birds been so hungry! They wished for a little rice. They knew a rat and his wife had filled up their home with rice for the whole winter. The birds envied the rats. The pigeon shouted rudely, "Share with us!" The rats said, "Go away!" The pheasant shouted, "Give me rice, or I'll take it!" But the rats _____ (laugh at, him). "It belongs to us!" they replied. The magpie thought, "Never will such methods succeed in getting rice!" So, he explained to the rats, "Good neighbors, for some of your rice would I be most grateful!" The rats approved of the magpie's good manners. No one could object to such a polite request! So impressed were the rats by his courtesy that they gave the magpie a big bag of rice. Thereafter, the courteous magpie became an honored symbol of Korea.

165 words, Reading Time: _____

1 주어진 표현을 사용하여 빈 칸을 완성하시오.

2 밑줄 친 표현을 도치가 일어나기 전의 기본 어순으로 바꾸어 쓰시오.

3 문맥상 fable 의 의미와 가장 가까운 표현을 고르시오.
   Ⓐ lesson   Ⓑ myth   Ⓒ legend   Ⓓ explanation

4 **Chain of Thought:** 다음 문장을 논리적 흐름에 따라 앞에서부터 이해해 봅시다.

(1) They knew / a rat and his wife had filled up / their home / with rice / for the whole winter.

⇨ 그들은 알고 있었다 [무엇을?] _____ [무엇을 채워 놓았느냐 하면] _____
[무엇으로 채워 놓았느냐 하면] _____ [왜 채워 놓았느냐 하면] _____

(2) The rats were so impressed / by his courtesy / that they gave the magpie / a big bag / of rice.

⇨ _____ _____ _____ _____ _____

규칙 1: 문장을 생각의 흐름에 따른 사고단위(Thought Unit)로 나누어 이해한다.
규칙 2: 명사 뒤에는 그 명사를 설명하는 형용사(구, 절)가 따라나올 것을 예상한다. 다른 뜻(부사구, 절)을 가진 어구가 나오면 전체 문장에 적합하도록 해석한다.
규칙 3: 문장을 뒤에서부터 해석하려고 하면 Chain of Thought에 따른 문장 이해에 혼란이 생길 수 있으므로 각별히 주의해야 한다. 뒷부분은 모두 가리고 앞에서부터 해당 부분만을 보면서 이해하도록 한다.

CHAPTER 12

시제
_Tenses

12-1 기본 시제: 현재, 과거, 미래

● Tense는 '시간과 관련된 동사의 변형된 형태'를 말한다. 즉, 현재형, 과거형, 과거분사형처럼 동사의 변형된 형태가 과거, 현재 등과 같은 '시간대의 제한된 범위(시제)'를 표현한다. 따라서, Tense를 시제로 번역하는 것은 부적절한 면이 있다.

1 현재*[Present]: 현실[present reality]과 현재의 사실[fact]

1) [말하는 순간의] 상태, 감정을 표현한다. (주로 be동사와 함께 사용)

Bradley **is** not here.

2) 현재 시제는 현재에(도) 사실(present reality, fact)인 상황을 표현한다.

Mr. Bean **reads** all the papers* in the morning.	현재에도 사실인 반복 또는 습관적인 상황 표현
London **is** the capital city of the United Kingdom.	현재에도 사실
Water **freezes** at 0 degree Celsius*.	현재에도 사실인 일반적 진리
A little learning **is** a dangerous thing.*	현재에도 사실인 일반적 진리

● 현재와 현재진행 시제의 비교*

She **eats** scrambled eggs with cheese.	'먹는다'는 사실 표현
She **is eating** scrambled eggs with cheese.	'현재 먹고 있다'는 상황, 행동 표현

● 진행형의 사용이 의미적으로 적합하지 않은 '상태를 나타내는 동사'의 경우에는 현재 시제로 진행형과 같은 현재의 상황과 동작을 표현한다.

I **think** you are right.	현재 그렇게 생각하고 있다는 상황 표현

| 영어의 12 시제 |

분류	현재	과거	미래
기본	A boy **sings**.	A boy **sang**.	A boy **will sing**.
진행	A boy **is singing**.	A boy **was singing**.	A boy **will be singing**.
완료	A boy **has sung**.	A boy **had sung**.	A boy **will have sung**.
완료+진행	A boy **has been singing**.	A boy **had been singing**.	A boy **will have been singing**.

▶ '시제'란 동사의 형태 변화(조동사의 첨가 포함)를 통해 시간대의 제한된 범위를 표현하는 것이다.
▶ [기본, 진행, 완료, 완료+진행의 4 시제] × [현재, 과거, 미래의 기본 3 분류] = 12개의 시제

2 과거 [Past] : History

- 과거 시제는 과거의 시점에서만 사실인 상황을 표현한다. *현재의 상황과 관련지어 말하는 것은 아님*

    The air **felt** still and cold.
    Yesterday morning Kitty **got up** at 7.
    Abraham Lincoln **was born** in Kentucky in 1809.

3 미래 [Future] : 예측, 기대, 의지

- 미래에 해야 할 일에 대한 결정 및 약속, 미래에 발생할 사건에 대한 기대, 예측, 가능성을 표현한다. (확정된 사실이라고 할 수는 없으며 예측, 기대, 의지 등을 표현한다.)
- 엄격히 말해 will과 be going to는 의미적 차이가 있지만, 현대 영어에서는 이론적인 의미 차이보다는 사용하는 사람이 개별적으로 느끼는 차이 및 어투에 따라 선택되어 사용되는 경향이 강하다.

    Situation 1 Linda: Did you do your homework?
                   Bill: Oh no, I forgot. **I'm going to / 'll** do it now.
    Situation 2 Linda: I decided to buy a new bicycle.
                   Bill: Wow, really?
                   Linda: Yep! Tomorrow **I'm going to / 'll** look for one.
    Situation 3 Linda: The phone is ringing.
                   Bill: I **will / am gonna*** get it.

▶ Situation 1: 즉흥적으로 결정한 미래의 일, Situation 2: 미리 결정한 미래의 일, Situation 3: 일반적으로 will이 선호된다고 알려진 경우

4 현재, 현재진행: 미래의 fact(사실)

- 현재 시제: 주어가 아닌 다른 누군가에 의해 이미 확정된 미래 상황

    미래 시제는 기본적으로 '예측'을 표현한다. 하지만, 미래의 일이라 하더라도 <u>학기 일정</u>, <u>비행 시각표</u> 등과 같이 이미 확정되어 '예측'이 아닌 'Fact(사실)'로 인정되는 것은 현재 시제를 사용하여 미래를 현재의 사실처럼 표현한다.

    The first train for Seoul **starts** at 6:45.
    Tomorrow **is** my 16th birthday.

▶ 현재로 미래를 표현하는 상황이 자주 발생하는 동사들: open, close, begin, start, end, finish, arrive, leave, come 등

■ 현재진행: 주어(행동의 실행자)의 의지로 이미 확정된 미래 상황

미래의 일이라고 하여도 예측이 아닌 확정된 사실(Fact)인 경우에는 현재 시제를 사용하지만, 행동의 실행자(주어)의 의지로 결정된 일은 현재진행의 형태로 표현한다.

Anna : What are you going to do next weekend?

Robin : Let me check my diary to see what is scheduled next week.
Uh, I'm visiting Uncle Dave's*.

■ 먼 미래에 관한 일은 변동이 생길 수 있으므로 현재(진행) 시제로 미래를 표현하는 상황은 '가까운 미래'에 관한 것이 적합하다. 학기의 시작과 같이 장기간에도 변동이 없을 것 같은 내용은 현재 시제로 미래를 표현할 수 있다.

The fall semester begins in September.

5 be going to, will, shall

will	be going to
일방적, 중립적인 느낌 / Willingness(자진해서 기꺼이 하려는 의지)를 강하게 표현한다.	상호적인(interpersonal) 느낌이 강하여 대화 중 친근감을 전달한다.
말하는 시점에 즉흥적으로 결정한 미래의 일을 표현한다.	미리 결정한 미래의 계획(plans), 의도(intentions)를 나타낸다.

▶ 이론적으로 will과 be going to는 의미 차이가 있으며 여러 책에서 (위 도표에서와 같이) 그 차이점을 설명하고 있지만, 실제로는 거의 아무런 의미 차이 없이 사용된다. 물론 will과 be going to를 엄격하게 구별하여 사용하는 사람도 있지만 그것 또한 단지 개인적인 선호도로 취급될 뿐이다. Be going to가 친근한 느낌이 있기는 하며, will을 강하게 발음하여 사용하면 의지가 강조됨을 느낄 수 있다. 논문과 같이 형식적인(formal) Writing에서는 will을 사용하는 것이 옳다.

▶ 영국식 영어에서도 will이 많이 사용되지만, 개인적인 선호도와 어투에 따라 shall도 사용된다.

▶ 미국식 영어에서는 의문문의 형태로 1인칭(I, we) 주어와 함께 공손한 제안을 할 때에만 제한적으로 shall이 사용된다.
ex. Shall we go? (이제 그만 갈까요?)

Check Up

1 현재 또는 과거 시제를 사용하여 문장을 완성하시오.

(1) The paper in most books _____ (come) from trees.

(2) In 1876 the United States _____ (have) its one-hundredth birthday.

(3) Newfoundland _____ (be) a large island in eastern Canada.

(4) Steve _____ (take) a day off yesterday because he _____ (not, be) very well.

(5) Whales and dolphins _____ (be) mammals that _____ (spend) their whole lives in the ocean.

2 둘 중 알맞은 표현을 골라 문장을 완성하시오.

(1) A: Do you think my shoes will be ready soon?
    B: Yes, they (will, are going) be ready anytime.

(2) A: What are you having for dinner?
    B: I (will, am going) to go to Sally's house. We (will, are going) to have a barbecue party tonight. Will you join us?

(3) I expect that Bob (will, is going) drop by later in the afternoon to deliver the documents.

(4) Sally (will, is going) to visit her grandmother on vacation. She hasn't seen her for ages.

(5) We (won't, aren't going) be able to make the flight tonight. We had an emergency* in the hospital, so we (will, are going) have to take a later flight.

3 빈 칸에 들어갈 동사의 시제가 나머지와 다른 하나를 고르시오.

(1) _____ ⓐ Life _____ uncertain voyage*.
             ⓑ I'm hungry because I _____ nothing this morning.
             ⓒ There _____ not a lot of doves in the city several years ago.

(2) _____ ⓐ She likes chocolate and _____ it every day.
             ⓑ It _____ twenty-four hours for the Earth to turn round on its axis*.
             ⓒ Peter and I _____ the house next month. It's our dream house.

(3) _____ ⓐ Dave _____ the tickets for the show tomorrow instead of us.
             ⓑ Do you know when human beings _____ on the moon for the first time?
             ⓒ Sally _____ her grandmother on vacation. She hasn't seen her for ages.

4 밑줄 친 동사의 형태가 나타내는 의미상 시제를 고르고, 문장을 해석하시오.

현재☐ 과거☐ 미래☐ (1) The final test is at the end of May.

현재☐ 과거☐ 미래☐ (2) This train starts at 11, and an hourly service will operate soon after.

현재☐ 과거☐ 미래☐ (3) The plane arrives in Seoul in ten or fifteen minutes.

현재☐ 과거☐ 미래☐ (4) The film **"Gone with the Wind"** opens across Korea on March 3.

5 Speak-out 다음 우리말을 영어로 세 번씩 말하시오. (현재, 현재진행 시제에 유의할 것)

(1) A: Kate는 보통 수업 시간에 제일 앞 줄에 앉습니다.
B: 그런데 오늘은 제일 뒷줄에 앉아 있습니다.

(2) A: 아래 그림을 잘 보세요. 요리사는 지금 무엇을 하고 있습니까?
B: 요리사는 스프를 맛 보고 있습니다.

(3) A: 눈을 감고 잘 들어 보세요. 저는 지금 무엇을 하고 있습니까?
B: 당신은 손뼉을 치고 있습니다.

6 Speak-out 다음 우리말을 영어로 세 번씩 말하시오. (미래를 나타내는 다양한 표현에 유의할 것)

(1) 나는 다음 주 아버지 생신에 아버지에게 카드를 보낼 거야.
(2) Smith씨는 보통 5시에 퇴근하지만, 오늘은 한 시간 일찍 퇴근할 겁니다.
(3) 나는 뉴욕행 네 시 비행기를 탈 계획이야.
(4) 그 미술관은 내일 아침 열 시에 문을 열 거야.

---

comments

- **현재** '현재 시제는 절대적인 진리, 일반적인 사실, 의견, 반복적인 상황, 습관적인 동작을 표현한다'라고 암기하는 학습을 하지 말고, '절대적인 진리, 일반적인 사실, 의견, 반복적인 상황, 습관적인 동작 등은 현재에(도) 사실이므로 현재 시제로 표현한다'라고 학습해야 한다. 세부사항을 개별적으로 암기하지 않고 근본적인 하나의 개념으로 이해하도록 접근하면 문법 학습이 독해, 청취, 영작, Speaking 영역에 실용적으로 활용될 수 있다.
- **paper** n. 종이, 신문 / 종이는 물질을 나타내는 명사로서 셀 수 없는 명사(부정관사와 결합 불가, 항상 단수 취급)로 분류하지만, 종이가 모여 신문이라는 하나의 상품을 구성할 때에는 셀 수 있는 명사로 취급한다.
- **Celsius** [sélsiəs] adj. 섭씨의 -n. 섭씨 온도 (18세기 스웨덴의 천문학자 Celsius가 물의 어는점(0°)과 끓는점(100°)을 100등분하여 만든 온도 측정 기준이다.) / **Fahrenheit** [fǽrənhàit] adj. 화씨의 -n. 화씨 온도 (Celsius 외에 또 다른 온도 측정 기준으로서 18세기 독일의 물리학자 Fahrenheit가 물의 어는점 (32°)과 끓는점(212°)을 180등분하여 만들었다.)
- **A little learning is a dangerous thing.** 어설프게 알고 있는 것이 더 위험하다
- **현재와 현재진행 시제의 비교** 현재 시제는 현재에도 사실인 일반적인 상황을 표현하고, 현재진행 시제는 과거나 미래와는 관계없이 현재에 진행되고 있는 상황의 표현에 집중한다. / She now eats scrambled eggs with cheeses. Now와 같은 수식어의 도움으로 과거에는 아니었지만 현재에 발생되는 상황을 표현할 수 있다. (암기하지 말고 표현의 감각을 느끼고 이해하도록 할 것)
- **gonna** [gɔ́:nə] 일상회화에서는 going to를 줄여 gonna라고 하기도 한다.
- **Uncle Dave's** Uncle Dave's house / 추측이 가능한 경우에는 장소를 나타내는 명사를 생략할 수 있다. ex. a barber's (shop)
- **emergency** [imə́:rdʒənsi] n. 비상 사태, 긴급 사태, 응급실
- **voyage** [vɔ́iidʒ] n. 항해, 여행
- **axis** [ǽksis] n. 축, 중심선

12-2 완료 시제

● 완료 시제가 사용되는 상황을 분류해 보면 **결과**, **경험**, **완료**, **계속** 등의 의미를 표현한다고 할 수 있다. 그러나, 이러한 분류를 분석적으로 학습하는 것은 문법을 위한 문법 학습이 될 수 있는 한편 Speaking 등을 위한 실용성에 방해가 될 위험이 있다. 분석적으로 생각하지 말고, 문맥과 어울리는 뜻을 자연스럽게 이해하는 연습을 하도록 한다.

1 현재완료 [Present Perfect]

■ 현재완료 시제는 용어 자체에서 보듯이 과거에 시작되어 현재에 완료된(completed, perfected*) 상황 및 행동을 표현한다. 즉, 과거 시제는 단지 과거의 사실만을 표현하지만 현재완료는 과거의 사실이 현재의 상황과 관련되어 있음을 나타낸다.

Julia **has learned** English *before*.	(So, Julia can speak English now.)
He **has been** to Africa a lot.	(So, he knows Africa well.)
He **went** to Africa.	아프리카에 갔다는 과거의 사실만 전달
This is the best book I **have** *ever* **read**.	(현재 이 순간까지도 최고의 책)

▸ Before, ever, never, often, once 등의 부사가 결과 및 경험의 의미와 잘 어울린다.

I **have** *just* **finished** b-TOEFL Grammar.	과거에 시작해서 현재에 완료

▸ 주로 already, just, now, yet 등의 부사가 완료의 의미와 잘 어울린다.

Tom **has been** absent from school two times.	(현재까지 포함해서 몇 번이나)
How long **have** you **lived** in Los Angeles?	(현재까지 계속해서 얼마 동안이나)
She **has collected** stamps for many years.	(She will probably continue.)

■ 완료형 문장에 나타나는 부사, 전치사들이라고 해서 완료형에만 쓰이는 것이 아님에 주의!

I **have lived** in L.A. *since* 2005.	Since는 항상 완료형과 함께 사용
I **lived** in L.A. *for* three years.	의미에 따라 과거, 완료, 미래 시제에 모두 사용

Richard **was** *already* late for the appointment with his girlfriend.
Do you know if she *ever* **read** any of his poems?
A quarrel between Bob and his brother **was** *just* about to end.

2 과거와 현재완료

I **didn't see** your hamster yesterday.	(어제 햄스터를 보지 못했다)
I**'ve not seen** your hamster for days.	(며칠 전부터 지금까지 햄스터를 보지 못했다)

We **got** a lot of rain last year, but we **haven't gotten** much rain this year.

3 과거완료 [Past Perfect]

- 'had + 과거분사'의 형태로 과거보다 앞선 시점에 일어난 동작이나 상황을 나타낸다. 흔히 '대과거'라고 부른다.

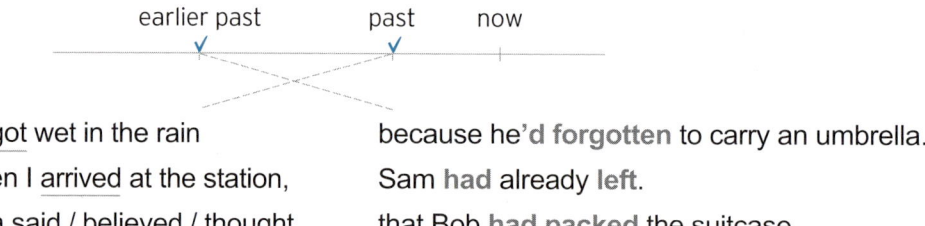

He <u>got</u> wet in the rain because he**'d forgotten** to carry an umbrella.
When I <u>arrived</u> at the station, Sam **had** already **left**.
Olga <u>said</u> / <u>believed</u> / <u>thought</u> that Bob **had packed** the suitcase.

Check Up

1 밑줄 친 표현에 유의하여, 다음 문장을 해석하시오.

(1) ⓐ She asked me, "What <u>did</u> you <u>do</u>?"
    ⓑ She asked me, "What <u>have</u> you <u>done</u>?"
(2) ⓐ They <u>reported</u> the situation to the President last Monday.
    ⓑ They <u>have</u> always <u>reported</u> the situation to the President on Mondays.
(3) ⓐ The TV show <u>began</u> when I <u>got</u> home.
    ⓑ The TV show <u>had begun</u> when I <u>got</u> home.
(4) ⓐ <u>Were</u> you disappointed that you <u>didn't receive</u> a better grade?
    ⓑ <u>Were</u> you disappointed that you <u>hadn't received</u> a better grade?

2 현재완료와 과거 시제를 사용하여 문장을 완성하시오.

(1) A: Can you speak Chinese well?
    B: No, not really. I _____ (study) it just for a few weeks.
(2) Tommy _____ (know) her since childhood and is going to marry her.
(3) A: What movie _____ (you, get) from the shop?
    B: **"Titanic"**. Have you seen it?
    A: No, I _____ (not, see) it. Let's watch it now.
(4) Jane and Kevin _____ (be) in the same class three years ago.
(5) Seoul is one of the most exciting cities that we _____ (ever, visit).
(6) Nell is never interested in music. No wonder* she _____ (not, be) inside a concert hall.

3 과거완료와 과거 시제를 사용하여 문장을 완성하시오.

(1) A: Did you meet Fiona at the party?
    B: No. She _____ (go) home when I _____ (arrive).
(2) According to his statement, it _____ (not, rain) there for months.
(3) Jill _____ (be) a fire officer before she _____ (become) a plumber*.
(4) A: Why didn't you come yesterday?
    B: My son _____ (be) sick all day, so we had to stay at home.
(5) The carpet on the floor _____ (wear) out because we _____ (not, be) careful with it.
(6) Robin felt very cold. He _____ (wonder) who _____ (leave) the window open.
(7) Jake was late. The teacher _____ (already, call) the roll* when he _____ (get) to class.
(8) They _____ (tell) us that they _____ (not, take) part in the contest before.

4 **Speak-out** 다음 우리말을 영어로 세 번씩 말하시오.

(1) A: 당신은 눈을 본 적이 있습니까?
    B: 지난 1월, 제 인생에서 처음으로 눈을 보았습니다.
(2) A: 3년 전에는 어디서 사셨나요?
    B: London에서 살았습니다.
(3) A: 푸른색 새 스웨터를 산 이후에 몇 번이나 그걸 입었니?
    B: 지난 달 동생 결혼식에서 한 번 입었어.
(4) A: Charlie가 오늘 아침부터 네게 네 번이나 전화를 했단다.
    B: 언제 전화를 했었는데요?
    A: 9:10, 10:25, 11:30, 그리고 1:50에 전화를 했어.

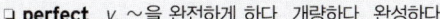

❏ **perfect** v. ~을 완전하게 하다, 개량하다, 완성하다
❏ **no wonder (that)** 'It is no wonder (that) ~' 과 같은 표현으로서 '~인 것은 조금도 이상하지 않다, 놀랄 일이 아니다' 라
고 해석한다.
❏ **plumber** [plʌ́mər] n. (수도, 가스 등의) 배관공, 연관공
❏ **call the roll** 출석을 부르다 / roll n. 출석부

12-3 진행 시제

진행 시제는 말하는 시점 이전부터 말하는 시점 이후까지 계속되고 있는 연속성을 나타낸다. 특히, 말하는 순간에 행동이 이루어지고 있음을 강조하는 어감을 느껴 보는 것이 중요하다. 또한 현재와 현재진행, 과거와 과거진행 시제의 의미 차이를 느껴 보는 것도 필요하다.

1 현재진행: be(현재형)+~ing

My grandfather **is making** a garden* right now.
They **are looking** into each other's eyes.
My sister **is** always **complaining** about trifles*.
▸ Always, constantly 등의 부사와 함께 불평이나 불만스런 감정을 표현한다.

Do you think they **are being** silly?   현재 바보 같이 군다는 표현
Do you think they **are** silly?   원래 바보 같다는 표현

2 과거진행: be(과거형)+~ing

■ 어떤 동작이나 상황이 말하고자 하는 과거의 시점 전후에 진행 중이었음을 나타낸다.

The light **turned** off all of a sudden while he **was reading** a book.
Sara **was walking** there when the accident **happened**.

3 미래진행: will be +~ing

■ 미래의 특정 시점에 벌어지고 있을 행동을 나타낸다.

This time tomorrow she **will be walking** along the Thames.
During the summer we **will be developing** the programs.

■ 미래와 미래진행
Can I call you then?
– Yes, I'**ll stay** at the office.   상대방의 말을 들은 뒤, 사무실에 있겠다는 뜻
– Yes, I'**ll be staying** at the office.   원래 그 시간에 사무실에 있을 예정이었다는 뜻

4 진행 시제가 불가능한 동사들 ◦LOOK

■ 일반적으로 감정·심리(mind), 소유(ownership), 감각(sense) 등 '상태를 나타내는 동사'의 경우 진행형을 사용하면 의미가 어색해질 수 있다.

know, understand, believe, remember, think, love, hate, like, appreciate, need, want / own, have, possess, belong / see, recognize, seem, appear, resemble, smell, taste 등

▶ 상태를 나타내는 동사라고 하여도 능동적인 상태의 변화(changing states), 의도적인 동작(deliberate actions)을 나타낼 때에는 진행 시제가 가능하다.

I **love** you.   I'm **loving** you.
He's rude.   He's **being** rude.
The food **tastes** good.   The food **is tasting** better and better. (음식이 점점 맛이 나고 있다)

Check Up

1 둘 중 알맞은 표현을 고르고, 큰 소리로 세 번씩 말하시오.

(1) Look at the airplane up in the sky. It (moves, is moving) very quickly.
(2) I (don't have, am not having) any kinds of sweets this week. I'm on a diet.
(3) Please, (answer, be answering) the phone. I (take, am taking) a bath.
(4) How about turning down the volume? It (is, is being) late, and other people (sleep, are sleeping).
(5) When I (ate, was eating) breakfast, I (memorized, was memorizing) new words.
(6) He just (ran, was running) around while I (got, was getting) dinner on the table.
(7) When the phone rang, Bill (slept, was sleeping) late and (dreamed, was dreaming) about video games.
(8) While the farmer (harvested, was harvesting) crops, a stranger (approached, was approaching) him.
(9) It (is raining, will be raining) all through the next weekend.
(10) Sam (was appearing, will be appearing) on a talk show this afternoon.

2   **Speak-out** 다음 우리말을 영어로 세 번씩 말하시오.

(1) 네게 무슨 일이 일어날지도 모른다.
(2) 문 뒤에서 무슨 일이 일어나고 있다.
(3) 유럽 여행을 하는 동안 나는 건축에 관심을 갖게 되었다.
(4) 누군가 들어오는 소리를 들었을 때 그는 아내에게 이야기를 하던 중이었다.

❏ **make a garden** 정원을 가꾸다, 정원을 만들다   ❏ **trifle** [tráifl] n. 시시한 일, 하찮은 일, 소액, 푼돈

12-4 시제의 일치

"Elvis는 Tina의 노래를 좋아한다고 말했다."에서와 같이 한국어에서는 주절의 시제가 과거일 때 종속절의 시제가 현재라고 하여도 의미 전달에 문제가 없다. 그러나 한국어와는 달리 영어에서는 주절과 종속절의 시제 관계가 매우 중요하다. 기본적으로 영어에서는 종속절의 시제가 주절의 시제와 같지만 의미에 따라 다양한 변형이 가능한데, 주절의 시제가 무엇이냐에 따라 가능한 종속절 시제의 종류가 한정된다. e-Grammar에서 '화법' 관련사항을 참고하자.

1 시제의 일치

■ 주절과 종속절을 포함한 문장에서 종속절의 시제는 주절의 시제에 따라 제약을 받는다.

주절 시제	종속절 시제
현재 또는 미래일 때	(논리적 관계가 성립된다면) 모든 시제 가능
과거일 때	과거 또는 과거완료

He **likes** steak, while his wife **prefers** fish. 　　　　　현재 – 현재
Sally **promises** that she **won't be** late again. 　　　　　현재 – 미래
I **have played** chess because my dad **plays**. 　　　　　현재완료 – 현재

The seven dwarves* **will do** whatever she **wants**. 　　　　미래 – 현재
You'll **realize** that you **have been** in love with her. 　　　미래 – 현재완료
I'm **going to be working** all day tomorrow, so I **won't have** time to shop.
　　　　　　　　　　　　　　　　　　　　　　　　　　　　미래진행 – 미래

I **heard** that he **was** a skillful mechanic. 　　　　　　　　과거 – 과거
We **were tired** because we **had been working** all day. 　　과거 – 과거완료진행
When I **began** watching the movie, I **remembered** that I **had seen** it before.
　　　　　　　　　　　　　　　　　　　　　　　　과거 – 과거, 과거 – 과거완료

2 주의해야 할 시제 표현

■ 종속절의 내용이 지속적인 사실, 습관, 진리를 나타낼 때에는 항상 현재 시제를 쓴다.
■ 시간, 조건을 나타내는 부사절에서는 항상 현재 시제가 미래 시제를 대신한다. (Ch.16-3 참고)

Dad **told** us a life in the service of others **is worth*** living.
The religion **orginated** in the city of Mecca, which **lies** near the Red Sea.
I **will go** abroad to find a job *when* this school year **finishes**.
Sam **will be** home at 7 o'clock today *if* he **starts** on time.

Check Up

1 알맞은 표현을 골라 문장을 완성하시오.

(1) Alice told me she (finds, found, will find) a very good job.
(2) When I (see, saw, will see) an ambulance outside, I knew something was wrong.
(3) She read in the book that George Washington (is, was, will be) the first president of the U.S.
(4) My friend will jump up and down when he (hears, heard, will hear) the news.
(5) Do you know Japan (is, was, will be) bombed twice with an atom bomb in 1945?
(6) You will sleep better at night if you (stop, stopped, will stop) drinking coffee.
(7) Jill will get bored if she (doesn't change, didn't change, won't change) her job soon.
(8) You'll feel good when you (get, got, will get) up early in the morning.

2 다음 문장이 바르게 쓰였으면 O표를 하고, 잘못 쓰였으면 ×표를 하시오.

_____ (1) Sam says he usually goes to church on Sundays.
_____ (2) Tina put on sweaters because it is so cold yesterday.
_____ (3) Mike and Kate think that they've done enough for today.
_____ (4) Debbie[débi] swears by the moon that she is always with him.
_____ (5) She learned from a biology class that frogs slept in winter.
_____ (6) They are planning to go on a world cruise if they win the lottery someday.
_____ (7) Sunlight left the sun's surface eight minutes before we see it.
_____ (8) Have you thought about whether you'll continue to study or get a job when you will graduate from college?

❏ **dwarf** [dwɔːrf] *n.* 난쟁이, 소인
❏ **worth** [wəːrθ] *adj.* ~할 가치가 있는, ~해 볼 만한 / Worth 는 항상 서술적 용법으로 사용되며 그 뒤에 (대)명사, 동명사구를 동반한다. (이러한 특성 때문에 worth를 전치사로 분류하기도 함)
ex. It is not worth a straw. (한 푼의 값어치도 없다)
It is not worth doing at all.

Grammar Review

1 다음 문장이 바르게 쓰였으면 O표를 하고, 잘못 쓰였으면 ×표를 하시오.

_____ (1) It was not safe to talk on the phone when you are driving the car.
_____ (2) Since 1994, the winter Olympic games is held every two years.
_____ (3) Samantha[səmǽnθə] said she bites her nails when she is nervous.
_____ (4) When Napoleon lost the war with Russia in 1812, he is sent to St. Helena.
_____ (5) After they will clear the house, living conditions will begin to improve.

2 다음 질문에 대한 적절한 답을 완전한 문장으로 말하시오.

(1) When will the football season begin in Korea?
  ➭ _____

(2) Have you visited any interesting places recently?
  ➭ _____

(3) What were you doing when I called you last night?
  ➭ _____

3 다음 글을 읽고, 빈 칸에 들어갈 알맞은 표현을 고르시오.

Mines are necessary to society. As long as people have been using metal tools, (1) _____ mines, and there will surely be mines in the future as well.
 Ⓐ there have been Ⓑ there has been

But as necessary as mines are, they are also very dangerous to the environment. Every day, (2) _____ dangerous chemicals into our environment. Most of
 Ⓐ mines are released Ⓑ mines are releasing

this pollution comes from mines that are no longer operating. When a mine shuts down, the mining company no longer makes any money from it. While the mining company (3) _____ to keep the mine clean up to that point,
 Ⓐ has paid Ⓑ had paid

they won't want to continue to pay to clean up the mine because they get nothing out of it. Without anyone to keep it clean, the mine will start releasing chemicals into the ground and into the water. Abandoned mines like this (4) _____ our environment far into the future.
 Ⓐ will be pollute Ⓑ will be polluting

Grammar Up

Time Limit: 6 min, _____ / 18

어법상 빈 칸에 들어갈 알맞은 표현을 고르시오.

1 I _____ when I saw her in a restaurant.
  (A) was surprised
  (B) surprised
  (C) to be surprised
  (D) will be surprise

2 Insects _____ huge amounts of crops every year.
  (A) have consumed
  (B) consume
  (C) they are consuming
  (D) they consumed

3 Pip _____ the Statue of Liberty in New York three years ago.
  (A) visits
  (B) will visit
  (C) visited
  (D) is visiting

4 He _____ about time while he is with Kate.
  (A) forgets
  (B) has forgotten
  (C) and forgets
  (D) forgetting

5 When Phil bought a new book, _____ his name on the back of it.
  (A) signing
  (B) to sign
  (C) he is signed
  (D) he signed

6 Discord between the two families _____ for over ten years.
  (A) it lasted
  (B) but to last
  (C) has lasted
  (D) have lasted

7 In the 1972 Olympics, Mark Spitz _____ a record seven gold medals.
(A) to win
(B) winning
(C) winner
(D) won

8 Leaf-cutting ants _____ their nests under the ground.
(A) built
(B) they built
(C) build
(D) they build

어법상 잘못된 부분을 고르시오.

9 The police still not have found the murder weapon.
  (A)   (B) (C)   (D)

10 The people in the store were buy groceries.
  (A) (B)   (C) (D)

11 That tree has stand there since my grandparents were little.
      (A)   (B)   (C) (D)

12 Yesterday one of my friend's dogs biting me, and I went to hospital.
        (A)   (B) (C)   (D)

13 Peter worked at a furniture store for ages, but now was a taxi driver.
        (A)   (B) (C) (D)

14 Our director, who reached 65 next year, intends to retire.
 (A)   (B)   (C) (D)

15 Mike felt sorry to have losing touch with some of his childhood friends.
         (A)   (B) (C)   (D)

16 When the telephone rang, Joan was listened to music.
 (A) (B)   (C)   (D)

17 They had to choice between leaving early and paying for a taxi.
      (A)   (B)   (C)   (D)

18 Throughout time, maps have be important to people around the world.
  (A)   (B)   (C) (D)

CHAPTER 13

조동사
_Modal Verbs

13-1 조동사의 개념, 역할 및 종류

조동사는 8품사의 항목에 없다. 이처럼 중요한 역할을 하는 단어가 왜 정식 품사의 항목에 이름을 올리지 못했는지 놀랍기만 하다. 일반적으로 조동사를 Helping Verbs(Auxiliary* Verbs)라고도 하지만, 전문 용어로는 Modal* Verbs(Modal Auxiliaries)라고 한다. Modal은 mood, mode, attitude*에서 유래된 말로 '동사의 분위기를 나타내는(expressing mood of a verb)'을 뜻한다. 조동사는 동사가 아니다. 조동사는 주어(행동의 실행자)의 행동(동사)에 포함된 태도, 분위기를 전달한다.

1 조동사의 개념

- 조동사가 없는 문장은 사실을 표현한다. Modal Verbs가 있는 문장은 말하는 사람의 attitude, mood, mode(태도와 분위기)와 같은 주관적인 생각, 감정을 전달한다.
- 조동사의 유무에 따른 문장의 의미 차이를 느끼며 영어를 학습하면 언어 감각을 높이는데 큰 도움이 된다.

  I go to church on Sundays. 일요일마다 교회에 간다는 습관 및 사실
  I **must** go to church on Sundays. 일요일마다 교회에 가야만 한다는 결의에 찬 태도 포함

2 조동사의 종류와 역할

- 2군 조동사: 기능적 역할 담당 – do, have, be
- 1군 조동사: 기능적, 의미적 역할 담당 – will, would, may, should, ought to 등
- 유사 조동사(구 형태의 조동사) – be going to, have to, used to, would rather 등

  ▶ 1, 2군 조동사를 함께 쓸 때에는 1군 조동사를 앞에 놓는다.
  ▶ 1군 조동사는 하나만 써야 하지만, 2군 조동사는 두 개 이상 함께 쓸 수 있다.
  ex. They **may have to** give up their rights. (may must는 틀림)

- <u>의미적 역할</u> 조동사 학습은 의미적 역할에 집중된다.
  ① 조동사의 의미(필요, 충고, 능력, 허가 등)와 관련된 화자의 '태도, 기분'을 표현한다.
  ② 조동사가 포함된 문장은 사실만을 나타내는 것이 아니므로, '확실성의 정도(degrees of certainty)'에 관한 의미가 포함되기도 한다.

- <u>기능적 역할</u> 태, 진행형, 시제, 부정문, 의문문, 강조의 문장을 만든다.

  Michel, I love you. → Michel, I **do** love you!
  You'**ll have been** teaching for twenty years next year, **won't** you?

  ▶ 술어전체(Complete Verbs): 조동사와 동사를 합하여 술어전체라고 한다.

Check Up

1 조동사를 찾아 그 종류(1군, 2군 조동사)를 구별하시오.

(1) Children under seven may enter the zoo for free.
(2) Are you sure that he has never been in jail*?
(3) An important policy should be announced in advance*.
(4) She must have had some difficulty adjusting* to a new environment.

2 다음 문장이 바르게 쓰였으면 O표를 하고, 잘못 쓰였으면 ×표를 하시오.

_____ (1) It is cold outside, so we should wore jackets.
_____ (2) Everyone cans enjoy this board game.
_____ (3) His theory be will proved wrong soon.
_____ (4) The documents may be not read without permission.
_____ (5) You should be careful when you cross the road.
_____ (6) You'll can find out the answer at the end of this course.

3 주어진 조동사를 넣어 문장을 다시 쓰고, 원래 문장의 의미와 비교하시오.

(1) Simon buys a limousine. (will)
   ➪ _____

(2) The man is a gardener at the white house. (may)
   ➪ _____

(3) Is the box wrapped*? (must)
   ➪ _____

(4) You see the mountains from here on a clear day. (can)
   ➪ _____

 comments

- **auxiliary** [ɔːgzíljəri] *n.* 보조자, 원조자, 조동사
- **modal** [móudl] *adj.* 법(mood)의, 형태상의, 형식의, 양식의
- **mood** [muːd] *n.* 심리 상태, 감정, 기분, 분위기
- **mode** [moud] *n.* 양식, 방법, 형태, 법(mood)
- **attitude** [ǽtitjùːd] *n.* 태도, 마음가짐, 견해, 자세
- **jail** [dʒeil] *n.* 감옥, 구치소
- **in advance** 미리, 앞에, 선금으로, 전방에, 선두에 서서
- **adjust** [ədʒʌ́st] *v.* 조절하다, 조화시키다, 맞추다
- **wrap** [ræp] *v.* (덮어) 싸다, 감추다

13-2 Degrees of Certainty

조동사가 포함된 문장은 기본적으로 화자의 태도, 분위기를 표현하므로 사실(fact) 표현보다는 추측이나 가능성(possibility)을 표현하는 경우가 많다. 강한 의미를 나타내는 조동사는 가능성이 높아 보인다.

1 현재 사실에 대한 추측

■ 화자가 현재의 어떤 사실에 대해 확신하는 정도(degrees of certainty)가 100%일 때에는 사실(fact)을 나타내는 현재형을 쓴다. 한편, 조동사를 사용하면 조동사가 갖는 의미에 따라 화자의 확신 정도를 다르게 표현할 수 있다. 다음 예문을 반복해서 말함으로써 감각을 익히도록 하자.

긍정	확신 정도	부정
My dog **is** happy.	100%	His cat **isn't** full.
	99%	His cat **couldn't be** full. His cat **can't be** full.
My dog **must be** happy.	95%	His cat **must not be** full.
My dog **may be** happy. My dog **might be** happy. My dog **could be** happy.	50%이하	His cat **may not be** full. His cat **might not be** full.

▶ Could의 경우에는 부정적 추측일 때와 긍정적 추측일 때 그 확신 정도가 다른 것에 주의한다!
▶ Could, might은 각각 can, may의 과거형이기도 하지만, 그 자체로 현재 시제의 조동사(추측의 의미)로 사용되는 경우가 더 많다. (Would도 마찬가지임)
▶ '미래'의 확신 정도(긍정)를 나타낼 때에는 must 대신에 should, ought to를 쓴다.
 ex. She **should** / **ought to** do well on the contest.

2 과거 사실에 대한 추측

■ 과거의 어떤 사실(확신 100%)을 표현할 때에는 과거형을 쓴다. 그 외에는 화자의 확신 정도에 따라 '조동사+have p.p.' 형태를 사용한다.

긍정	확신 정도	부정
Ann **was** kind.	100%	Tom **wasn't** sad.
	99%	Tom **couldn't have been** sad. Tom **can't have been** sad.
Ann **must have been** kind.	95%	Tom **must not have been** sad.
Ann **may have been** kind. Ann **might have been** kind. Ann **could have been** kind.	50%이하	Tom **may not have been** sad. Tom **might not have been** sad.

▶ 'Might have p.p.'와 'could have p.p.'는 가정법 형태로서 '(과거에) ~할 수 있었을 텐데'라는 의미를 갖는다. 그러나 상황에 따라 화자의 확신 정도가 약하거나 '~할 수 있었지만 하지 않았다'는 뜻을 나타내기도 한다.
 ex. I **could have called** her, but I didn't.

▸ 'Should have p.p.'는 과거에 하지 못한 것에 대한 아쉬움, 후회를 표현한다.
　ex. I **should have discussed** the problem with you. (당신과 상의했어야 했는데)

Check Up

1 주어진 상황을 읽고, 추측하는 문장을 완성하여 세 번씩 말하시오. (현재 사실에 대한 추측)

SITUATION INFORMATION	There is a blue car parked outside. I wonder who came home. **Daddy** drives a blue car. **Mommy** drives a yellow car. **Sue** also drives a blue car and visits occasionally.

(1)　It must be _____　　　It couldn't be _____
　　It might be _____

SITUATION INFORMATION	Look out the window. The window is wet. The sky is blue, and it is not **raining**. **The garden hose** is turned on. **The sprinkler*** turns on automatically at different times of the day.

(2)　It must be _____　　　It couldn't be _____
　　It could be _____

2 주어진 상황을 읽고, 추측하는 문장을 완성하여 세 번씩 말하시오. (과거 사실에 대한 추측)

SITUATION INFORMATION	Someone ate my apple. I wondered who ate it. **The dog** was sleeping on the couch. **The hamster** was out of the cage. **The cat** was licking* its face.

(1)　It must be _____　　　It couldn't be _____
　　It might be _____

SITUATION INFORMATION	My blue jacket was gone. I wondered who borrowed it. **Fred** is too big to wear my jacket. **Jake** likes to wear my clothes. **Sam** wears the same size as I do.

(2)　It must be _____　　　It couldn't be _____
　　It could be _____

❏ **sprinkler** [sprínklər]　*n.* 물 뿌리는 장치, 물 뿌리는 사람　　❏ **lick** [lik]　*v.* ~을 핥다, 핥아 먹다

13-3 필요, 조언, 의무, 책임

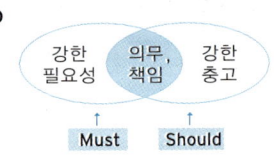

Must와 should는 그림에서 보듯이 서로 다른 뜻을 나타내는 동시에 비슷한 뜻을 나타내기도 한다. 따라서, 구별하여 쓰기도 하고 혼용하여 쓰기도 한다. Must는 necessity, should는 advisability가 기본 정의이다. 즉, must는 '피할 수 없는 상황'을 should는 '피할 수는 있지만, 해야 좋은 상황'을 표현한다. 기본적으로 둘의 의미 차이를 확실히 이해해야 하지만 일상회화에서는 엄격하게 구분하지 않고 사용하기도 한다.

1 Necessity*, Obligation* [필요*, 의무, 책임]

■ 학습 조동사 must, have to, have got to*

You **must** / **have to** / **need to** pay back your debts before next month.
Ken **had to** drop by* a supermarket to buy some groceries on his way home.
Must you play the music so loudly? It's 1:30 a.m.
He(**'s**) **gotta** score* an A on this test to pass the course.   ('s gotta = have got to)

▸ Must는 과거형이 없으므로 had to로 대체하여 사용한다. (Have to는 '추측'의 의미로 사용하지 않는다.)

■ Must는 기본적으로 '필요' 외에도 '추측'을 표현한다.

A: I'm coughing and sneezing, blowing my nose, and running a fever.
B: Well, you **must** have a bad cold. You'd better go and see a doctor.

■ must have p.p. : '(과거에 대한) 논리적 결론, 강한 추측'을 표현한다.

A: I grew up in the Amazon jungle.
B: Really? You **must have had** fun we can't imagine.

2 must의 부정 [금지 vs. 필요성의 부정]

■ 학습 조동사 must not ≠ don't have to, don't need to

금지	We **must not** / **mustn't** read them.	(~해서는 안 된다)
강한 필요	We **must** / **have to** / **need to** read all the books Dr. Hall mentioned to us.	
필요 부정	We **don't have to** / **don't need to** do it.	(~할 필요가 없다)

▸ Have to는 조동사의 일종으로 취급하지만, need to에서 need는 일반동사이다.
▸ British English에서는 need가 부정문에서 조동사로 쓰이기도 한다.
  ex. They **needn't** know where I am.
   You **needn't** worry.

3 Advisability*, Obligation [충고*, 의무, 책임]

- 학습 조동사: should, ought (not) to, had better (not), should (not) have p.p.

They **should** / **ought to** / **had better** watch what they are doing more closely.
Drivers **shouldn't** / **oughtn't (to)** / **had better not** phone when they are driving.

▸ Ought to는 부정문, 의문문에서는 잘 쓰이지 않는다. (부정문에서는 to를 생략하기도 함)
▸ 조언 : should, ought to ↔ had better : 경고

I **should have bought** apples while I was at the grocery store. (~했어야 했는데)

▸ Should는 자체적으로 과거형이 없으며, 'should have p.p.' 형태를 사용하여 '과거에 실행하지 못한 일에 대한 후회와 유감'의 뜻을 나타낸다.

4 had better vs. would rather

- would rather, would prefer는 '선호'의 뜻을 나타낸다.

I have to look after my sisters, so I'**d rather** stay at home.   (= would prefer to stay)
Kids **would rather** play than study.   (= prefer to play rather than study, prefer playing to sudying)

▸ would rather, would perfer는 1인칭 주어와 함께, had better는 2, 3인칭 주어와 함께 쓰이는 경우가 많다.
　ex. I'**d rather** go fishing.   　You'**d better** stay at home.

5 should vs. must

- Must는 '피할 수 없는 상황'을, should는 '피할 수는 있지만 해야 좋은 상황'을 표현
- Must류는 지시하는(받는) 느낌이 강하고, should류는 조언하는(받는) 느낌이 강하다.

Men **must** serve in the army in Korea.
You **should** go and see the movie, *Gone with the Wind.* It's a great film.

Check Up

1 둘 중 알맞은 표현을 골라 문장을 완성하시오.

(1) I'm feeling sick. I (must, get) go to hospital.
(2) Think about why you (must, have) to study hard first.
(3) The computer (must, has) be switched off before we leave the lab.
(4) You (should, had) practice writing every day.
(5) The battery (had, ought) to be changed once a month.
(6) They (had, ought) better put off their departure till tomorrow.

2 🔵 Speak-out 다음 우리말을 영어로 옮겨 큰 소리로 세 번씩 말하시오.

(1) 당신은 그의 담장에 대해 무슨 말을 해야만 합니다.
→ _____

(2) 당신은 추가 비용(additional costs)을 지불해야만 할 것입니다.
→ _____

(3) 당신은 코트를 입을 필요가 없습니다.
→ _____

(4) 사냥꾼들은 허가 없이 사슴을 죽이면 안됩니다.
→ _____

3 빈 칸에 들어갈 알맞은 표현을 보기에서 고르고, 완성된 문장의 의미를 느끼며 세 번씩 말하시오.

보기 | should have been   shouldn't have eaten
      shouldn't have listened   should have spent

(1) Robbie _____ to Jack. He has a big mouth*.
(2) Probably it was an accident, but she _____ more watchful.
(3) We're out of money now. We _____ our money more carefully.
(4) Harry has a bad toothache. He _____ so much chocolate.

4 🔵 Speak-out Should/Had better를 사용하여 상황에 맞는 충고의 문장을 만들어 큰 소리로 세 번씩 말하시오.

(1) Cindy is really a late riser. Advise her not to sleep late.
→ _Cindy_ _____

(2) Many people are hurt by what Alex said. Advise him to be careful with his words.
→ _____

(3) It is very dangerous for kids not to wear their seatbelts. Advise parents to make their children wear their seatbelts in the car.
→ _____

---

comments

❑ **necessity** [nəsésəti] n. 필요성, 필요한 일, 필연적인 일
❑ **obligation** [àbləgéiʃən] n. 의무, 구속, 책임, 책무
❑ **advisability** [ædvàizəbíləti] n. 타당성, 권할 만함, 옳은 그름
❑ **필요**(must) (매우 필요하기 때문에) ~해야만 한다 / 따라서 '의무, 책임'의 의미를 나타낸다.
❑ **충고**(should) (강력히 충고하므로) ~해야만 한다 / 따라서 '의무, 책임'의 의미도 나타낸다.
❑ **have got to** Have got to는 Writing에서는 사용하지 않는다.

현재 시제에서만 쓰이며, ('ve) gotta [gátə]와 같이 have의 부분이 매우 약하게 발음되므로 종종 have를 생략해 버리기도 한다.

❑ **drop by** (예고 없이, informally) 잠깐 들르다 (by는 전치사) /
She and Danny will **drop by** later. (by는 부사)
❑ **score** v. (~의 점수를) 얻다(= gain, get), 점수를 매기다
ex. She **scored** 100 in the final test.   (100점을 받았다)
    They **are scoring** the test.   (점수를 매기고 있다)
❑ **have a big mouth** 입이 가볍다, 말이 많다

13-4 능력, 허가, 부탁, 제안

● 기본적으로 can은 ability(능력)를 나타내고 may는 permission(허가)을 나타낸다. Can은 '~할 수 있다, 해도 된다'는 뜻에서도 보듯이 '가능성'의 의미도 포함하고 '허가'의 의미도 느낄 수 있다. 현대 영어에서는 '허가'의 의미로 can과 may가 전혀 차이 없이 쓰이지만, may의 뜻을 엄격하게 구별하는 사람들도 있으므로 공손하게 허가의 뜻을 표현할 때에는 may를 쓰도록 한다.

1 Ability, Possibility : can, be able to

She **can** read Latin* even though she is only four.
She **couldn't / was unable to** read or write when she left school at 17.
They **seemed able to** work together efficiently.
One *should* **be able to** lower oneself.   (should can: ×)
Being able to speak English is a requirement for the job.   (Canning: ×)

▶ Be able to는 형식적인(formal) 느낌이 강하므로 일상회화에서 현재 시제를 표현할 때에는 많이 사용하지 않는다.

■ Could는 can의 과거형으로 쓰이기도 하지만,
  could 자체가 현재의 추측, 확실성의 정도를 나타내거나 ex. He **could be** very lonely.
  'could have p.p.'의 형태로 과거의 추측을 나타내거나 ex. He **could have been** very lonely.
  couldn't가 불가능성(impossibility)을 나타내기도 한다.   ex. He **couldn't be** very lonely.

■ Could가 현재인지 혹은 과거인지, 어떠한 뜻을 나타내는지는 문맥의 흐름을 통해 쉽게 파악할 수 있다.

We **could** do a great deal in our country to educate people.

▶ 위의 문장은 과거의 능력(~할 수 있었다) 또는 현재의 가능성(~할 수 있을 거야)의 의미로 해석할 수 있다. '~할 수 있었다'의 의미를 정확히 전달하기 위해서는 were able to를 써야 한다.

Pop Quiz 다음 문장에서 could가 나타내는 시제가 무엇인지 고르고 해석하시오.

현재☐ 과거☐ (1) My dog **could** be happy.
현재☐ 과거☐ (2) She **could** stand by herself when she was only one year old.
현재☐ 과거☐ (3) We **could** see the sun rise over the horizon.
현재☐ 과거☐ (4) My old car **couldn't** hold six persons.
현재☐ 과거☐ (5) His invention was helpful to those who **couldn't** hear.
현재☐ 과거☐ (6) Sam **couldn't** be hungry.
현재☐ 과거☐ (7) Sam **couldn't** have been hungry
현재☐ 과거☐ (8) The company said they **could** have kept the quality competitive.

2 공손한 부탁 [polite request]

- 주어가 1인칭인 경우

    <u>May / Can / Could</u> I use the phone?

    ▸ 'Might I ~' 도 가능하지만 지나치게 형식적인 표현이므로 거의 사용하지 않는다.

- 주어가 2인칭인 경우 (상대방의 허가를 구함)

    <u>Will / Would / Can / Could</u> you help us lift this couch?
    <u>Would / Do</u> you mind if I open the door?
    <u>Would / Do</u> you mind opening the door?

3 허가 [permission]

- You **may / can** read this story book.
    Anyone who loves taking pictures **may / can** join our club.
    Only those who have a ticket **are allowed to / are permitted to** enter the theater.

    ▸ 엄격히 말해 허가를 나타낼 때에는 may를 사용해야 하지만 일상회화에서는 may와 can이 혼용된다. 그러나 기초 학습 단계에서는 may를 사용하는 연습을 하도록 하자.

4 제안 [suggestion]

- **Let's** always hang out* together, shall we?
    I'm totally exhausted. **Let's not / Don't let's** go dancing. *Let's의 부정*
    You look tired. **Why don't** you take a day off?
    Shall we go? (이제 그만 갈까요?) / **Shall we** dance?

5 **used to, would:** (현재와 비교하여) 예전엔 그랬지

- **used to**   과거의 습관적인 '행동' 및 '상황' (일상회화에서 주로 사용)
    would   과거의 습관적인 '행동' 만 표현

    I **used to / would** keep a diary in English in my high school days.
    I **used to / would** drink beer; now I drink wine.
    There **used to** be a lot of tigers in Korea.   *현재는 호랑이가 거의 없음*
    There **were** a lot of tigers in Korea.   *과거 사실만을 전달할 뿐 현재 상황은 알 수 없음*

- **be used to + (동)명사: '~에 익숙해져 있다'** (be동사 대신 get, become 사용 가능)

    You should try to **get used to** getting up early.   *(일찍 일어나는데 익숙해지다)*

6 상황과 어투에 따른 조동사의 선택

My teacher said that I **had to** see a doctor.   Giving Advice

▶ 언어란 표현하는 방법과 상황 등에 따라 그 의미와 강도가 달라진다. 따라서, 전달 방법에 따라 must, need to, have to / should, ought to, had better / could, might 등이 유사한 분위기로 '조언'의 뜻을 전달할 수 있다.

Check Up

1 [조동사의 현재형·과거형 종합] 빈 칸에 알맞은 표현을 넣으시오.

현재형	의미	과거형
will	future / willingness / request	(1)
would	request / preference / repeated action in the past	would have p.p.
can	ability, possibility	could
could	request	×
	certainty (50% ↓)	(2)
may	polite request / permission	(3)
	certainty (50% ↓)	may have p.p.
might	certainty (50% ↓)	might have p.p.
must	necessity / obligation	×
	certainty (95%)	(4)
should	advisability	(5)
	obligation	×

2 'd는 had 또는 would가 축약된 형태이다. 다음 문장에서 'd가 무엇인지 밝히시오.

_____ (1) I think you'd better send the files as soon as possible.
_____ (2) She'd rather buy some apples than some bananas.
_____ (3) He'd always climb up the tree when he was a little boy.
_____ (4) You'd better not carry your pet dog to a public place.
_____ (5) He'd give me a ride to my house when it rained.
_____ (6) If it's all the same to you, I'd rather work at home.
_____ (7) We'd seen it before.

3 밑줄 친 could가 나타내는 시제를 고르고 해석하시오. (Present는 Future를 포함)

Present☐ Past☐ (1) She's a little bit busy. She could be working late tonight.
Present☐ Past☐ (2) Look at the drawer*. Your keys could be in it.
Present☐ Past☐ (3) Bill could see that something was terribly wrong.
Present☐ Past☐ (4) He was jailed two years ago and could be released next month.
Present☐ Past☐ (5) No one could understand that Ellen preferred to be alone.
Present☐ Past☐ (6) The boy couldn't have been more than fourteen years old.

4 두 문장의 의미가 유사하면 S(same)를 쓰고, 다르면 D(different)를 쓰시오.

(1) _____ ⓐ May I play the harmonica over there?
　　　　　　ⓑ Can I play the harmonica over there?
(2) _____ ⓐ Mr. Brown used to live in Florida.
　　　　　　ⓑ Mr. Brown would live in Florida.
(3) _____ ⓐ Let's go out to eat.
　　　　　　ⓑ Shall we go out to eat?

5 ▸Speak-out 다음 우리말을 영어로 옮겨 큰 소리로 세 번씩 말하시오.

(1) 물 좀 마셔도 될까요?
　　➡ _____
(2) 창문 좀 닫아 주시겠습니까?
　　➡ _____
(3) 그는 배가 고프지 않음에 틀림없다.
　　➡ _____
(4) 그는 돈이 많지 않음에 틀림없다.
　　➡ _____
(5) 청소년(adolescent*)은 담배나 술을 살 수 없습니다.
　　➡ _____
(6) 그들을 추수감사절 파티에 초대하는 게 어때요?
　　➡ _____

---

comments

☐ **Latin** [lǽtən] *n.* 라틴어/고대 로마인들이 사용했던 언어이다. 지금은 더 이상 실용 언어로 사용되지 않지만, 다른 언어에 어원으로 차용되어 쓰이는 경우가 많다. (영어의 총 어휘 중 60% 차지) 어휘와 문법이 까다롭기로 유명하여 라틴어를 공부하느라 진땀을 흘린 위인들의 재미있는 일화가 많다.

☐ **hang out** ~와 어울리다, 사귀다, 가까이 지내다 (out은 부사)
☐ **drawer** [drɔ́ːər] *n.* 서랍, 장롱
☐ **adolescent** [æ̀dəlésnt] *n.* 10대 청소년 —*adj.* 청춘의, 젊은, 청년기의, 미숙한

Grammar Review

1 두 문장의 의미가 유사하면 S(same)를 쓰고, 다르면 D(different)를 쓰시오.

(1) _____ ⓐ Martin can read and write Greek well.
ⓑ Martin is able to read and write Greek well.

(2) _____ ⓐ The actress might not have committed suicide.
ⓑ The actress couldn't have committed suicide.

(3) _____ ⓐ You should practice your drums only before 10:00 p.m.
ⓑ You ought to practice your drums only before 10:00 p.m.

2 다음 문장이 바르게 쓰였으면 ○표를 하고, 잘못 쓰였으면 ×표를 하시오.

_____ (1) The store may or not may sell batteries.
_____ (2) You had not better eat something between meals.
_____ (3) Would you mind proofread this report?
_____ (4) Pat must not have read the instructions before he proceeded.
_____ (5) We should doing something for the environment right now.

3 다음 글을 읽고, 빈 칸에 들어갈 알맞은 표현을 고르시오.

Signs must convey much information in few words. Let us see an example. Here is a road that (1) _____ be open but now is closed. At the end of the
　　　　　　　　　　　　　　　　Ⓐ would　Ⓑ used to

road is a large red sign. It says: STOP. DO NOT ENTER. Those four simple words convey a complex message. It means: "You have to stop here. You must go no farther. You (2) _____ enter, because you do not have permission.
　　　　　　　　Ⓐ may　Ⓑ may not

Of course, you can enter. But if you enter, then you will be in trouble." Someone who sees the sign thinks, "Should I enter here? No, I had better go back. The sign (3) _____ be there for a good reason, and I ought to obey its warning."
　Ⓐ must　Ⓑ has to

Do you see how much four words say? The sign's color makes the message even stronger. Red means danger. So, the red sign makes it clear that you may not, must not, should not, and (4) _____ enter here – all in just four words.
　　　　　　　　　　　　Ⓐ had not better　Ⓑ had better not

Grammar Up

Time Limit: 6 min, _____ / 18

어법상 빈 칸에 들어갈 알맞은 표현을 고르시오.

1 If you are to get there by noon, you _____ now.
- (A) start
- (B) must start
- (C) will start
- (D) must have started

2 You _____ left and right before you cross the road.
- (A) looked
- (B) could looked
- (C) should look
- (D) must have looked

3 She was embarrassed at not _____ her own address.
- (A) can remember
- (B) canning remember
- (C) be able to remember
- (D) being able to remember

4 According to the report, either he or she must _____.
- (A) be a liar
- (B) to be a liar
- (C) is a liar
- (D) being a liar

5 Jane can understand her father's thinking, but _____ agree with him.
- (A) she
- (B) cannot be
- (C) she cannot be
- (D) she cannot

6 When you catch a cold, _____ better rest at home rather than play outside.
- (A) you
- (B) you should
- (C) you should be
- (D) you had

어법상 잘못된 부분을 고르시오.

7 They all anticipated that land prices might went down further.
         (A)   (B)   (C)   (D)

8 I avoid drinking coffee because it can keeps me awake at night.
            (A)   (B)   (C)   (D)

9 Would you mind to hand me a book on the top shelf?
   (A)   (B)   (C)   (D)

10 Can I got a refund for this sweater which I bought yesterday?
         (A)   (B)   (C)   (D)

11 They never said whether or not they will returns today.
              (A)   (B)   (C)   (D)

12 This course will helps you develop your writing skills.
   (A)   (B)   (C)   (D)

13 He must was sick, for he did not come to work today.
           (A)   (B)   (C)   (D)

14 Weeds that appear in gardens should are removed before other plants suffer.
         (A) (B)   (C)   (D)

15 One can still saw holes where foundations for ancient buildings were dug.
                 (A)   (B)   (C)   (D)

16 An invitation should included your name, the date, and the time.
   (A)   (B)   (C)   (D)

17 No one can proves that something really happened billions of years ago.
   (A)   (B)   (C)   (D)

18 Our world is mostly water, as you can seeing from the map of the world.
                (A)   (B)   (C)   (D)

Grammar in Context

The Color of Lifejackets and Lifeboats

Things like lifejackets and lifeboats must be designed very carefully. Since a person's life may depend on these things, they should be made of the best possible materials. Every part of a lifejacket or lifeboat must be thought about carefully. For example, have you ever noticed that lifejackets are almost always an orange color? There's a good reason for this.

Lifejackets and lifeboats have to be made from bright colors that can be seen easily. Dark colors like brown or green are not good because they can be hard to see against the dark background of the ocean. Lifejackets used to be made from bright yellow material. This color was very easy to see in the ocean, and so the air force and the navy both used yellow lifejackets for their pilots. But they began to notice that sharks were attracted to the yellow of the lifejackets, so the pilots would call this color "yum yum yellow". Certainly nobody would want to wear something that attracted sharks, so the lifejackets were changed to orange.

174 words, Reading Time: _____

1 앞에서 세 번째 (1군) 조동사를 찾아 쓰시오.

2 뒤에서 네 번째 술어(전체)를 찾아 쓰시오. (종속절의 술어전체도 포함할 것)

3 문맥상 materials 의 의미와 가장 가까운 표현을 고르시오.
   Ⓐ clothes
   Ⓑ ideas or information
   Ⓒ solid substances
   Ⓓ things needed in a particular activity

4 **Chain of Thought:** 다음 문장을 논리적 흐름에 따라 앞에서부터 이해해 봅시다.

   (1) Lifejackets and lifeboats have to be made / from bright colors / that can be seen easily.
   ➡ 구명 조끼와 구명 보트는 만들어져야 한다 [무엇으로?/왜?] _____ [어떤 밝은 색이냐 하면]
   _____

   (2) Nobody would want / to wear something / that attracted sharks, / so / the lifejackets were changed / to orange.
   ➡ _____ _____ _____ _____ _____

규칙 1: 문장을 생각의 흐름에 따른 사고단위(Thought Unit)로 나누어 이해한다.
규칙 2: 명사 뒤에는 그 명사를 설명하는 형용사(구, 절)가 따라나올 것을 예상한다. 다른 뜻(부사구, 절)을 가진 어구가 나오면 전체 문장에 적합하도록 해석한다.
 규칙 3: 문장을 뒤에서부터 해석하려고 하면 Chain of Thought에 따른 문장 이해에 혼란이 생길 수 있으므로 각별히 주의해야 한다. 뒷부분은 모두 가리고 앞에서부터 해당 부분만을 보면서 이해하도록 한다.

CHAPTER 14

법과 가정법
_Mood and Subjunctive Mood

14-1 법과 명령법

말의 내용을 전달하는 방법(Mood, Mode, Manner)을 크게 세 가지로 분류하면 직설법(있는 그대로 전달), 명령법(일방적으로 전달), 가정법(우회적으로 전달)으로 구분할 수 있다. '직설법(Indicative* Mood*)'이란 '있는 그대로 말하는 방법(사실의 전달)'이다. 의문문과 감탄문도 직설법에 포함된다. '명령법'은 용어 자체가 강압적인 분위기를 나타내지만, 화자가 일방적으로 말하는 방법으로서 요청이나 제안과 같은 친근한 분위기를 전달하는 경우에 더 많이 쓰인다.

1 명령법[Imperative* Mood]

- 요청, 제안, 명령을 표현한다. 광고, 슬로건, 지시문 등에서도 자주 사용한다.

    Freeze!   (꼼짝 마!)
    Don't be afraid.   (걱정하지 마세요)
    Keep it away from children under 5.   (5세 이하의 어린이들의 손이 닿지 않게 보관하세요)
    It's now or never, so make up your mind.*   동등한 절에 명령문이 나오는 경우
    Do be careful before you jump out.   강조
    Do me a favor, **please**. / **Could you** do me a favor?

    ▶ 공손함을 나타내기 위해 please 또는 could you를 첨가할 수 있다.

- 부가의문문

    Give me a hand, **will you/won't you**?
    Turn down the stereo, **can't you/could you**?

    ▶ 명령문의 부가의문문은 숨겨진 주어 you의 '의향, 의지'를 물을 수 있는 will/can you?를 사용한다.
    ▶ Will/Can you? 외에 would/could/won't/can't you?를 활용하여 다양한 의미를 전달할 수 있다.
    ▶ Won't/Can't you?와 같은 부정의 부가의문문은 더 강한 감정을 표현한다.

- Let us ~* : 말하는 사람과 듣는 사람이 함께 하려는 제안

    Let's go outside. – Yes, let's. / No, let's not.
    ▶ Let us ~ 로 표현하면 형식적인(formal) 느낌이 강하다.

    Let's not lose hope. / **Don't let us** lose hope.
    Let's do it together, **shall we**?

- Let someone ~* : 제안, 요청, 허가

    Let me tell you what I saw yesterday.   (내가 어제 본 걸 들어봐)
    Let the news be known, **will you**?
    ▶ 그 뉴스가 알려지도록 내버려 두는 게 어떨까요? (= Let them know the news.)

    (You) **Don't let her** go by herself.
    ▶ 강조하기 위해 you를 삽입할 수도 있다.

Check Up

1 다음 문장이 바르게 쓰였으면 ○표를 하고, 잘못 쓰였으면 ×표를 하시오.

_____ (1) Let don't them lean out of the window.
_____ (2) Wait here for a minute, shall you?
_____ (3) Don't forget to repot your plant, will you?
_____ (4) Let's turn off all the lights except those on the Christmas tree.

2 Speak-out 다음 우리말을 영어로 옮겨 세 번씩 말하시오.

(1) 즐거운 휴가 보내세요.
(2) 우리 본심으로 돌아갑시다.
(3) 다시는 그러지 마세요, 그렇지 않으면 어려움에 처할 겁니다.
(4) 제발 이렇게 늦은 시간에 개들이 크게 짖지 않도록 해 주세요.

3 다음은 Potato Onion Sandwich를 만드는 법이다. 순서대로 나열하여 조리법을 완성하시오.

① Before it is cool, mash it up* very well. ② Spread the potato salad on bread.
③ Boil a potato for 15 minutes. ④ Mix these ingredients* well.
⑤ Add a tablespoon of mayonnaise and two tablespoons of milk.
⑥ Peel the potato and put it into a bowl.

_____ ⇨ _____ ⇨ _____ ⇨ Slice a quarter of an onion thinly and combine it with the potato. ⇨ _____ ⇨ _____ ⇨ Add salt and pepper to taste. ⇨ _____ ⇨ Enjoy your creation.

---

comments

- **indicative** [indíkətiv] *adj.* 직설법의, 나타내는, 가리키는 / **indicate** [índikèit] *v.* 가리키다, 지시를 내리다
 ex. Often physical appearance is **indicative** of how a person feels. (사람이 어떻게 느끼는지를 나타낸다)
- **mood** *n.* (동사의) 법 / **mode** (*n.* 방법, 방식)의 변형
- **imperative** [impérətiv] *adj.* 명령법의 -*n.* 명령법, 명령법의 동사
- **It's now or never, so make up your mind.** 지금이 아니면 (앞으로는) 이루어 질 수 없어요, 그러니 결심을 하세요.
- **Let us ~** 일반적으로 명령문에는 주어 you가 생략되어 있다고 여겨진다. 그러나, 'Let us ~'의 문장에서는 '나는 ~할 텐데 당신도 함께 합시다'라는 의미를 전달한다고 볼 수 있으므로 us가 행동의 실행자(주어)처럼 느껴진다. / 부가의문문을 만들 때에는 '함께 하자는 제안'을 하는 shall we?를 사용하거나, (나는 ~할 텐데) 당신도 하겠느냐를 묻는 will you?를 사용할 수 있다.
- **Let someone ~** 주어 you가 생략되어 있다고 여겨진다. 따라서 부가의문문을 만들 때 'Let's dance, shall we?'처럼 shall we?를 쓸 수 없으며, 일반 명령문과 같이 will you?를 사용해야 한다.
- **mash up** 으깨다, 짓이기다 (up은 부사)
- **ingredient** [ingríːdiənt] *n.* (혼합물의) 성분, 요소, (요리의) 재료

14-2 가정법의 기본

● 가정법(Subjunctive* Mood)이란 이룰 수 없는, 이루지 못한 일에 대한 **서글픔, 아쉬움, 안타까움, 불안감** 등을 표현한다. 대부분 if절의 내용이 가정법 문장의 핵심 내용이라고 생각하지만, if절은 단지 주변 상황을 제시할 뿐이다. 주절 즉, 주절 안의 동사가 조동사의 도움을 받아 가정법의 의미를 나타낸다는 사실을 꼭 기억하자!

1 가정법 문장 만들기

- 가정법이란 실현이 불가능함을 노골적으로 표현하지 않고 우회적으로 표현하는 방법이다. 또한, 상대방으로 하여금 화자가 우회적으로 말하고 있음을 정확히 알도록 한다.
- 모든 문장의 의미 변화는 동사의 형태 변화로부터 유발된다. 따라서, 현재에 불가능한 내용을 우회적으로 표현하더라도 듣는 이가 화자의 의도를 정확히 알도록 하기 위하여 <u>현재의 내용을 현재 시제가 아닌 다른 시제로 나타낸다</u>. 그리고 화자의 mood, attitude를 표현하기 위하여 조동사를 첨가한다.

I buy you a car.
→ I {will + bought} you a car.
→ I **would buy** you a car.   가정법 형태 완성

▶ 현재와 반대되는 상황을 조동사가 포함된 과거 시제로 전달한다. 즉, '형태적 시제'와 '의미적 시제'가 다르다. 조동사는 주로 would가 쓰이며, 의미에 따라 could와 might가 사용되기도 한다.

- **if절 안의 시제** 주절의 시제와 맞춘다.

I'll buy a car if I have enough money.   직설법/현재의 상황 설명, 아쉬움 없음
→ ① I **would buy** a car if I **had** enough money.   가정법 과거/현재의 아쉬운 감정
→ ② I **would have bought*** a car if I **had had** enough money. 가정법 과거완료/과거의 아쉬운 감정

▶ ① 주절(과거) – if절(과거) / '충분한 돈이 있었다면 차를 샀을 텐데'로 해석하면 안 된다!
  ② 주절(과거완료) – if절(과거완료) / '충분한 돈이 있었다면 차를 샀을 텐데'로 해석한다.

▶ 주절의 시제와 if절 안의 시제가 다른 '혼합 시제의 가정법'도 있다. (Ch.14-4 참고)

형태적 시제 vs. 의미적 시제

☼ 가정법에서는 형태적 시제와 의미적 시제가 일치하지 않는다는 사실에 주의한다. 따라서, 정확한 의미를 파악하기 위해서는 형태적 시제와 의미적 시제를 혼동하지 않아야 한다.

- 가정법 과거
  현재 사실의 반대/<u>미래 또는 현재에 이루지 못하는 일에 대한 아쉬움, 불안감</u>을 <u>과거 시제로 표현</u>
- 가정법 과거완료
  과거 사실의 반대/<u>과거에 이룰 수 없었던 일에 대한 아쉬움</u>을 <u>대과거 시제로 표현</u>

> **Pop Quiz 1** 다음 문장을 가정법(과거 사실의 반대)으로 바꾸고, 큰 소리로 세 번씩 말하시오.
>
> (1) I took a shower.
>   ⇒ _____
>
> (2) She met my friend.
>   ⇒ _____
>
> (3) We were able to buy a new suit.
>   ⇒ _____
>
> (4) Robbie and Lucy cheered for our team.
>   ⇒ _____

2 were

If he **were** not an accountant, he **would have to hire** one.

If she **were** / **had** not **been** there, she **would have saved** her own life.

We **would have been able to go** / **could have gone** on a picnic if it **had been** sunny yesterday.

▶ 가정법 과거에서 if절 안의 be동사는 were를 쓴다. 한편, 가정법 과거완료에서는 주어가 사람인 경우에는 had been을 써야 하지만 were도 자주 사용되며, 사물인 경우에는 주로 had been을 쓴다.

3 직설법 vs. 가정법

If they **come**, please **let** me know.   (=They might come. / 직설법 – 올 확률이 있음)

If they **came**, they **could meet** Carl.   (=They will not come. / 가정법)

If they **had come**, they **would have met** Carl.   (=They didn't come. / 가정법)

> **Pop Quiz 2** 다음 직설법 문장을 가정법으로 바꾸고, 큰 소리로 세 번씩 말하시오.
>
> (1) If I had time yesterday, I called her.
>   ⇒ _____
>
> (2) If we were there, we might be able to help.
>   ⇒ _____
>
> (3) If Kevin buys new guitar strings*, he will play for the class.
>   ⇒ _____
>
> (4) If you don't have a secretary, you have to type the reports yourself.
>   ⇒ _____

Check Up

1 다음 문장을 읽고, 질문에 yes 또는 no로 답하시오.

(1) If chicken were on the menu, he would not have fish.
  ⓐ Is chicken on the menu? _____
  ⓑ Does he have fish? _____
(2) If they had enough time, they could build a patio*.
  ⓐ Do they have enough time? _____
  ⓑ Can they build a patio? _____
(3) She would go to the moon if she were given an opportunity.
  ⓐ Is she given the opportunity? _____
  ⓑ Does she go to the moon? _____

2 다음 가정법 문장이 바르게 쓰였으면 ○표를 하고, 잘못 쓰였으면 ×표를 하시오.

_____ (1) Ted can change the tire if he had a spare one.
_____ (2) Christine could shop now if the store were open.
_____ (3) If you work overtime, you could make extra money.
_____ (4) If I spoke Spanish, I wouldn't need a translator.
_____ (5) If she had tasted it, she would liked it.
_____ (6) If you have been at the party last night, you could have met Bob.

3 🔊 Speak-out 다음 우리말을 영어로 옮겨 큰 소리로 세 번씩 말하시오. (가정법 과거)

(1) Sally는 집에 있으면 항상 전화를 받는다.
   ➡ _____
(2) Sally가 집에 있다면 그녀는 전화를 받을 텐데.
   ➡ _____
(3) 내가 차에 대해 충분히 알고 있다면 직접 고칠 수 있을 텐데.
   ➡ _____
(4) 거기에 의사가 없다면 상황은 더 심각할 텐데.
   ➡ _____
(5) Tom이 그녀에게 사과를 하면 그녀는 그를 용서해 줄 텐데.
   ➡ _____
(6) Ellen이 백만 달러를 가지고 있다면 세계 여행을 할 수 있을 텐데.
   ➡ _____

(7) 공기가 없다면 인간은 몇 분 이내에 죽을 것이다.
→ _____

(8) 네가 작은 차를 산다면 휘발유 비용을 아낄 수 있을지도 모를 텐데.
→ _____

4 밑줄 친 if가 직설법의 if이면 R(real)을 쓰고, 가정법의 if이면 UR(unreal)을 쓰시오.

_____ (1) If it were sunny, we would play football.
_____ (2) If it doesn't rain, the party will be outdoors.
_____ (3) If this car were a truck, it could carry a lot of wood.
_____ (4) If the paper touches an acid, it will turn red.
_____ (5) If I had used a computer, I could have finished the work sooner.
_____ (6) If you met aliens* from outer space, what would you do?

5 Speak-out 다음 우리말을 영어로 옮겨 큰 소리로 세 번씩 말하시오. (가정법 과거완료)

(1) 내일 날씨가 좋다면 우리는 동물원에 갈 거야.
→ _____

(2) 오늘 날씨가 좋다면 우리는 동물원에 갈 텐데.
→ _____

(3) 어제 날씨가 좋았다면 우리는 동물원에 갔을 텐데.
→ _____

(4) 내 차를 가지고 있었다면, 큰 소리로 라디오에 맞춰 노래를 불렀을 텐데.
→ _____

(5) Sally가 알람을 맞춰 두었더라면, 그녀는 수업에 늦지 않았을 텐데.
→ _____

(6) 네가 우유를 냉장고에 넣어 두었더라면, 우유는 상하지 않았을 텐데.
→ _____

(7) Marcie가 그 일에 지원을 했었다면, 그들이 그를 고용했었을까?
→ _____

(8) 그들이 그 주식(stock)에 투자를 했었더라면, 그들은 부자가 되었을 텐데.
→ _____

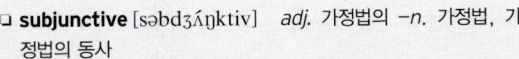

❏ **subjunctive** [səbdʒʌ́ŋktiv]   *adj.* 가정법의 -*n.* 가정법, 가정법의 동사
❏ **would have bought**   will + had bought
❏ **string** [striŋ]   *n.* 끈, 줄, (활의) 시위, (악기의) 현(絃)

❏ **patio** [pǽtiòu]   *n.* 테라스 (스페인식 건물에서 건물의 바닥과 같은 높이로 하여 정원이나 길가로 내민 부분으로 의자와 탁자를 내다 놓고 식사나 휴식을 하는 장소로 이용할 수 있다.)
❏ **alien** [éiljən]   *n.* 외계인, 외국인 -*adj.* 외국인의, 다른

14-3 가정법의 다양한 표현법

가장 기본적인 가정법 문장은 주절만으로 또는 if절과 함께 Subjunctive Mood를 나타내는 형태이다. 이 때, Subjunctive Mood를 확실히 전달하기 위해 조동사를 첨가하는 한편 현재 상황은 과거 시제로 과거 상황은 과거완료 시제로 표현한다. Subjunctive Mood를 전달하기 위한 또 하나의 방법은 동사의 원형을 사용하는 것이다.

1. 동사 원형으로 Subjunctive Mood 표현

It is essential that *he* submit the application early as possible.
The doctor recommended that *she* drink 15 cups of water if she desperately wanted to get rid of the cold.

▶ 원서를 빨리 제출하지 않으면, 충분한 물을 마시지 않으면 심각한 상황이 벌어질 것 같은 불안감을 전달한다(가정법). 주절에 제안, 요구, 필요를 나타내는 단어가 오는 경우가 많다. 일상회화에서는 should drink로 쓰기도 한다.

My advice is that one depends on learning by example and through imitation.

▶ 주절에 제안, 요구, 필요를 뜻하는 단어가 나온다고 하여 문장의 의미에 따라 직설법을 써야 하는 경우도 있다. 위의 예문은 단순한 사실을 전달하므로 depend가 아닌 depends를 써야 한다.

■ 제안, 요구, 필요의 의미를 나타내는 단어
  advise, ask, demand, desire, insist, propose, recommend, request, suggest 등의 동사
  proposal, recommendation, advice, suggestion 등의 명사
  best, crucial, essential, important, urgent 등의 형용사

2. wish vs. hope

■ 'wish that ~'은 사실과 반대되거나 실현 가능성이 없는 일에 대한 아쉬움을 표현한다.
■ Hope는 실현될 가능성이 있는 일에 대한 기대와 소망을 나타낸다. (직설법)
■ wish(ed) that + 가정법 과거 　　　　주절과 동일한 시제를 가리킨다.
　wish(ed) that + 가정법 과거완료 　　주절보다 과거 시제를 가리킨다.

We all wish you could come to the party. (너는 못 올 테니 아쉽구나)
We hope you will come to the party tonight. (네가 오기를 기대하고 있다/직설법)

I wish it were true. (= It would be nice if it were true.)
I wish it had been true. (= It would be nice if it had been true.)
They wished that they wouldn't repeat the same mistake.
They wished that they hadn't repeated the same mistake.

■ Wish가 that절을 이끌지 않는 구문에서는 강한 희망을 표현한다.
She wishes to go away for the weekend. (주말에 멀리 떠났으면 좋겠다)

I wish you both a good journey. (좋은 여행이 되세요)
I wish you well. (건강하길 바래요)

> **Pop Quiz 1** 다음 문장이 나타내는 상황을 보기에서 고르고, 해석하시오.
>
> |보기| ⓐ 현재 또는 미래에 이루어질 수 없는 일에 대한 아쉬움, 불안감 표현
> ⓑ 과거에 이루어질 수 없었던 일에 대한 아쉬움 표현
>
> _____ (1) I wish I <u>had</u> a younger sister.
> _____ (2) I wish that I <u>were</u> better looking.
> _____ (3) I wish that I <u>could work</u> miracles.
> _____ (4) Do you ever <u>wish</u> you <u>would be</u> a President?
> _____ (5) All the people in town <u>wish</u> he <u>would come</u> soon.
> _____ (6) Now I <u>wish</u> I <u>had followed</u> her advice.
> _____ (7) She <u>wishes</u> she <u>had been</u> a little more ambitious.
> _____ (8) She <u>wishes</u> he <u>could have helped</u> her more than he did.

> **Pop Quiz 2** 다음 우리말을 영어로 세 번씩 말하시오.
>
> (1) 그것이 사실이 아니면 좋을 텐데. (2) 그것이 사실이 아니었으면 좋을 텐데.
> (3) 나는 그것이 사실이 아니기를 바랬다. (4) 나는 그것이 사실이 아니었기를 바랬다.

3 as if, as though

- as if / as though + 가정법 과거   주절과 동일한 시제를 가리킨다.
  as if / as though + 가정법 과거완료   주절보다 과거 시제를 가리킨다.

  Sally acts **as if** there **were** not enough time. (There is enough time.)
  Sally acted **as if** there **were** not enough time. (There was enough time.)
  He is talking **as if** he **had witnessed** the accident. (He didn't witness the accident.)
  He was talking **as if** he **had witnessed** the accident. (He hadn't witnessed the accident.)

4 but for, without / with

- Without, but for는 '~이 없(었)다면'을 의미하고, with는 '~이 있(었)다면'을 나타낸다.
- But for는 일상회화에서는 거의 사용하지 않는다.

  With a bit more time, we **would visit** more places.   가정법 과거
  ▶ 시간이 조금 더 있다면 / 현재 사실의 반대

Without/But for her advice, I'**d be** through with my girlfriend. 가정법 과거
▸ 당신의 충고 없이는 여자친구와 헤어지게 될 텐데. (그러니 제발 도와줘.) / 현재 상황의 불안감 표현

Without/But for your help, I **would not have found** it possible. 가정법 과거완료
▸ 당신의 도움이 없었다면 그것이 가능하다는 것을 알지 못했을 겁니다. / 과거의 불안했던 감정의 회상

5 혼합 시제의 가정법

구분	기본 시제의 가정법		혼합 시제의 가정법		의미
	주절	if절	주절	if절	
가정법 과거	과거	과거	과거	대과거	과거의 일 때문에 생긴 현재의 결과는?
가정법 과거완료	대과거	대과거	대과거	과거	현재의 상황을 보니, 과거의 결과는?

■ 과거의 상황 때문에 일어난(종속절 대과거) 현재의 결과(주절 과거시제)에 대한 아쉬움 표현
  I didn't drink a lot of milk, so I am not tall now.
  → If I **had drunk** a lot of milk, I **would be** tall.

■ 현재의 상황(종속절 과거시제)을 기준으로, 과거의 상황(주절 대과거)에 대한 아쉬움 표현
  She was late for the class, because she is not diligent.
  → If she **were** diligent, she **would** not **have been** late for the class this morning.

Check Up

1 다음 문장의 표현 방법을 고르시오.

직설법☐ 가정법☐ (1) It'll be absolutely important that we cooperate for the plan.
직설법☐ 가정법☐ (2) They insisted that their apartment was searched.
직설법☐ 가정법☐ (3) The company may ask that applicants write a test.
직설법☐ 가정법☐ (4) Our proposal that she be present in the meeting was ignored.

2  'wish that ~'을 사용하여 다음 우리말을 영어로 세 번씩 말하시오.

(1) 내가 불어를 할 수 있다면 좋을 텐데.
(2) Richard가 좀 더 용감한 소년이라면 좋을 텐데.
(3) Bill은 어제 음악회에 참석하기를 바랬었다.
(4) Mary는 봄에 태어났었기를 바랬었다.

3 🔊 **Speak-out** 'as if/as though ~'를 사용하여 다음 우리말을 영어로 세 번씩 말하시오.

　(1) Joel은 마치 다이어트 중이지 않은 것처럼 많이 먹는다.
　(2) Brown 부인은 마치 우리 엄마인 것처럼 행동했다.
　(3) 그녀는 마치 거기에 오래 살았던 것처럼 런던에 대해 이야기한다.
　(4) Ann은 마치 지난 밤 귀신을 보았던 것처럼 행동을 했다.

4 문장의 표현법이 나머지와 <u>다른</u> 하나를 고르시오.

　(1) _____　ⓐ I wish you luck at the interview.
　　　　　　　　ⓑ I hope you and your friends have a great time in Seoul.
　　　　　　　　ⓒ My grandmother wishes she would be back in her hometown, Kaesong.

　(2) _____　ⓐ The man investigated around the broken window very thoroughly, as if he had been an FBI* agent.
　　　　　　　　ⓑ It rains cats and dogs* as if it'll swallow up everything in the world.
　　　　　　　　ⓒ Ms. Ann would burst into tears as though she felt every emotion of the main character in the movie.

5 🔊 **Speak-out** 다음 우리말을 영어로 세 번씩 말하시오.

　(1) 그녀의 배려와 관심이 없다면 나는 아무런 기회도 갖지 못할 텐데.
　(2) 비자를 받는 데 지체가 없었다면 그녀는 일찍 출발할 수 있었을 텐데.
　(3) 당신의 도움이 없었다면 그는 완주하지(finish the race) 못했을 텐데.

6 🔊 **Speak-out** 혼합 가정법을 사용하여 다음을 한 문장으로 바꾸고, 큰 소리로 세 번씩 말하시오.

　(1) Ken didn't practice hard. He isn't a world-leading tennis player.
　(2) Paine went to school in Florida. We cannot have a chat over tea.
　(3) Mr. Brown is overweight. He had a lot of candies and chocolate.
　(4) The flowers by Joanna's bed are withering*. She didn't water them.

comments

❏ **retrospect** [rétrəspèkt]　n. 회고, 회상 (a review, survey, or contemplation of things in the past) / in retrospect 되돌아 보면, 회고하면 (looking backward or reviewing the past)
❏ **FBI** 미(美) 연방 수사국(1908년 법무부 검찰국으로 발족하였으며, 제2차 세계대전 당시 국내 첩보 활동이 활발해지자 간첩죄 등의 수사에서 크게 활약하였다. FBI의 정식 명칭은 Federal Bureau of Investigation이다.)
❏ **It rains cats and dogs.** 비가 억수같이 쏟아지다 (서로 으르렁거리는 개와 고양이처럼 많은 비가 요란스럽게 내리는 상황을 묘사하는 말이다.)
❏ **wither** [wíðər]　v. 시들다, 말라빠지다, 활기를 잃다

14-4 주의해야 할 조건절

① 'Wish that ~'은 오직 가정법에만 쓰이지만 ② if, as if/as though 등은 가정법과 직설법에 모두 사용된다. 한편, ③ unless, in case (that), whether or not, even if, as long as 등은 의미적으로 가정법 문장이 가능하지 않으므로 직설법에만 쓰인다.

1 직설법 조건절

Unless you are trying to lose weight to please yourself, then it's going to be tough to keep your motivation level high.

▸ Unless는 직설법에서만 사용하며 가정법에서는 'if ~ not'을 사용한다!

In case (that) you don't know the way here, get the map from the internet home page.
Even if/Whether or not a military coup* is taking place* in that country, we don't care and will travel there.
I don't care who you are or what you are **as long as** you love me. (~하는 한 / = if, provided that)

2 as if, as though

직설법	Jake looks **as if/as though** he **is** another rookie*.	(Probably he is another rookie.)
직설법	They're acting **as if/as though** they **haven't been** here before. (Probably they haven't been here before.)	
직설법	She <u>acts</u> **as if/as though** she **is** rich.	(Probably she is rich.)
가정법	She <u>acts</u> **as if/as though** she **were** rich.	(She is not rich.)
가정법	She <u>felt</u> **as if/as though** she **had known** him.	(She didn't know him.)
가정법	She <u>speaks</u> English well, **as if/as though** she **had been born** in the United States. (She was not born in the United States.)	

3 if의 생략과 도치

■ If절에 were, had p.p.가 포함된 경우에는 도치가 가능하다. 이 때, if가 생략되면서 주어와 동사의 어순이 바뀌게 된다.

Were I in your shoes, I would not make such a decision.
(← If I <u>were</u> in your shoes, I would not make such a decision.)

Had she not been ill then, she would have gone to the exhibition.
(← If she <u>had</u> not <u>been</u> ill then, she would have gone to the exhibition.)

Check Up

1 다음 문장의 표현 방법을 고르고, 해석하시오.

직설법□ 가정법□ (1) He looks as if he had not broken his leg yesterday.
직설법□ 가정법□ (2) You wouldn't believe it unless you were there.
직설법□ 가정법□ (3) In case you need a day off, please talk to us in advance.
직설법□ 가정법□ (4) Whether or not it rains, Tina will practice figure-skating on the outdoor ice rink this coming Sunday.

2 Speak-out 다음 우리말을 영어로 옮겨 큰 소리로 세 번씩 말하시오

(1) 그녀는 마치 모국어(mother tongue)가 아닌 것처럼 한국어를 말한다.
   ⓐ (그녀의 모국어는 한국어가 아닐지도 모른다.) _____
   ⓑ (그녀의 모국어는 한국어이다.) _____
(2) Tom의 아버지는 마치 육군 장군처럼 명령을 했다.
   ⓐ (Tom의 아버지는 육군 장군일지도 모른다.) _____
   ⓑ (Tom의 아버지는 육군 장군이 아니다.) _____

3 Speak-out 다음 문장을 if를 생략하여 큰 소리로 세 번씩 말하시오.

(1) If there were a golf course, we could play golf.
(2) If Sarah were walking very fast, she couldn't notice the sign which says "Stop."
(3) If Charles had been here, we would have finished it more quickly.
(4) If the market had sold beans, I would not have bought rice.

4 Speak-out 의미에 맞게 A와 B를 연결하고, 큰 소리로 세 번씩 말하시오.

A	B
(1) She treats me	ⓐ nothing could live on the earth.
(2) Without the sun,	ⓑ as if I were a three-year-old child.
(3) I wish	ⓒ I would have stopped to look at them.
(4) Had I seen the birds,	ⓓ the world were always what I wish it to be.

□ **military coup** 군사 쿠데타 / coup[kuː] n. (불시의) 일격, 공격
□ **take place** (사건 등이) 일어나다 (= happen)
□ **rookie** [rúki] n. 풋내기, 신인선수, 신입사원 (어떤 일을 처음 시작하여 경험이 부족한 사람을 가리켜 부르는 말이다.)

Grammar Review

1 다음 문장이 바르게 쓰였으면 ○표를 하고, 잘못 쓰였으면 ×표를 하시오.

_____ (1) Were the movies worth watching, I watch them.

_____ (2) If she knew his telephone number, she would call him.

_____ (3) Had I known the road was closed, I will not have gone there.

_____ (4) If I had not eaten so much at the party, I would not have a stomachache.

_____ (5) If New York is a country, it would be the ninth largest economy in the world.

_____ (6) Harry major in engineering if he were certain he could get a job in the space industry.

2 다음 글을 읽고, 빈 칸에 들어갈 알맞은 표현을 고르시오.

It would be interesting to meet an alien! If you met an alien in the street, what would you say? Imagine!

You: Are you an alien?
Alien: Look at me! If I were from Earth, (1) _____ green skin?
　　　　Ⓐ would I have　Ⓑ will I have

You: Why are you here?
Alien: It was a mistake! If I had known what I was doing, I would not have come to Earth!

You: What happened?
Alien: I used the wrong computer program! I thought it would be nice to visit Mars. But I used the program for Earth instead! (2) _____ careful,
　　　　Ⓐ If I have been　Ⓑ If I had been
　　　　I would not be here!

You: Don't you like Earth?
Alien: No! It's too hot and wet! And the air is too thick! (3) _____ an alien,
　　　　Ⓐ Were you　Ⓑ You were
　　　　could you breathe this air? It is (4) _____ in a steam bath! I wish I
　　　　Ⓐ as if I were　Ⓑ if I were
　　　　were on Mars! Let me out of here!

Grammar Up

Time Limit: 6 min, _____ / 18

어법상 빈 칸에 들어갈 알맞은 표현을 고르시오.

1 If I _____ your letter then, I would be with you now.
  (A) received
  (B) would receive
  (C) have received
  (D) had received

2 If you really loved Steve, you _____ him go away.
  (A) would not let
  (B) do not let
  (C) to let
  (D) did not let

3 His face wouldn't be so bad if it _____ some character.
  (A) has
  (B) had
  (C) would have
  (D) had had

4 _____ up earlier, she would not have missed the plane.
  (A) She got
  (B) She has gotten
  (C) Were gotten
  (D) Had she gotten

5 The sun goes on shining after your death as if nothing _____.
  (A) happens
  (B) had happened
  (C) would happen
  (D) happen

6 I wish that I _____ my mother, who passed away last year, once again.
  (A) had seen
  (B) will see
  (C) could see
  (D) am seeing

7 _____ for good friends, life would have been filled with a feeling of loneliness.

(A) Were it not
(B) Had it not been
(C) If it is not
(D) If it has not

8 Would you believe me _____ you that a cat wanted to make friends with a mouse?

(A) if
(B) I told
(C) that I told
(D) if I told

어법상 잘못된 부분을 고르시오.

9 They would be <u>angry</u> <u>if</u> we <u>don't</u> invite them <u>to</u> the party.
                       (A) (B)   (C)   (D)

10 <u>No one</u> would go out in the middle of the <u>speech</u> if his talk <u>is</u> <u>a little</u> more interesting.
    (A)   (B)   (C) (D)

11 If you <u>have</u> not put them <u>in</u> the refrigerator, they <u>would</u> have gone <u>bad</u>.
          (A)   (B)   (C)   (D)

12 This cake would taste <u>better</u> if it <u>has</u> more <u>sugar</u> in <u>it</u>.
                  (A)   (B)   (C) (D)

13 <u>But</u> flowers and trees, <u>the world</u> <u>would</u> be very <u>unhappy</u>.
   (A)   (B)   (C)   (D)

14 <u>If</u> he <u>worked</u> hard <u>when young</u>, he would <u>live</u> better now.
 (A)   (B)   (C)   (D)

15 If it <u>is</u> not <u>for</u> the Internet, we <u>would</u> not be able to do many <u>things</u>.
      (A)   (B)   (C)   (D)

16 Alice smiled <u>because</u> the rabbit looked <u>as if</u> he <u>is</u> about <u>to speak</u>.
              (A)   (B) (C)   (D)

17 The poet <u>would</u> be sixty-seven <u>years old</u> now if <u>she</u> had not <u>kills</u> herself.
         (A)   (B)   (C)   (D)

18 <u>As if</u> I <u>had studied</u> English harder, I could <u>speak</u> English <u>well</u>.
 (A)   (B)   (C)   (D)

CHAPTER **15**

수동태
_Passives

15-1 효과적인 수동태 문장의 사용

말을 전달하는 방법에는 ①있는 그대로 전달하는 방법(직설법), ②일방적으로 전달하는 방법(명령법), ③우회적으로 전달하는 방법(가정법)이 있다. 또 다른 방법으로는 ⓐ적극적인 목소리로 전달하는 방법(Active Voices)과 ⓑ소극적인 목소리로 전달하는 방법(Passive Voices)이 있다. 꼭 기억할 것은 늘 당당한 자세가 좋다는 것이다. 억지로 겸손하려는 것은 거만하거나 비굴한 것이다. 자신감이 있으면 자연스럽게 겸손할 수 있고 당당할 수 있다. 영어의 문장에서도 특별한 상황이 아니면 능동태를 사용하도록 하자.

1 수동태와 능동태*의 기본 차이점

■ 능동태는 직접적이고(direct), 경제적이며(economical), 개인적인(personal) 느낌이 강한 반면, 수동태는 간접적이고(indirect), 객관적이며(objective), 형식적인(formal) 느낌이 강하다.

We **cannot repay** your travel expenses unless you submit receipts.
Travel expenses **cannot be repaid** unless receipts are submitted.

You **have not paid** your bill.
This bill **has not been paid**.

▶ 위의 예는 수동태 문장을 쓰는 것이 더 적합하다. 능동태 문장은 직접적, 개인적인 어감이 강하므로 무례한 표현이 될 수도 있지만, 수동태 문장은 간접적, 우회적, 객관적인 표현이기 때문이다.

2 반드시 수동태를 써야 하는 경우

■ 능동태로는 표현이 불가능하거나 어색하여 수동태를 써야만 하는 경우

Dave **was born** in October.
His mother **bore** Dave in October.   (×)

Are you **done**?   (다 마치셨나요?)
Are you **finished** with your meal?   (식사를 다 마치셨나요?)

▶ 형태상 수동태로 보이지만, 여기서 done과 finished는 분사 형태의 형용사이다. 두 번째 문장은 'Did you finish your meal?'로 바꿔 쓸 수 있다.

3 행위의 주체(자)보다 행동을 받는 대상을 더 강조할 때

I **was shocked** by his death.
▶ 비교: His death shocked me.

He **is disappointed** with the result.
▶ 비교: The result disappoints him.

4 행동의 주체자를 밝히지 않는 것이 적합한 경우

- 행동의 주체자에 대해 관심이 없거나, 숨기는 것이 좋거나, 모르거나, 중요하지 않은 경우

  His grandfather **was killed** in World War II.
  The man **has been jailed** for more than ten years.
  Jill **was fined** fifty dollars for the violation of the traffic law.
  The result of the survey **will be** carefully **analyzed**.
  Snuppy, the world's first cloned* dog, **was created** in 2005.
  John Lennon **was murdered** at his apartment in New York on December 8, 1980.

- 수동태 문장은 대화체보다는 글에서 사용 빈도가 높다. 특히 교과서, 보고서 등 행위의 주체자보다 과정이나 결과가 강조되는 경우에 쓴다.

  Active Voice ◄——— conversation ——— fiction ——— journalism ——— science ———► Passive Voice

Check Up

1 짝지어진 능동태 문장과 수동태 문장을 보고, 의미 차이가 있는지 또는 어떤 형태가 더 적합한지 토론해 보시오.

(1) ⓐ The house was designed for blind people.
    ⓑ They designed the house for blind people.

(2) ⓐ The mooing* of cows would be heard in a nearby field.
    ⓑ She would hear the mooing of cows in a nearby field.

(3) ⓐ A mistake was made by him.
    ⓑ He made a mistake.

(4) ⓐ I'm very impressed with your work.
    ⓑ Your work really impressed me.

2 **Speak-out** 다음 우리말을 영어로 세 번씩 말하시오. (수동태를 사용할 것)

(1) 새로운 아이디어들이 그 책에서 제시되었다.
(2) 지금까지 실종된 어린이에 대한 아무런 증거도 발견되지 않고 있다.
(3) 세미나는 얼마나 오래 계속될까요?

3 다음은 Charlotte Perkins Gilman의 전기를 쓰기 위해 수집한 자료의 일부분이다. 수동태로 표현해야 할 부분을 모두 고르시오.

ⓐ bear in 1860
ⓑ formally educate only four years
ⓒ marry in 1884 & give birth to a daughter
ⓓ hospitalize in Philadelphia because of depression
ⓔ release after a month from the hospital
ⓕ soon ill again, so leave her husband & move with her daughter to California
ⓖ recover and go on to write many books
ⓗ "The Yellow Wallpaper" / publish in *New England Magazine* in 1982
ⓘ diagnose* with breast cancer in 1932
ⓙ die three years later at age 75

4 위의 자료를 기초로 하여 Charlotte Perkins Gilman의 전기문을 완성하시오.

One of the most famous female authors in America during the late 19th and early 20th centuries, Charlotte Perkins Gilman (1) _____ in 1860. Her family was poor and she (2) _____ only four years. She (3) _____ in 1884 and (4) _____ a daughter. After the baby was born, however, Gilman developed a severe depression. She (5) _____ in Philadelphia because of it. After a month in hospital, Gilman (6) _____, but soon she (7) _____ ill again. This time, she (8) _____ her husband and (9) _____ with her daughter to California. There, she (10) _____ and (11) _____ on to write many books. Gilman is best known for her autobiographical short story "The Yellow Wallpaper," about a woman with depression. It (12) _____ in *New England Magazine* in 1982. Gilman (13) _____ with breast cancer in 1932 and (14) _____ three years later at age 75.

❏ **수동태와 능동태** 기본적으로 능동태와 수동태의 의미는 동일하며, 형태적으로도 긴밀히 연결되어 있다. 그러나 능동태와 수동태는 서로가 개별적이고 독립적인 문장이므로, 수동태를 능동태로부터 파생된 형태라고 생각하지 않도록 주의한다. 즉, 능동태 문장이 있어야만 수동태 문장을 만들 수 있다는 오해를 하지 않도록 한다.

❏ **clone** [kloun] v. 복제하다, 똑같이 만들다
❏ **moo** [mu:] v. 소가 (특히 어린 송아지가) 음매 하고 울다
 —n. 음매 하고 우는 소리
❏ **diagnose** [dáiəgnòus] v. (병)을 진단하다

15-2 주의해야 할 수동태

동사의 형태를 'be+p.p.'로 쓰기만 하면 수동태가 가능하다고 생각하기 쉽지만, ①동사의 의미에 따라 수동태가 부적합한 경우도 있으며, ②수동태의 의미를 능동태의 형태로 표현하는 경우도 있다. 특히, 두 번째의 경우는 한국어와 영어의 의미 차이 때문에 학습하는데 많은 혼동이 있을 수 있다. 그 외에도 ③전치사의 목적어, 4형식 문장, 원형부정사를 포함한 문장, that절의 수동태 표현에 대한 학습을 할 때에는 주의가 필요하다.

1 수동태가 부적합한 동사들

■ '목적어'가 있고 동작(actions)의 의미를 나타내면 수동태 문장이 가능하다. 타동사라고 하여도 '상태(state)'를 나타낼 때에는 수동태 문장이 어색하다. (진행 시제가 안 되는 동사들과 유사)

have, get, let, fit, lack, resemble, suit 등

I **resemble** my girlfriend. (O)	→	My girlfriend **is resembled** by me. (×)
In my view, he **lacks** patience. (O)	→	In my view, patience **is lacked**. (×)
Rabbits **have** red eyes. (O)	→	Red eyes **are had** by rabbits. (×)

2 형태는 **Active**, 의미는 **Passive**인 자동사

■ 한국어와 영어의 의미적 차이로 인해 자동사인데도 불구하고 수동태로 써야 할 것 같은 혼동이 생길 수 있다.

open, close, lock, sell, rent, happen, occur, take place, rise, fall, disappear 등

Mike's store **opens** at nine and **closes** at seven.	(열리다, 닫히다)
Mike's store is **open** now.	(열려 있는, 형용사/opened는 틀림)
Mike **opens** his store at nine.	(열다)
The book **sells** well because it is very interesting.	(특별한 노력을 하지 않아도 잘 팔린다)
The book **is being sold** well because he is a naturally good salesman.	(그의 수완으로 인해 잘 팔린다)
The book **is sold** out, so it is out of stock.	(사람들이 모두 사버려서 재고가 없다)
This building **rents** easily.	(잘 임대된다)
The accident **happened** due to lack of carefulness.	was happened는 틀림
Marcie **fell** from the horse.	was fallen는 틀림

3 '자동사+전치사+목적어'의 수동태

People **refer to** our economy as a free market.
→ Our economy **is referred to** as a free market.

▶ 타동사만이 수동태를 만드는 것이 아니라, 전치사의 목적어도 수동태의 주어가 될 수 있다.

4 4형식 동사와 수동태

- 간접/직접목적어를 사용한 두 개의 수동태가 가능하지만, 간접목적어인 사람을 주어로 하는 것이 보다 자연스럽다. 직접목적어를 주어로 할 경우에는 전치사 to 또는 for*를 간접목적어 앞에 둔다.

    Has anyone taught you language skills?
    → Have you been taught language skills?
    → Have language skills been taught to you?

    He bought her a bundle of flowers the other day.
    → She was bought a bundle of flowers the other day.
    → A bundle of flowers was bought for her the other day.

5 원형부정사와 수동태

- 수동태에서는 원형부정사가 to-부정사가 된다.
    see, watch, hear, feel, notice 등 / make

    We saw the children play over there.
    → The children were seen to play over there.
    People made him leave the room.
    → He was made to leave the room.

- Let은 수동태를 만들지 못하며 allow, permit을 사용하여 수동의 의미를 나타낸다.

    My mother doesn't let me eat before I wash my hands.
    → I'm not allowed to eat before I wash my hands.

6 that절과 수동태

- That절이 동사의 목적어로 쓰였을 때 각각 두 개의 수동태가 가능하다.
    think, know, believe, feel, expect, agree, hope 등

    Everyone believes that the little girl is a great poet.
    → It is believed that the little girl is a great poet.
    → The little girl is believed to be a great poet.

Check Up

1 다음 문장이 바르게 쓰였으면 O표를 하고, 잘못 쓰였으면 ×표를 하시오.

_____ (1) Suddenly the book was fallen from the shelf.
_____ (2) Whom do you resemble, your father or mother?
_____ (3) Nothing astonishing was occurred at all.
_____ (4) What time does the department store open?
_____ (5) Does your car drive well?
_____ (6) Balloons were burst here and there.
_____ (7) The imports have sharply been risen for the last five years.
_____ (8) Digital photography has been become more and more popular.

2 주어진 문장을 목적어가 강조되는 수동태로 바꾸고, 큰 소리로 세 번씩 말하시오.

(1) She could teach us a lot about how to succeed.
→ We _____
→ A lot _____

(2) The photographer offered her 200 dollars to be a model.
→ She _____
→ 200 dollars _____

(3) He was telling James a mysterious story.
→ James _____
→ A mysterious _____

(4) The president asked Jill several questions at the meeting.
→ Jill _____
→ Several questions _____

3 같은 의미가 되도록 빈 칸에 알맞은 표현을 쓰시오.

(1) jump　　ⓐ The trainer makes her dog _____ through a hoop.
　　　　　ⓑ Her dog _____ through a hoop.

(2) swell out　ⓐ You could see its body _____ in a minute.
　　　　　　ⓑ Its body _____

(3) reach　　ⓐ Her hard work made her _____ the top.
　　　　　　ⓑ She _____

(4) tremble   ⓐ Robbie even felt a tiny thing _____ in the breeze.
              ⓑ A tiny _____
(5) ring   ⓐ All of them heard the bell _____, didn't they?
              ⓑ _____

4 주어진 문장을 수동태로 바꾸고, 큰 소리로 세 번씩 말하시오.

(1) They say that Ms. Hooper has visited many countries.
   ⇢ It is _____
   ⇢ Ms. Hooper _____

(2) We think she has been to Russia and China.
   ⇢ It is _____
   ⇢ She _____

(3) Some people suppose that she went to the Arctic*, too.
   ⇢ It is _____
   ⇢ She _____

(4) Everyone feels that she should write about her travels.
   ⇢ It _____

(5) People anticipate that her stories will be exciting.
   ⇢ It _____
   ⇢ Her stories _____

5 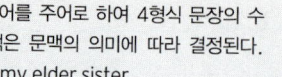 다음 우리말을 영어로 세 번씩 말하시오.

(1) 그 서점은 10시에 문을 엽니다.
(2) 그 서점은 열려 있습니다.
(3) 그 카페는 5시에 문을 닫습니다.
(4) 그 카페는 닫혀 있습니다.
(5) 이 방을 임대하고 싶은데요?
(6) 이 방은 어제 (누군가에 의해) 임대되었습니다.
(7) 이 방은 한 달에 400 달러에 임대됩니다.

❏ 전치사 **to** 또는 **for** 직접목적어를 주어로 하여 4형식 문장의 수동태를 만들 때 전치사의 선택은 문맥의 의미에 따라 결정된다.
ex. This letter is written **to** my elder sister.
    (내가 나의 손위 언니에게 편지를 썼다는 뜻)

This letter is written **for** my elder sister.
(나의 손위 언니를 위해 내가 대신 편지를 썼다는 뜻)

❏ **the Arctic** [á:rktik] n. 북극(지방, 권)

15-3 수동태와 기타 사항

수동태에 관한 학습을 수동태 문장 만들기에 집중하면 수동태 학습은 전혀 하지 않은 것과 같다고 해도 과언이 아닐 것이다. 수동태 영어 문장을 말과 글로 사용할 수 있기 위한 학습이 중요하다. 특히, 한국 사람들은 영작에서 수동태 문장을 많이 사용하는 경향이 있다. TOEFL과 같은 Essay Writing에서는 기본적으로 능동태 문장을 기본으로 해야 하며, 필요한 경우 수동태 문장을 효과적으로 활용할 수 있어야 한다.

1 행위자

- 능동태는 어떤 행위자가 무슨 행동을 했는지에 대한 관심의 표현이고, 수동태는 행위 자체나 그 결과에 대한 관심을 표현한다.

  Tom repaired my car.
  주어=행위자 (누가 ~을 하다)

  My car was repaired.
  주어≠행위자 (무엇이 ~되다)

2 행위자를 생략하는 경우와 밝히는 경우

- 수동태를 활용한 표현은 행위 자체 또는 그 결과를 강조하는 표현이므로 행위자가 누구인지는 중요하지 않다. 따라서 행위자 표현(by someone)은 대부분 생략된다.

  German, French, and Italian are spoken in Switzerland (**by people**).

- 수동태로 표현하는 것이 효과적인 경우: 주어의 길이가 길어질 때

  We were awakened **by the buzzer sounding loudly in the middle of the night**.
  The boy is called a liar **by those who have been deceived several times**.

- 행위자를 밝히는 경우: 관계대명사절의 구조에서와 같이 행위자를 생략할 수 없을 때 또는 행위자를 밝히는 것이 내용의 전달에 필요하고 행위자를 알고 있을 때

  I'm wondering **by whom** the secret was revealed.　　관계대명사가 행위자를 포함하고 있음
  Harry Potter was written **by J. K. Rowling**.
  He had been poisoned **by his girlfriend**.
  He was brought up* **by an aunt**.

- with + 행동의 도구 (by + 행동의 실행자)

  Moisture must be drawn out first **with salt**.
  ▶ Salt must draw moisture out first. (소금이 가장 먼저 습기를 흡수함에 틀림없다)

  A circle was drawn in the dirt **with a stick**.
  ▶ Someone with a stick drew a circle in the dirt. (막대기로 먼지 위에 원을 그렸다)

3 수동태와 12시제

The tree **might be cut** for firewood.   The tree **has** not **been cut** for firewood.

▶ 기본적으로 수동태는 현재, 과거 외의 다른 시제와도 자유롭게 결합한다.
  그러나 미래진행(will be being p.p.), 완료진행(have been being p.p.)과는 잘 결합하지 않는다.

4 get + p.p. LOOK

- 일상회화에서는 be동사 대신 get을 사용하여 수동태를 만들 수 있다.
- 주로 사람이 주어이며 계획되지 않은 상황에 사용된다. 즉, 우연적이고 예상하지 못한 행동(action)이나 변화(change)가 있을 수 있는 상황에서 쓰인다.
- 부정문과 의문문을 만들 때에는 조동사 do의 도움을 받는다.

Tokyo Dome **was built** in 1988.   got built는 틀림. 미리 계획된 일에는 사용하지 않음
I **got fined** for crossing a road in L.A. last year. **Have** you **gotten fined** like that?
When **do** you **get paid**?

▶ get washed, get shaved, get (un)dressed, get changed / get engaged, get married, get divorced / get started(= start), get lost(= lose one's way)

Check Up

1 다음을 수동태로 옮기려고 한다. 행위자를 생략하는 것이 자연스러우면 O표를 하고, 생략하지 않는 것이 자연스러우면 ×표를 하시오.

_____ (1) People use hammers to drive* nails.
_____ (2) They might make a mistake in calculation of the time.
_____ (3) Harry has translated his novel into 30 languages.
_____ (4) They broadcast the soccer game all over the world.
_____ (5) A dentist has checked Ted's teeth once a year.
_____ (6) Will the editor divide the material into three parts?
_____ (7) Someone had reserved a double room for her under the name of Diana.
_____ (8) Charles Darwin wrote *the Origin of Species* explaining a theory of evolution.

2 🔊 Speak-out 목적어가 강조되는 수동태 문장으로 바꾸고, 끊어 읽기에 유의하여 큰 소리로 세 번씩 말하시오. (행위자의 생략과 표현에 주의할 것)

(1) Farmers grow rice in Korea.
↳ Rice _____

(2) Everyone predicts a good harvest this year.
↳ A good harvest _____

(3) Do you connect the computer to the power supply?
↳ Is the computer _____

(4) The brave firefighters soon extinguished the fire.
↳ The fire _____

(5) Has someone finally rescued the prince from the wizard*?
↳ _____

(6) J. R. R. Tolkien, a towering figure in fantasy literature, wrote and published *the Lord of the Rings* in 1954-55.
↳ _____

3 둘 중 알맞은 표현을 골라 문장을 완성하시오.

(1) Bob is driven to work (by, with) his friend every day.
(2) The music was amplified* (by, with) microphones.
(3) Most of the damage was caused (by, with) the stubborn captain.
(4) Christmas trees are decorated (by, with) candles, fairy lights, and colored beads.

4 🔊 Speak-out 다음 우리말을 영어로 옮겨 큰 소리로 세 번씩 말하시오.

(1) 털이 긴 그 개는 일년에 두서너 번 털을 깎는다. (get shaved)
↳ _____

(2) 왜 사람들은 결혼을 할까요? (get married)
↳ _____

(3) 다행스럽게도 소녀는 길을 잃지 않고 집으로 무사히 돌아왔다. (get lost)
↳ _____

- **bring up** 키우다, 가르치다, 훈육하다 (up은 부사)
- **drive** v. (말뚝·못 등)을 박다, (지식·교훈 등)을 주입시키다, (의견·생각 등)을 강력히 밀고 나가다
- **wizard** [wízərd] n. 마법사, 마술사, 요술쟁이 −adj. 마술의, 마법사의, 불가사의한
- **amplify** [ǽmpləfài] v. 확대하다, 증대하다, 증폭하다

Grammar Review

1 다음 문장이 바르게 쓰였으면 O표를 하고, 잘못 쓰였으면 ×표를 하시오.

_____ (1) Harry said he was not tell about the report at all.
_____ (2) Kelly lives in Los Angeles, but she born in Minnesota.
_____ (3) Thirty-nine reservations have already are confirmed.
_____ (4) Do you know how many stops are planning on our bus trip?
_____ (5) It believes that Mr. Larson had a home in the Rocky Mountains.
_____ (6) The air that surrounds the Earth can divide into four main layers.
_____ (7) *Les Miserables* is scheduled at the student hall tonight. Shall we go together?
_____ (8) In the 18th century, the Native Americans' way of life had changed by Europeans.

2 주어진 표현을 사용하여 문장을 완성하시오. (시제와 태에 유의할 것)

(1) Neil can play the trumpet. He _____ (say) to be very good at it.
(2) As we're listening, the speaker _____ (stop) by a question from the audience.
(3) When the warship Virginia _____ (launch) in 1862, no one _____ (know) it would become very famous.
(4) Jennie arrived late for the concert. For half an hour, she _____ (catch) in a traffic jam.
(5) The man _____ (suspect) of committing a crime, but the police _____ (not, yet, find) evidence enough to arrest him.
(6) Maybe this photo of Abraham Lincoln _____ (take) before 1860 or 1861. That was when he _____ (grow) his famous beard.
(7) A very rare bird _____ (see) in the woods near our town last week. We know about it because someone _____ (photograph) it.
(8) Although they _____ (find) the report three years later, it _____ (lack) certain vital information.
(9) The island _____ (belong) to Korea, but many children in Japan _____ (teach) that it is a part of their territory with the name of Tomato.
(10) John Franklin, an English-Canadian explorer, _____ (lead) a famous expedition to the Arctic but _____ (disappear) there along with all his men.

3 같은 의미가 되도록 빈 칸에 알맞은 표현을 쓰시오.

(1) bind   ⓐ The wizard _____ his hands with rope tightly.
            ⓑ His hands _____

(2) use   ⓐ We _____ the form of "be+past participle" in the passive.
           ⓑ The form of "be+past participle" _____

(3) build   ⓐ Bob and his friends _____ the house last year.
            ⓑ The house _____

(4) divide   ⓐ Mom _____ the cake into eight slices.
             ⓑ The cake _____

4 다음 질문에 대한 적절한 답을 완성된 문장으로 말하시오. (자신의 생각을 표현할 것)

(1) When will the new textbook be published?
     ➡ _____

(2) Have the foreign heads of state been welcomed by the mayor of the city?
     ➡ _____

(3) Has the TOEFL test been prepared by the ETS?
     ➡ _____

(4) Who was considered to be a great pilot?
     ➡ _____

(5) Who was awarded the first Nobel Prize? (Marie Curie)
     ➡ _____

5 다음 글을 읽고, 빈 칸에 들어갈 알맞은 표현을 고르시오.

       Have you seen a solar eclipse? For a very long time, people were scared by it because solar eclipses (1) _____ by the public. Nowadays, however,
                                                  Ⓐ were not understood   Ⓑ were not understand
scientists have discovered a lot of things about the cause and effect of the eclipse, and people are familiar with solar eclipses. A solar eclipse (2) _____ as the
                                                                    Ⓐ happens   Ⓑ is happened
moon passes directly between the sun and the earth. When the whole sun (3) _____ up, we call it a total eclipse. Sometimes, a part of the sun is
    Ⓐ covers   Ⓑ is covered
covered. That is called a partial eclipse. An eclipse (4) _____ more than
                                                 Ⓐ never lasts   Ⓑ is never lasted
about seven and a half minutes. Now, how about observing a solar eclipse with your own eyes?

Grammar Up

Time Limit: 6 min, _____ / 18

어법상 빈 칸에 들어갈 알맞은 표현을 고르시오.

1 If something _____ into 10 equal parts, each part is a tenth.
- (A) divide
- (B) divides
- (C) is divided
- (D) are divided

2 Hydrogen _____ as a highly flammable gas.
- (A) knowing
- (B) to know
- (C) known
- (D) is known

3 The seven largest pieces of land _____ continents.
- (A) are called
- (B) were called
- (C) are call
- (D) calling

4 _____ first invented by King Sejong, the greatest Korean king of all.
- (A) Hangeul
- (B) Hangeul is
- (C) Hangeul was
- (D) Hangeul has

5 _____ delivered before noon every day.
- (A) Our mail
- (B) Our mail is
- (C) Our mail was
- (D) When our mail

6 Mount Kilimanjaro _____ local people as the "Mountain of Cold Devils."
- (A) knew to
- (B) was known for
- (C) was known to
- (D) was known as

7 Ancient people _____ into the night sky and saw shapes in the stars.
(A) looked
(B) was looked
(C) were looked
(D) was looking

8 Janet, a smart African American girl, _____ as the best student by all students.
(A) chosen
(B) has chosen
(C) has been chosen
(D) and has been chosen

어법상 잘못된 부분을 고르시오.

9 Each of the stories is required 20 minutes to read.
　(A)　　　　　　(B)　　　(C)　　(D)

10 Major events can often be anticipating.
　(A)　　　(B)　(C)　　(D)

11 I'm interested by science, and I want to be a great scientist.
　　　　　(A)　　　(B)　　(C)　　　　(D)

12 If I post the letter today, he will be gotten it tomorrow.
(A) (B)　　　　　　　　　　(C)　　(D)

13 Yesterday our teacher was arrived five minutes late.
　(A)　　　　　　(B)　　　(C)　　(D)

14 Mother didn't know that the cake had already eaten by the children.
　　　　(A)　　(B)　　　　　　(C)　　(D)

15 Romeo and Juliet was wrote not by Hemingway, but by Shakespeare.
　　　　　(A)　(B)　(C)　　　　　　　(D)

16 On the day before Christmas, the stores crowd with a lot of customers.
(A)　　　(B)　　　　　　　　　(C)　　　(D)

17 Cars, buses, and trucks are used roads, but trains run on tracks.
　　　(A)　　　(B)　　　(C)　　　　(D)

18 By painting, your home can keep in good condition.
(A)　　　(B)　　　　　(C) (D)

Grammar in Context

Government Budget

A lot of money is required to run the government of a large city. Los Angeles, for example, has a budget of several billion dollars a year. This money is raised in several ways. The first way is through taxes. Nearly everything in a city has a tax on it. The money a person makes is taxed. When a car or house is sold, taxes are paid. If money is exchanged between two people in any way, there is probably a tax involved.

Cities also make money through lotteries. In a lottery, tickets are sold to the public, typically for a few dollars for each ticket. The winner of the lottery receives a large amount of money, but the money the winner receives is not all of the money from the lottery. A large portion of it is kept by the city government. Furthermore, the winner is required to pay taxes on the money that he or she won in the lottery, so an even bigger percentage of the money is returned to the city government.

176 words, Reading Time: _____

1 앞에서 다섯 번째 술어(전체)를 찾아 쓰시오.

2 뒤에서 네 번째 술어(전체)를 찾아 쓰시오. (종속절의 술어전체도 포함할 것)

3 다음 문장이 참이면 T를 쓰고, 거짓이면 F를 쓰시오.
   _____ (1) When people buy and sell something, there may be a tax involved.
   _____ (2) The winner of the lottery receives all of the money from the lottery.
   _____ (3) When a person wins the lottery, he or she has to pay taxes on a lottery ticket.

4 **Chain of Thought:** 다음 문장을 논리적 흐름에 따라 앞에서부터 이해해 봅시다.
   (1) A lot of money is required / to run the government / of a large city.
   ⇨ 많은 돈이 요구된다 [왜?] _____ [어떤 정부이냐 하면] _____
   (2) The winner is required / to pay taxes / on the money / that he or she won / in the lottery.
   ⇨ _____ _____ _____ _____

규칙 1: 문장을 생각의 흐름에 따른 사고단위(Thought Unit)로 나누어 이해한다.
규칙 2: 명사 뒤에는 그 명사를 설명하는 형용사(구, 절)가 따라나올 것을 예상한다. 다른 뜻(부사구, 절)을 가진 어구가 나오면 전체 문장에 적합하도록 해석한다.
[경고] 규칙 3: 문장을 뒤에서부터 해석하려고 하면 Chain of Thought에 따른 문장 이해에 혼란이 생길 수 있으므로 각별히 주의해야 한다. 뒷부분은 모두 가리고 앞에서부터 해당 부분만을 보면서 이해하도록 한다.

CHAPTER 16

명사절, 부사절
Noun Clauses and Adverb Clauses

16-1 명사절 (1): 의문사절과 whether/if절

● 명사절은 ①의문사로 시작하는 절과 ②that, whether, if로 시작하는 절로 구분한다. 명사절은 주어, 보어, 목적어, 전치사의 목적어 역할을 한다. 그러나, that절과 if절은 전치사의 목적어로 사용하지 않는다.

1 의문사가 이끄는 명사절

■ 의문사로 시작하는 명사절은 의문사가 없는 의문문을 간접의문문으로 바꾼 것과 같다.

의문문	명사절의 형태
Who is she?	who she is
Whose book is that?	whose book that is
Whom has she waited for all day long?	whom she has waited for all day long
How far is it from here to Denver?	how far it is from here to Denver
Which one does he like?	which one he likes
What should they do?	what they should do
When did it happen?	when it happened
Where did she learn English?	where she learned English
Why did you say so?	why you said so

We're talking about **who(m)** she has waited for all afternoon, but no one knows **who** he is. So, we decide to ask her about him.
Who(m) I invite is none of your business. (= It's none of your business who(m) I invite.)
This is **how much** I've done today.

2 whether/if절: '~인지 아닌지'

■ Whether와 if는 동의어로 취급한다. 엄밀히 구분하면, whether는 다른 선택이 있다고 여겨지는 경우를 나타내기 때문에 or 또는 or not과 함께 쓰는 경우가 많다. 그러나, if는 다른 선택이 있다고 하더라도 그것이 무엇인지 모를 때 사용한다.

She asked **if** I had left with Stacy, and I said no.
I don't know **whether** he stays at a hotel **or** at his home.
We didn't know **whether** to believe him **or not**. (= whether we could believe him or not)
Whether or not she can come is another matter.
The question is **whether** the place is worth a visit.
She refused to comment on **whether** we should accept the proposals. (if는 안 됨)

▶ 주어, 보어의 경우 if 보다 whether가 선호되고, 전치사의 목적어가 될 때에는 반드시 whether를 써야 한다!
▶ I'll buy a house **whether** I don't get married. (조건의 부사절을 이끄는 whether / '~이라 할지라도')

Check Up

1 둘 중 알맞은 표현을 고르고, 끊어 읽기에 유의하여 큰 소리로 세 번씩 말하시오.

(1) Can you tell me (who, what) Pat's telephone number is?
(2) I have no idea (whose, which) the colored pencil on the floor is.
(3) Ken wants to get a better job, and that is (how, why) he's learning computers.
(4) (When, Where) you are from or (what, whether) you are doesn't matter.
(5) I don't care (if, whom) Ann is going to take English class next semester.
(6) All they worry about is (whether, if) or not their son is all right.
(7) Give me two days to decide on (if, whether) I'll change the old couch for a new one.
(8) The police have really done everything to find out (what, if) he died of natural causes or was murdered.

2 다음 문장에서 명사절을 찾아 밑줄을 긋고, 그 역할을 보기에서 골라 쓰시오.

보기 | 주어   보어   목적어   전치사의 목적어

_____ (1) What he does in his spare time is not obvious*.
_____ (2) Sometimes Mr. Cosby[kósbi] used to forget where he put his keys.
_____ (3) This is why all the plans have failed miserably in spite of their efforts.
_____ (4) The bear is looking into the jar to see if there is honey.
_____ (5) The only question is whether there live fish in the pond or not.
_____ (6) How serious the situation has become is being shown on the live TV show.
_____ (7) The police finally discovered whether the footprints left on the floor were the suspect's*.
_____ (8) At first she worried about who would like her poems, but she became one of the most beloved* poets in history.

3 **Speak-out** ( ) 안의 정보를 묻는 의문문을 만들고, 다시 명사절로 바꾸어 문장을 완성하시오. 그리고, 완성된 문장을 큰 소리로 세 번씩 말하시오.

(1) Ted is going to leave for Chicago (in October).
   QUESTION _____
   NOUN CLAUSE Tell me _____

(2) Dean has been (in San Diego) since last week.
   QUESTION _____
   NOUN CLAUSE   Do you know _____
(3) (Jill) is good at dealing with* the problem.
   QUESTION _____
   NOUN CLAUSE   Please tell me _____
(4) The relationship broke up (because of a lack of a common interest).
   QUESTION _____
   NOUN CLAUSE   Nobody knows _____

4 Speak-out 주어진 의문문을 명사절로 바꾸고, 완성된 문장을 큰 소리로 세 번씩 말하시오.

(1) Did he take the pictures?
   → I wonder if _____
(2) Does Sam live with his parents?
   → Let's ask Sam whether _____
(3) Did you lock the door to your bedroom?
   → Do you remember _____
(4) Did she eat my chocolate cake?
   → _____ is still a mystery.
(5) Do you like Steve?
   → _____ is not important to me.

5 Speak-out 다음 우리말을 영어로 옮겨 큰 소리로 세 번씩 말하시오.

(1) 선생님은 내게 4 곱하기 2가 무엇인지 물었다.
   → _____
(2) 우리는 그가 서울을 잘 알고 있는지 아닌지 모른다.
   → _____
(3) 그녀는 안경을 어디에 두었는지 잊어 버렸고, (우리가) 그것을 찾는데 이틀이 걸렸다.
   → _____

❏ **obvious** [ábviəs] *adj.* 분명한, 명백한
❏ **suspect** [sʌ́spekt] *n.* 용의자
❏ **beloved** [bilʌ́vid] *adj.* 가장 사랑하는, 소중한
❏ **deal with** ~을 다루다, 처리하다, 취급하다 (with는 전치사)

16-2 명사절 (2): that절

That이 이끄는 명사절은 주어, 보어, 목적어의 역할을 한다. 명사절에서 that절은 기본적인 학습에 속한다. 그러나, 영어는 가장 기본적이고 일반적인 내용이 결국에는 가장 어렵게 느껴지는 경우가 많다. 예를 들어 get, take, have, do, make와 같은 가장 기본적인 단어를 정복하는 것이 난해한 단어를 정복하는 것보다 훨씬 더 어렵다. 난해한 단어는 사용 범위가 좁지만 일반적인 단어는 그 쓰임새가 다양하고 방대하기 때문이다.

1. Speaking, Writing 시험과 that절의 활용

1) that*절이 주어 및 보어로 쓰일 때

So, **it** is clear **that** we need better organization. 　　　　it – 가주어, that절 – 진주어

What I'm thinking is **that** everyone should learn how to be happy. 　　　　보어

The thing is (**that**) when you meet the right person, the past won't matter.

The point is (**that**) love can make the wisest look foolish.

▸ 자신의 견해에 대한 주목을 요할 때 사용하는 표현이다.
▸ answer, conclusion, fact, point, problem, question, thing, truth 등
▸ 일상회화에서 보어 역할을 하는 that절의 that은 대부분 생략된다. (목적어로 쓰일 때에도 마찬가지임.)

2) that절이 목적어로 쓰일 때

I believe (**that**) we are all equal.

I agree (**that**) the topic is worth continuing to study.

▸ 자신의 의견이나 주장을 제시할 때: I를 주어로 하여 현재 시제로 표현한다.

I don't think **that** computer science and mathematics are mutually* exclusive*.

I don't expect **that** I have the power to change anyone's mind.

▸ 부정을 할 때에는 상대방의 의견이 아니라 자신의 의견을 부정하는 것이 좋다. 즉, that절의 내용을 부정하지 않도록 한다.
I **think** that computer science and mathematics are **not** mutually exclusive. (×)
She insists that any opinion through the internet must be allowed even in the case of blackmailing, but **I think she is not** right. (×) → ~ but **I don't think** she **is** right. (better)

2. 전치사와 that절

- 일반적으로 that절은 전치사의 목적어로 사용하지 않는다. 전치사 다음에 that절이 나오는 경우에는 전치사를 탈락시킨다. (Ch.18-1 참고)

We're **sorry about** the delay.

We're **sorry that** the plane is late.

Are you **aware of** some differences between beef and pork?

Are you **aware that** there are some differences between beef and pork?

I was **surprised at** his knowledge of Korean history.

I was **surprised that** he knew so much about Korean history.

Sue has no **idea of** his problems.

Sue has no **idea that** he has problems.

He is perfect, **except that** he's too boring. (~을 제외하고)

▶ Except that, except when 등은 부사절을 이끄는 접속사이다. 그러나 정확한 문법적 설명은 아니지만, that절이 전치사 except의 목적어가 된다고 설명하기도 한다. (Except 만으로도 접속사로 쓰일 수 있음)

Check Up

1 다음 문장에서 that절을 찾아 밑줄을 긋고, 그 역할을 보기에서 골라 쓰시오.

보기 | 주어   보어   목적어

_____ (1) It is clear that the myth had many different sources.

_____ (2) Her father suggests that she should not go far from the hotel.

_____ (3) The fact was that I was always interested in the story of animals.

_____ (4) She explained that she was a sales manager from Qwerty Computer Corp*.

_____ (5) It was true that the boy was extremely embarrassed.

_____ (6) He claims that the committee would willingly* accept the view.

_____ (7) The answer is that the tree should be uprooted before the queen arrives.

_____ (8) People in town think it best that they wait until the investigation is complete before they jump to conclusions.

2 **Speak-out** 다음을 that을 사용하여 한 문장으로 바꾸어 큰 소리로 세 번씩 말하시오.

(1) Jake lost the race so near the finish. He was disappointed.
   ↪ Jake was disappointed that _____

(2) They're a great success in Edinburgh. They're glad.
   ↪ They're glad that _____

(3) I was late for the weekly meeting. I'm sorry.
→ I'm _____

(4) Sally received a bundle of flowers from her boyfriend. She's happy.
→ _____

3 다음 대화문을 읽고, 내용에 맞게 A와 B를 연결하시오. 그리고, B를 영어로 옮겨 큰 소리로 세 번씩 말하시오.

> *Dad*: Vacation is coming, and every family is deciding where to go. Where do you think is the best place?
> *Sue*: I like the beach, so I would go there. It is fun to go swimming and to make sand castles.
> *Mom*: Well, I prefer to go to a big city because I can go shopping and go to the theater.
> *Ted*: Maybe I will rent a boat and travel down a river. On the river, everything is peaceful and quiet.
> *Dad*: The big city, beach, and river all sound good, but I'd like to stay home during vacation. My idea of a good vacation is to stay home and listen to beautiful music!

A   **B**

(1) Dad •   • ⓐ 나는 매일 다른 식당에서 저녁 식사를 할 수 있어.
                   (The point is that ~)

(2) Mom •   • ⓑ 그것은 비용이 들지 않아. (The thing is that ~)

(3) Ted •   • ⓒ 조개 껍데기와 조약돌(pebble)을 모을 수 있어.
                   (I think that ~)

(4) Sue •   • ⓓ 강에서 낚시와 수영을 할 수 있어. (I think that ~)

comments

❑ **that** 명사절을 이끄는 다른 접속사와는 달리 that은 그 자체의 의미를 갖지 않는다. 따라서 종종 생략되기도 한다. 그러나, 주어나 보어로 쓰인 경우에는 that을 생략하면 문장 전체의 구조적 혼란이 생길 수 있다.

❑ **mutually** [mjúːtʃuəli] *adv.* 서로, 상호간에, 합의하여

❑ **exclusive** [iksklúːsiv] *adj.* 배타적인, 양립할 수 없는, 독점적인

❑ **Corp.** Corporation의 줄임말 / corporation [kɔ̀ːrpəréiʃən] *n.* 법인, 조합, 주식회사

❑ **willingly** [wíliŋli] *adv.* 기꺼이, 쾌히, 자진해서

16-3 부사절 (1): 시간, 조건

부사는 동사, 형용사, 부사, 구, 절을 수식하는데, 부사절은 절 또는 동사를 수식한다. 절의 핵심어는 동사이므로 절을 수식한다는 것이 동사를 수식한다는 것과 유사하기도 하다. 부사절은 일종의 수식어구로서 문장의 뒤에 위치하는 것이 기본이며, 강조를 위해 문장의 앞에 위치할 수 있다.

1 as, when, while: '~할 때, ~하는 동안에'

The race began **as/when/while** the clock was striking 12.
As/When/While the clock was striking 12, the race began.*
When Bill is nervous, he sweats a lot.
Sally is going to share a flat with Ann **while** she is in London.
It began to snow **as/while** Dave was running.

2 after, before, until, as soon as: 시간의 전후 관계

After he was informed about the schedule, he went out.
It took about three hours **before** Jill got the parcel*.
I considered her very selfish **until** I met her.
As soon as we get the tickets, we'll send them to you.

▶ After, before는 전치사와 부사로도, until은 전치사로도 사용된다.
I promise that I'll follow you two days **after**.   부사/시간(이틀 후에)
Let's discuss how to do it **after** a ten-minute break.   전치사/시간(10분의 휴식 뒤에)
After you, please.   전치사/시간(먼저 하세요/가세요)

3 since: 과거의 어느 때 이후의 시간

"**Since** I arrived in Seoul in 1997, I **have held** two jobs." said the man.
Conditions for the prisoner **have been improved since** the officer was changed.

▶ Since를 포함한 문장에서는 **주절 동사의 형태가 항상 완료 시제**여야 한다.

4 if, even if, unless, as/so long as: 어떤 사건, 행동이 일어나기 위한 조건

If A is true, B is false.
If A and B both are true, I'll treat* you to lunch.
I won't marry you **even if** you're a millionaire.   (= whether* or not you're a millionaire)

▶ Even if ('~이든 말든')는 특정한 조건이나 상황에 관계없음을 뜻한다.

A: He'll leave you **unless** you try to lose weight. (= if you don't try to lose weight)

B: Never mind.* I assure you that he doesn't care how much I weigh **as/so long as** he loves me. (= on condition that he loves me)

▸ As/So long as는 '~하는 한'으로 해석한다.

5 시간, 조건의 부사절과 시제

You'll feel a lot better **if** you take a rest for a while.

As soon as he realizes what he has done, he will apologize.

The little boy may inherit his grandmother's possessions **when** she dies.

▸ 시간, 조건을 나타내는 부사절에서는 내용상 미래 시제라고 하여도 항상 현재 시제로 표현한다.

Check Up

1 둘 중 알맞은 표현을 고르고, 큰 소리로 세 번씩 말하시오.

(1) I normally make dinner (while, since) she is watching TV.

(2) (After, Until) he spent a night in bitter cold, he got a bad cold.

(3) I have to go, but I'll always stay in your mind (as long as, unless) you love me.

(4) "(Even if, If) it rains, you should dry clothes indoors." said Mom.

(5) The dog stared after her with its tail wagging* (until, since) she disappeared around a corner.

2 밑줄 친 표현의 쓰임이 나머지와 다른 하나를 고르시오.

(1) _____
ⓐ The war had ended before the winter came.
ⓑ Tomorrow or one day after will be OK.
ⓒ I'm sorry, but I can't remember whether I've been there before.

(2) _____
ⓐ He wrote his name after Sally's at the bottom of the paper.
ⓑ The company was the best at making shoes in Korea until maybe the 1970s.
ⓒ Mr. Robinson waited for her until it got dark.

(3) _____ ⓐ There are 100 days left until the festival starts.
ⓑ My brother was born several weeks before Christmas.
ⓒ He's reluctant to go out after he seriously injured his legs a few years ago.

3 Speak-out 주어진 표현을 사용하여 문장을 완성하여 큰 소리로 세 번씩 말하시오.

(1) If Jill _____ (meet) her friend tomorrow, she will go skating.
(2) Caroline will answer the door, as soon as you _____ (knock).
(3) What will you do if someone you don't know _____ (ask) for help?
(4) Anita should be willing to work long hours until she _____ (become) a surgeon*.
(5) Once they _____ (ascertain) he is not a spy, they will agree to release him.
(6) David will give you a hand with readiness* as long as you _____ (be) his friend.

4 Speak-out 다음 우리말을 영어로 옮겨 큰 소리로 세 번씩 말하시오.

(1) 전공을 결정할 때에는 고려해야 할 많은 것들이 있다.
⇨ _____
(2) 중학교를 졸업한 이후로 나는 그 선생님을 뵌 적이 없다.
⇨ _____
(3) 내가 나가 있는 동안 그가 오면 그에게 잠깐 기다리라고 말해 주세요.
⇨ _____
(4) 시간이 허락한다면 나는 8월에 뉴욕에 계신 삼촌을 방문할 것이다.
⇨ _____

---

comments

❏ **부사절의 위치** 기본적으로 부사절은 문장 뒤에 위치한다. 그러나 부사절의 내용을 강조하고 싶을 때에는 문장 앞에 둘 수 있다. 기초 영작 학습 단계에서는 부사절을 문장 뒤에 쓰도록 연습한다.
❏ **parcel** [pá:rsəl] n. 꾸러미, 소포, 한 무더기
❏ **treat** [tri:t] v. 대접하다, 환대하다, 한턱 내다
❏ **whether** Whether는 명사절 외에 부사절을 이끌 수 있는데, 부사절 접속사(~이든 말든)로 사용될 때에는 even if와 같은 뜻을 갖는다.
ex. This happens whether / even if the children are in a nuclear family or a large family.
❏ **Never mind.** 괜찮다, 걱정 마라
❏ **with its tail wagging** 꼬리를 흔들면서 / wag [wæg] v. 흔들다, 요동하다, 까딱거리다 / 전치사 with는 분사구와 결합하여 동시동작(~한 채, ~하면서)을 나타낸다. 이 때, 분사 앞에 위치한 명사는 분사의 의미상 주어가 된다.
ex. with his arms folded (그의 팔짱을 낀 채)
❏ **surgeon** [sə́:rdʒən] n. 외과의사
❏ **with readiness** 쾌히, 기꺼이

16-4 부사절 (2): 이유, 대조, 목적, 결과

● 부사절은 다양한 의미를 가지고 다른 절(동사)을 수식한다. 본 Unit에서는 시간, 조건을 나타내는 부사절 외에 이유, 대조, 목적, 결과를 나타내는 다양한 부사절의 종류와 쓰임에 대해 살펴봄으로써 일상회화에서의 활용 범위를 넓힐 수 있도록 한다.

1 as, because, since : 이유 [reason]

Everyone in the village liked her **as** she was so cute and kind.
I had a stomach disorder*, **because** I ate too much.
Since we did our best, let's wait for the result.

▸ 일반적으로 because를 가장 많이 사용한다.
▸ Since는 이유를 소개하며 문장을 시작할 때 쓰이는 경우가 많으므로 주로 문장 앞에 쓴다.
▸ As와 since는 시간을 나타내는 부사절에서도 쓰인다.

2 though, although, even though, while : 대조 [contrast]

Tim will be blamed **though**/**although** he lied for good reasons.
Though/**Although** he was born disabled, he is never discouraged.
Even though she was really tired, she couldn't take a rest.

▸ 예상하지 못한 결과(~에도 불구하고)의 뜻을 나타낸다.

Peter was a good student, **while** his brother was not.

▸ While은 직접적인 대조(반면에)의 관계를 표현한다.
▸ While은 시간을 나타내는 부사절에서도 사용한다.

3 so that, in order that : 목적 [purpose]

She has to earn lots of money **so that** she can support* her dalmatians*.
He was preparing to move to a big city **so that** he could get a better job.
We would like to email a newsletter to all who have an email address **in order that** we can decrease our mailing charges.

▸ So that/In order that절은 주로 현재 시제 또는 will/would, can/could와 함께 쓰이며, 일상회화에서는 that이 생략되기도 한다.
▸ In order that은 형식적인(formal) 느낌이 강하므로 so that을 사용하는 경우가 더 많다.

4 so/such ~ that : 결과 [result]

It's **such** a good price **that** they decide to buy it at once.
His voice was **so** loud and clear **that** it was heard in the distance.

▶ So는 형용사/부사와 함께 쓰고, such는 명사와 함께 쓴다. 이 때, 어순에 주의한다.
 so + 형용사/부사 + that vs. such + a/an + 형용사/부사 + 명사

Check Up

1 🗣 Speak-out 주어진 접속사를 사용하여 한 문장으로 바꾸어 큰 소리로 세 번씩 말하시오.

(1) All my belongings fell onto the ground. The lock on my suitcase broke. (as)
➡ _____

(2) Sue is willing* to help other people. She is a kind girl. (because)
➡ _____

(3) Sharks eat sick fish and animals. They keep oceans clean. (since)
➡ _____

(4) Jim quit his job. The work was not interesting any longer. (because)
➡ _____

2 🗣 Speak-out 주어진 접속사를 사용하여 다음 문장을 바꾸어 큰 소리로 세 번씩 말하시오.

(1) Tom is not tall, but he is a good basketball player. (though)
➡ _____

(2) It was very cold outside, but Bob went out without a coat. (though)
➡ _____

(3) Some clothes are quite expensive, but they sell out in a minute. (although)
➡ _____

(4) The company is famous for its strict hiring policies*, but he is going to apply for a job. (even though)
➡ _____

3 빈 칸에 들어갈 알맞은 표현을 고르시오.

(1) Today is sunny, while yesterday was _____.
　ⓐ clear　　　　　　　ⓑ rainy
　ⓒ warm　　　　　　　ⓓ also sunny

(2) The bread smells good, while it tastes _____.
　ⓐ very bad　　　　　　ⓑ something good
　ⓒ like an apple　　　　ⓓ even better

(3) Helen likes to get up early, while Jack likes _____.
　ⓐ to get up early　　　ⓑ to go to a zoo
　ⓒ to play　　　　　　　ⓓ to sleep late

(4) Tom is only eleven years old, while he sometimes acts _____.
　ⓐ well　　　　　　　　ⓑ better
　ⓒ like an adult　　　　ⓓ like a child

4 Speak-out 주어진 표현을 사용하여 다음 문장을 바꾸어 큰 소리로 세 번씩 말하시오.

(1) He hurried. He didn't want to be late. (so that)
　→ _____

(2) Sue opens the window. She wants the air to be refreshed. (so that)
　→ _____

(3) Because the traffic is heavy, they cannot arrive on time. (so ~ that)
　→ _____

(4) Because the weather was fine, we could not just stay in. (so ~ that)
　→ _____

(5) As the car is small, a few of them have to walk. (such ~ that)
　→ _____

(6) Since he seldom talked about himself, I hardly knew about him.
　(such ~ that, a man of few words)
　→ _____

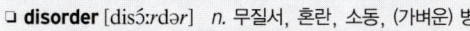

❑ **disorder** [disɔ́ːrdər] *n.* 무질서, 혼란, 소동, (가벼운) 병
❑ **support** [səpɔ́ːrt] *v.* 부양하다, 먹여 살리다, 받치다
❑ **dalmatian** [dælméiʃən] *n.* 달마시안, 달마티아 개 (부드럽고 하얀 털에 검정색 얼룩을 가진 개이다.)
❑ **willing** [wíliŋ] *adj.* 기꺼이 ~하는, ~하기를 사양치 않는 (주로 'be willing to+부정사'의 형태로 사용되는 경우가 많다.)
❑ **policy** [páləsi] *n.* 정책, 방침, 수단, 방법

Grammar Review

1 빈 칸에 공통으로 들어갈 접속사를 보기에서 고르시오.

보기 | if   whether   since

(1) _____ ⓐ He didn't ask _____ they agreed with what he was doing.
　　　　　　　ⓑ You can ask a dealer for a discount _____ you pay cash or buy on credit.

(2) _____ ⓐ _____ Steve phones me, tell him I'll be back at 9 p.m.
　　　　　　　ⓑ Are you sure _____ those children are the same ones that broke the window in your house?

(3) _____ ⓐ _____ she has lots of experience on every level, she'll do it well.
　　　　　　　ⓑ There hasn't been any contact at all between the two families _____ the war that began 14 years ago.

2 다음 문장이 바르게 쓰였으면 O표를 하고, 잘못 쓰였으면 X표를 하시오.

_____ (1) Brian wants to show the article to her but can't remember where is it.
_____ (2) If you open the windows, the paint fumes will disappear more quickly.
_____ (3) We all know about that he has plenty of experience with them.
_____ (4) Kelly couldn't avoid the accident though the brake couldn't stop the car.

3 다음 글을 읽고, 빈 칸에 들어갈 알맞은 표현을 고르시오.

　　Dr. Brown is a guest speaker in our class today. We just found out (1) _____
　　　　　　　　　　　　　　　　　　　　　　　Ⓐ when she is　Ⓑ when is she
going to speak, but we do not know what she will talk about. Maybe she will talk about what kind of jobs are in her field. Graduation is near, and I worry about where I will work. Sometimes I am (2) _____ that it is hard to sleep at night.
　　　　　　　　　　　　Ⓐ such worried　Ⓑ so worried
Since there are few good jobs, it would be good to know where they are. I am told that industries are not hiring many people. Hiring has slowed there, (3) _____
　　　　　　　　　　　　　　　　　　　　　　　　　　Ⓐ if　Ⓑ because
we are in a recession. But no one has told me what the state government is doing. I hear that state jobs are available. A state job would be great, (4) _____
　　　　　　　　　　　　　　　　　　　　　　　Ⓐ though　Ⓑ despite
competition probably will be heavy. Let's see what Dr. Brown says!

Grammar Up

Time Limit: 6 min, _____ / 18

어법상 빈 칸에 들어갈 알맞은 표현을 고르시오.

1 The baby slept soundly _____ the music was playing.
   (A) with
   (B) in
   (C) while
   (D) if

2 _____ depends on how hard you work.
   (A) All you to perform
   (B) How well you perform
   (C) You perform well
   (D) Although you perform

3 The question is _____ the work or not.
   (A) I will continue
   (B) though I will continue
   (C) whether not I will continue
   (D) whether I will continue

4 _____ astronomers know a lot about Venus, its clouds are still a mystery.
   (A) By
   (B) Despite
   (C) There are
   (D) Although

5 _____, he loved to build model airplanes like any other boy.
   (A) To be a boy
   (B) Be a boy
   (C) While he was a boy
   (D) He was a boy

6 The surgeons washed their hands _____ they entered the operating room.
   (A) and if
   (B) while
   (C) and after
   (D) before

7 None of them in the room knows _____ a new sales manager.
   (A) who will be
   (B) whom will be
   (C) that who will be
   (D) who he will be

8 _____ postponed, the class was canceled as well.
   (A) The exam
   (B) The exam was
   (C) When the exam
   (D) When the exam was

어법상 잘못된 부분을 고르시오.

9 I will <u>go</u> to the office today, <u>when</u> <u>it</u> is a <u>holiday</u>.
      (A)   (B) (C)   (D)

10 <u>Though</u> <u>you</u> need <u>a</u> calculator, you can use <u>mine</u>.
       (A)   (B)   (C)   (D)

11 The coach <u>explained</u> <u>to us</u> <u>because</u> he had won the race <u>in detail</u>.
                 (A)   (B)   (C)   (D)

12 <u>Vermont</u> is <u>snowy</u> in <u>winter</u>, it is enjoyed <u>by</u> skiers and boarders.
       (A)   (B)   (C)   (D)

13 Olga <u>and</u> Mike <u>are playing</u> tennis <u>they</u> have a paper <u>due</u> tomorrow.
            (A)   (B)   (C)   (D)

14 <u>Since</u> no one <u>came</u> to save him, so <u>he</u> began <u>to explore</u> the island.
       (A)   (B)   (C)   (D)

15 Kevin <u>wondered</u> <u>while</u> she <u>set off</u> on a trip <u>to</u> India.
             (A)   (B)   (C)   (D)

16 <u>Even</u> <u>going up</u> a ladder is <u>easy</u>, looking down can <u>be</u> difficult.
       (A)   (B)   (C)   (D)

17 The point <u>that</u> we should waste no time <u>because</u> the results <u>are due</u> <u>at</u> the end of the week.
                 (A)   (B)   (C)   (D)

18 The ship changed <u>its</u> course <u>so which</u> it could help <u>another</u> ship <u>in trouble</u>.
                        (A)   (B)   (C)   (D)

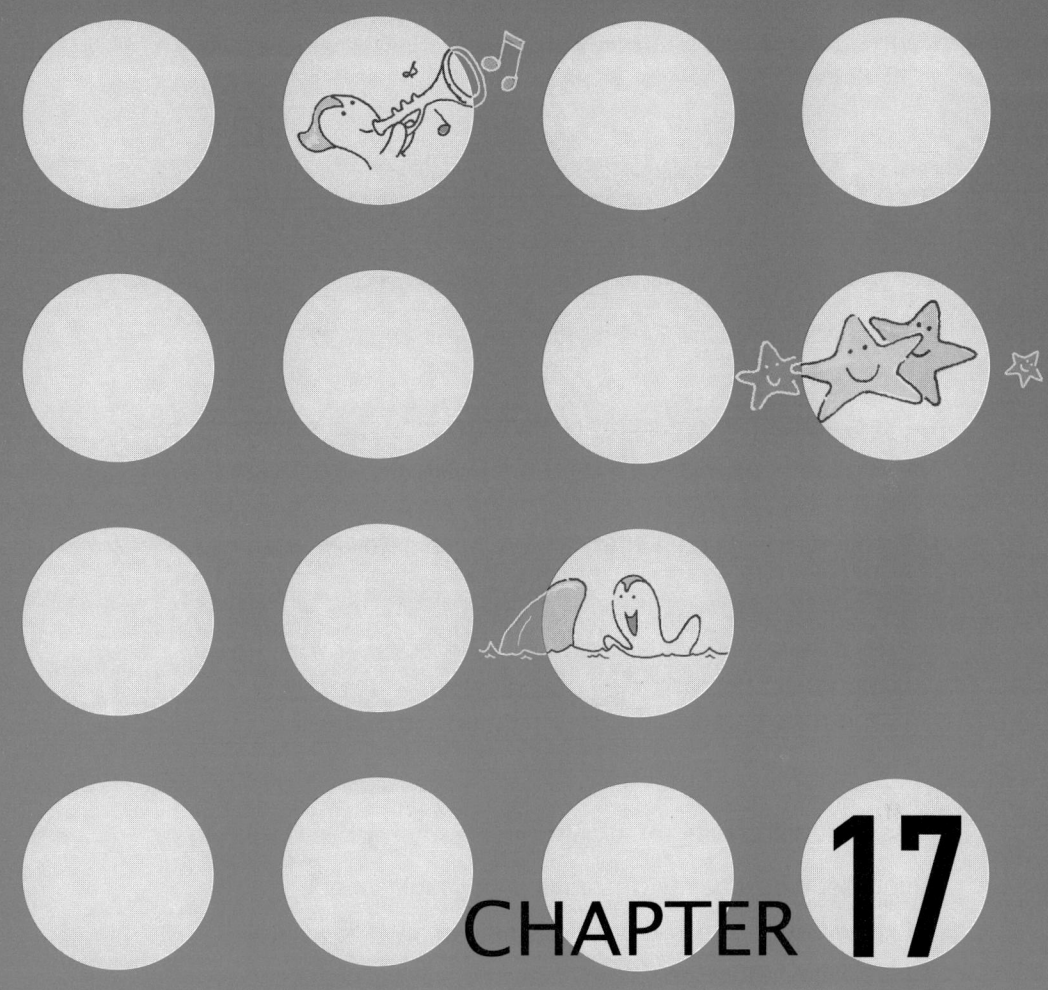

CHAPTER 17

형용사절
Adjective Clauses

17-1 관계대명사절의 형태와 역할

● 형용사절(관계대명사절)의 역할은 명칭에서 보듯이 명사를 수식하는 것이며 따라서 명사 바로 뒤에 위치한다. 한편, 관계대명사는 형용사절 안에서 일종의 대명사와 같이 주어, 보어, 목적어, 전치사의 목적어 역할을 한다.

1 선행사, 격 그리고 관계사절 [Relative* Clauses]

- 격은 주격, 소유격, 목적격을 말한다. 주격보어는 주격에 속한다.
- 관계대명사의 격은 관계대명사절 안의 성분으로 결정된다.

I know Ginny. + **She** was my classmate in my high school.
　　　　　　　　　　[주격]

I know Ginny, **who** was my classmate in my high school.

▸ 선행사 Ginny가 목적어라고 하여 목적격 관계대명사인 whom을 사용하지 않도록 한다.

Fred turns out to be a fraud*. + We have always trusted **him**.
　　　　　　　　　　　　　　　　　　　　　　　　　[목적격]

Fred **whom** we have always trusted turns out to be a fraud.

▸ Fred가 주어라고 하여 주격 관계대명사인 who을 사용하지 않도록 한다.
▸ 문법적으로는 틀리지만, 일상회화에서는 whom을 who로 대체하기도 한다.

2 I know **her who** was my classmate in my high school.

I know her who was my classmate in my high school.
→ I know Ginny who was my classmate in my high school.　　(better)
→ I know the lady who was my classmate in my high school.　　(better)

▸ 목적격 대명사 her 뒤에 주격 관계대명사 who가 이어지면 조금 어색하게 들린다. 이러한 경우에는 her를 일반명사 (a girl, a lady, a person, the one) 또는 고유명사(Ginny 등)로 바꾸는 것이 자연스럽다.

- 일반적으로 he, her, them 등의 인칭대명사는 관계대명사의 수식을 받는 것이 어색하게 들릴 수 있다.

They (who are) waiting to see the doctor may go in now.
→ Those (who are) waiting to see the doctor may go in now.　　(better)
This is he who called you last night.
→ This is the one/the man who called you last night.　　(better)

▸ 선행사 they, he는 형식적이거나 또는 거만한 느낌이 들 수 있다.

He who laughs last laughs best.　　(속담 – 마지막에 웃는 자가 제대로 웃는 자이다)

3 주격 관계대명사와 동사의 일치

I know some people that speak five languages.
The cap that is in the locker is mine.

4 관계대명사의 종류

분류	주격	목적격	소유격
사람	who, that	whom(/who), that, Ø	whose*
사물, 동물	which, that	which, that, Ø	whose, of+which

Let the person that/who made this mess clean it up.
Let the voters choose the government that/which/Ø they want.
Bob is a person whose energies are activated by a chat.
 ← Bob is a person. His energies are activated by a chat.

May I eat the cookies that/which are on the table?
The food that/which/Ø we had on the flight was not bad. (기내 식사가 나쁘지 않았어)
 ← The food was not bad. We had the food on the flight.

Look at the house whose roof is painted green.
= Look at the house of which the roof is painted green.
= Look at the house the roof of which is painted green.
 ← Look at the house. Its roof is painted green.

5 전치사의 목적어

- '전치사+전치사의 목적어'는 하나의 사고단위를 형성하므로 전치사의 목적어가 이동하면 전치사도 함께 이동하는 것이 기본 원칙이다. 따라서, 전치사는 자신의 목적어인 관계대명사와 함께 형용사절 앞으로 이동한다.

- 일상회화에서는 관계대명사만 이동시킨 표현도 즐겨 쓴다.

    Here comes a bus. We've been waiting for it.
    → Here comes a bus for which we've been waiting.   Writing 시험에서 선호
    → Here comes a bus which/that/Ø we've been waiting for.

    Do you remember Jessica? I told you about her.
    → Do you remember Jessica about whom I told you?   Writing 시험에서 선호
    → Do you remember Jessica who(m)/that/Ø I told you about?

6 관계대명사 that이 선호되는 경우

- That은 문장에서 없어서는 안 될 정보를 제공할 때 쓰이며 who, which는 계속적 용법(없어도 될 정보)을 제공할 때 쓰이는 것이 기본이다. 회화에서는 엄격한 구분없이 that을 사용하기도 한다.
- That은 '이~, 저~'와 같이 지시 대상의 범위를 제한하는 느낌이 강하다. 따라서, 선행사에 the only, the very, the same, all, every, some, any, no 등과 같이 제한하는 의미를 가진 수식어가 포함된 경우에는 that이 사용되는 경우가 많다.

He was **the only person who** didn't agree with me.   (acceptable)
He was **the only person that** didn't agree with me.   (better)

Check Up

1 다음 문장이 바르게 쓰였으면 O표를 하고, 잘못 쓰였으면 ×표를 하시오.

_____ (1) The clothes that is in the locker are mine.
_____ (2) I know the man, who speak five languages.
_____ (3) I saw the girl who was leaning against the wall.
_____ (4) She loves him who loves her.
_____ (5) Please return the book you borrowed last week.
_____ (6) We know the man whom is a teacher.
_____ (7) There is someone which you actually want to meet.
_____ (8) Do you remember Jessica about that I told you?
_____ (9) There is no one that the little girl would depend on.
_____ (10) Here comes a bus for that we've been waiting.
_____ (11) The woman who she lent me five dollars was kind and very friendly.
_____ (12) They decide on the furniture that are set next to the window.
_____ (13) The picture sold for one million dollars which were painted by an anonymous* artist.

2 다음 우리말을 영어로 세 번씩 말하시오.

(1) 이 쪽은 나의 친한 친구 중 한 명인 Alice입니다.
(2) 우리 모두는 파란 모자를 쓴 David을 좋아한다.
(3) 그녀는 내가 맞서 경기해 본 최고의 선수이다.

(4) Peter는 금요일 밤마다 방송되는 TV 쇼를 보는 것을 즐긴다.
(5) 우리는 텍사스에 있는 그 대학을 방문할 예정이다.
(6) Daniel은 무언가 내가 분명하게 알아 들을 수 없는 말을 했다.

3 🔊 Speak-out 다음 우리말을 영어로 세 번씩 말하시오.

(1) 네가 찾고 있는 열쇠가 담요 아래에 있다.
(2) 겨우 네 살인 Tom은 하모니카를 연주할 수 있다.
(3) 그가 다니는 학교는 한국에서 가장 좋다.
(4) 나는 지난 일요일에 네가 추천한 영화를 봤다.
(5) 당신 옆에 앉아 있던 사람이 개를 가지고 있었습니까?
(6) 오늘은 진열된 모든 신발들이 할인됩니다.

4 🔊 Speak-out 다음 우리말을 영어로 세 번씩 말하시오.

(1) 그는 Michelle[miːʃél]이라는 여자로부터 전화를 받았다.
(2) Brown씨는 그의 트럭이 길을 막고 있는 운전수에게 소리쳤다.
(3) 우리는 우리가 달리는 속도를 측정했다.
(4) 당신은 자유롭게 말을 할 상대를 가지고 있나요?
(5) 그녀는 내가 들어본 적이 없는 아주 작은 마을에서 왔다.

5 🔊 Speak-out 알맞은 관계대명사를 고르고, 끊어 읽기와 이어 읽기에 유의하여 큰 소리로 세 번씩 읽으시오.

> Do you know Sam, / about (who, whose, whom, that) I spoke yesterday? It is hard / to get to know Sam, / who never stops moving. He is the kind / of person / (who, whose, whom, which) is always / in a hurry. He always has / 20 things / that he must do. He has to write a paper / that is required / for his history class. He has to visit Susan, / who is in the hospital. Then he must see Bill, / (who, whose, whom, which) CD player / he borrowed, to return it / to him. Next, / he needs to look up something / (who, whose, whom, that) he needs / on an internet site. After that, / he has to practice / with the band / that he plays in. He never stops! When does he find time / to sleep?

- **relative** [rélətiv]　*adj.* 관계 있는, 관련되어 있는　*–n.* 친척, 일가, (문법) 관계사, 관계대명사
- **fraud** [frɔːd]　*n.* 사기꾼
- **whose**　Whose가 형용사의 역할과 같은 소유격을 대신하는 경우에는 whose가 포함된 관계사절을 관계형용사절이라 하는 것이 옳지만, 일반적으로 관계대명사절을 설명할 때 함께 포함시키고 있다.
- **anonymous** [ənánəməs]　*adj.* 작자(저자) 불명의, 익명(가명)의, 이름을 안 밝히는

17-2 관계대명사 what

선행사를 포함하고 있는 관계대명사 what은 결과적으로 **명사절** what과 형태나 역할에 있어서 차이점이 없다. 관계대명사 what이 만들어지는 과정을 학습은 하지만, 명사절의 what과 같은 것으로 인식하는 것이 활용하기에 쉽다. Wh-ever가 이끄는 관계사절도 what과 마찬가지로 명사절로 생각하는 것이 쉽지만, wh-ever절은 부사절로도 사용된다는 사실을 기억하자.

1 관계대명사 what이 만들어지는 과정

The things are perfectly true. + He said the things.
→ The things that he said are perfectly true.
→ What he said is perfectly true. 　　　　　　　　　　　주어 (그가 말했던 것)

Being alone is what I actually want. 　　　　　　　　　보어
Diana couldn't believe what she watched last night. 　목적어
His theory is just based on what he has personally experienced. 　전치사의 목적어

▶ 굳이, 의미적으로 차이점을 비교한다면 일반명사절의 what은 '무엇'이라는 의미가 강하다.
　ex. We don't know what love means.

2 강조의 what

- 일상회화에서는 전달하려는 의미를 강조하기 위해 'what ~+be동사' 구문을 사용하기도 한다.

  What Mike did *is* (to) choose five universities to apply to.
  = Mike chose five universities to apply to.

  What I need to do *is* (to) write to Chris immediately.
  = I need to write to Chris immediately.

3 관계사 + -ever [wh-ever 관계사절]

- '한계를 제한하지 않는다'는 의미를 나타낸다.

- whatever 　무엇이든　　　　　　　　　= anything that ~, no matter what ~
  whenever 　언제 ~하든, ~할 때마다　　= at any time, every time, each time

- 접속사로서의 역할과 동시에 종속절 안에서 명사(명사절인 경우) 또는 전치사구(부사절인 경우)의 역할을 한다. 즉, 형용사절을 이끄는 관계사가 선행사를 포함하여 명사절 또는 부사절로 사용되는 경우라고 할 수 있다.

  whatever you do = anything (that) you do
  wherever you go = at any place to which you go

명사절	**Whoever** was born in America can be an American citizen.	(Anyone who ~)
명사절	Why did they complain about **whatever** I proposed?	(anything that ~)
부사절	**Whomever** you invite, I don't care.	(No matter whom ~)
부사절	**Whatever** other people said, Sam stuck to* his own views.	(No matter what ~)
부사절	Be sure to phone me **however** late you are.	(no matter how late ~)
부사절	In Canada, **wherever** I went, I came across* Charlie.	(at any place where ~)

Check Up

1 ▶ Speak-out 다음 우리말을 영어로 옮겨 큰 소리로 세 번씩 말하시오.

(1) 이 피아노는 내가 항상 꿈꾸던 것이다.
↪ _____

(2) Olga는 그가 말하는 것을 주의 깊게 들었다.
↪ _____

(3) 내가 본 것은 나를 뼈 속까지 오싹하게 했다.
↪ _____

(4) 우리가 걱정하는 것은 내일 비가 올 것인지 않을 것인지이다.
↪ _____

2 밑줄 친 부분을 대신할 수 있는 접속사를 보기에서 골라 쓰시오.

보기 | whatever   whoever   wherever   whenever

_____ (1) No matter who won the lottery, we would share the wealth.
_____ (2) You can choose anything that you want to have.
_____ (3) At any time when I wash my car, it rains.
_____ (4) Find the secrets of life from any page where you turn to.

3 다음 문장에서 종속절이 하는 역할을 고르시오.

명사☐ 형용사☐ 부사☐ (1) In Canada, we escape to the wood whenever we'd like to.
명사☐ 형용사☐ 부사☐ (2) Whatever happens, I will deliver this letter to your father.
명사☐ 형용사☐ 부사☐ (3) Read the entire first two pages of whatever you've selected.

❏ **come across** 우연히 만나다 (across는 부사)   ❏ **stick to** 고집하다, 고수하다, 충실히 지키다 (to는 전치사)

17-3 관계부사절

● 관계부사절이라 하여 부사절로 착각하지 않도록 한다. 관계사절(관계대명사절, 관계부사절)은 명사를 수식하는 형용사의 역할을 한다. 관계부사절에서 관계부사는 '접속사+부사구'를 포함하고 있다. 관계부사절은 명사 뒤에서 형용사 역할을 하지만, 동사 뒤에서는 명사절로 취급될 수도 있는 것이 매우 특이하다. What이 관계사절이지만 명사절로 취급되는 것과도 유사하고, 선행사가 생략되면 의문사가 이끄는 명사절과 같은 역할을 한다.

1 관계부사와 관계부사절 만들기

■ 관계부사는 접속사+부사(구)의 역할을 한다.
즉, 형용사절을 이끄는 종속접속사인 동시에 전치사구(전치사+관계대명사)를 포함한다.

The hotel was awful. + I stayed in the hotel.
→ The hotel *in which* I stayed was awful.   관계대명사절-명사 수식
→ The hotel *where* I stayed was awful.   관계부사절-명사 수식

2 관계부사절은 원래 형용사절. 그런데 명사절?

■ She told me the reason. + She resigned her position for the reason.
→ ~the reason which/that/∅ she resigned her position for.   관계대명사절-형용사 역할
→ ~the reason *for which* she resigned her position.   관계대명사절-형용사 역할
→ ~the reason *why* she resigned her position.   관계부사절-형용사 역할
→ She told me *why* she resigned her position.   명사절(직접목적어)
→ She told me the reason she resigned her position.

▶ 마지막 두 문장은 why와 the reason이 동일한 의미를 나타내고 있어서 의미 중복을 피하기 위해 둘 중 하나가 생략된 형태이다. 특히, 마지막 문장은 전치사 for가 빠진 형태로써 문법적으로는 옳지 않지만 관계부사절이 간략하게 되는 과정에서 발생하는 특이한 경우의 형용사절이라고 할 수 있다.

3 관계부사절의 종류

선행사의 의미	관계부사절 형태	관계대명사절 형태
시간(time)	when ~	in/on/at which
장소(place)	where ~	in/on/at/to which
이유(reason)	why ~	for which
방법(way, manner)	how ~	in which

4 선행사가 생략되지 않는 경우

- 선행사가 the place, the time, the reason, the manner 등과 같이 일반적인 의미를 가질 때에는 생략하는 것이 좋지만, 특정한 의미의 명사인 경우에는 생략할 수 없으므로 관계부사를 생략하는 것이 좋다.

  Do you remember March 20th when we met for the first time?
  → Do you remember when we met for the first time?   (중요한 의미 상실, when이하는 명사절임.)
  → Do you remember March 20th we met for the first time?

  Do you remember the day when we met for the first time?
  → Do you remember when we met for the first time?
  → Do you remember the day we met for the first time?

- 관계부사가 how인 경우 선행사 또는 관계부사 중 어느 하나를 반드시 생략해야 한다.

  Could you show me the way I should cook rice?   (O)
  Could you show me how I should cook rice?   (O)
  Could you show me the way how I should cook rice?   (×)

Check Up

1 ▶ Speak-out 밑줄 친 표현을 알맞은 관계부사로 바꾸어 큰 소리로 세 번씩 말하시오.

(1) This is the time at which the mall is most crowded.
(2) The town in which Raul grew up was very small and quiet.
(3) Do you know the reason for which she divorced* her husband?
(4) There was a period in which dinosaurs* dominated the Earth.
(5) She explained in which we can distinguish men from animals.
(6) A habitat* is a place in which a particular type of plant or animal lives.

2 다음 문장이 바르게 쓰였으면 O표를 하고, 잘못 쓰였으면 ×표를 하시오.

_____ (1) The room in where she died in 2003 has been preserved.
_____ (2) Wasn't that the winter when we took the boys camping?
_____ (3) Many people love the smooth way how he plays the drums.

_____ (4) I cannot remember the reason for why Richard wanted us to leave.
_____ (5) Soon afterwards she reached a stage where she began to enjoy her work.

3 밑줄 친 접속사가 이끄는 절의 종류가 명사절이면 NC(Noun Clauses)를 쓰고, 형용사절이면 AC(Adjective Clauses)를 쓰시오.

(1) _____ ⓐ Uncle Ted built the house <u>where</u> we now live.
    _____ ⓑ You'll never imagine <u>where</u> Robbie and I are going.
(2) _____ ⓐ If you wonder <u>how</u> he did it, ask him.
    _____ ⓑ Ms. Ann broke down describing <u>how</u> her son died.
(3) _____ ⓐ Do you know the reason <u>why</u> Mark isn't in class today?
    _____ ⓑ I don't know <u>why</u> men like motorcycles.
(4) _____ ⓐ I've never been told <u>when</u> we begin our summer vacation.
    _____ ⓑ My favorite month is February <u>when</u> we celebrate Valentine's Day.

4 🔊 **Speak-out** 다음 우리말을 영어로 옮겨 큰 소리로 세 번씩 말하시오.

(1) 2002년은 대한민국과 일본에서 월드컵이 열린 해이다.
    ⇨ _____
(2) 이 곳은 실제로 작은 사원이 서 있던 곳이다.
    ⇨ _____
(3) 나는 그가 초대를 거절했던 어떤 이유도 생각할 수 없다.
    ⇨ _____
(4) 경험은 당신이 무엇인가를 배우기 위한 가장 좋은 방법이다.
    ⇨ _____
(5) 내가 2년 동안 머물렀던 Florida는 쾌적한 기후로 유명하다.
    ⇨ _____
(6) 일년 중 날씨가 가장 좋은 때는 8월이다.
    ⇨ _____

---

comments

❏ **divorce** [divɔ́:rs] *v.* 이혼하다, 분리하다
❏ **dinosaur** [dáinəsɔ̀:r] *n.* 공룡
❏ **habitat** [hǽbitæt] *n.* 생태 환경, 거주 환경, (동·식물의) 서식지, (표본 등의) 채집지, 거주지

17-4 쉼표와 관계사절

관계사 앞에 '쉼표가 없으면' 선행사의 의미를 올바로 전달하기 위하여 관계사절이 반드시 필요한 경우이다. 이와 달리, 관계사 앞에 '쉼표가 있으면' 관계사절의 내용이 없어도 내용 전달에 지장은 없지만 추가적 정보를 활용하여 대화를 더욱 생동감 있게 진행할 수 있다.

1 쉼표와 관계사절

1) 관계사 앞에 쉼표가 없는 경우(제한적 용법): 필수적인 정보(essential information) 전달

One might miss **the moment when** he or she was young.

▸ 관계사절의 정보가 없으면 the moment가 어떤 순간인지를 상대방이 알 수 없다.

2) 관계사 앞에 쉼표가 있는 경우(계속적 용법): 추가적인 정보(additional information) 전달

The reason, **why** I visited them, was because I was invited.
Ms. Stuart, **who** is a pet sitter*, is really proud of her job.

▸ Ms. Stuart가 누구인지를 대화 참여자들이 이미 알고 있으며, 관계사절의 정보가 없어도 의사 소통에 아무런 지장이 없다.

● 계속적 용법으로 쓰인 관계사는 생략할 수 없다.

This guy is the man (**that**) I have mentioned to you before. that 생략 가능
The chair, **which** you're sitting on, costs one hundred million dollars. which 생략 불가

Check Up

1 다음 두 문장의 의미를 비교하시오.

(1) I reached a lamp that was on the table.
(2) I reached a lamp, which was on the table.

2 주어진 문장과 의미가 같아지도록 둘 중 알맞은 표현을 고르시오.

(1) She has a son whose wife is a doctor.
 = (Only some, All) of her daughters-in-law are doctors.
(2) My books, which are very old, are valuable.
 = (Only some, All) my books are old.

❏ **pet sitter** 애완용 동물을 돌보아 주는 사람

17-5 형용사절, 명사절, 부사절 비교

'부사절'은 접속사를 삭제하여도 완전한 문장으로 남는다. 그러나, '관계사절(형용사절)'은 접속사를 삭제하면 불완전한 문장이 되는 것이 특징이다. 즉, 관계사절을 이끄는 종속접속사는 접속사의 역할을 하면서도 관계사절 안에서 주어, 보어 또는 목적어의 역할을 동시에 수행한다. 한편, '명사절'은 접속사를 삭제할 때 완전한 문장으로 남는 경우가 있고 그렇지 않은 경우가 있다.

1 관계사절과 명사절, 부사절의 비교

■ 다음 문장 안에 있는 종속절에서 종속접속사를 삭제하면

① 부사절	**Now that** he failed the test, he has to take it again.		Complete
② 형용사절	The student **who** is sitting next to Fred is my son.		Incomplete
③ 형용사절	Here are the keys **that** you were looking for.		Incomplete
④ 명사절	I can assure you **that** your child is well cared for.		Complete
⑤ 명사절	I don't know **who** she is.		Incomplete

▶ ① 밑줄 친 부분은 완전한 문장 / now that ~한 일이 벌어져서, ~하기 때문에
② 주어가 없으므로 불완전한 문장. Who가 주어의 역할을 하면서 동시에 종속접속사의 역할을 함.
③ 전치사의 목적어가 없기 때문에 불완전한 문장. Which가 for의 목적어 역할을 하면서 동시에 종속접속사의 역할을 함.
④ 밑줄 친 부분은 완전한 문장 / They well care for your child.
⑤ 보어가 빠져 있으므로 불완전한 문장. 관계대명사절과 유사하게 접속사 who가 보어의 역할을 하면서 동시에 종속접속사의 역할을 함. **의문사가 이끄는 명사절에서 일어나는 현상**.

2 관계사절의 접속사, 명사절의 접속사

명사절 접속사	형용사절 접속사	비 고
if		부사절에서도 사용
whether (or not)		부사절에서도 사용 (= even if)
that	that	
which	which	
who, whom, whose	who, whom, whose	
how	how	
what	what	형용사절의 what은 결과적으로 명사절과 동일
when	when	부사절에서도 사용
where, why	where, why	

Grammar Review

1 종속된 절을 찾아 밑줄을 긋고, 그 역할을 보기에서 골라 쓰시오.

보기 | 명사   형용사   부사

_____ (1) The news that Charlie is getting married astonished me.
_____ (2) The watch that I got fixed has just stopped working again.
_____ (3) I've not changed my belief that he is the right person to lead us.
_____ (4) Which of them do you think would be the best?
_____ (5) There are lots of skyscrapers in Seoul, one of which has more than 60 stories.
_____ (6) It's the day when the press conference is.
_____ (7) Do you check when the press conference is?
_____ (8) When Tom was a little boy, he hoped to become a movie star.
_____ (9) The police officer asked if I was at home, and I said yes.
_____ (10) Whenever I'm in the basement and the phone rings, I don't run to answer it. If the message is important, the person will call back.

2 다음 글을 읽고, 빈 칸에 들어갈 알맞은 표현을 고르시오.

The couple (1) _____ just moved in next door look like quiet neighbors.
　　　　　　Ⓐ that　Ⓑ that they

They seem like the best neighbors that we could hope for. The man comes home from the factory where he works at night as a security guard, and sleeps during the day. That means they have a home (2) _____ must be quiet
　　　　　　　　　　　　　　　　　　　　　Ⓐ it　Ⓑ that

during the day. His wife also needs a quiet place where she can do editing at home for a publisher. They have one daughter who is away at school, where she studies commerce, and their pet, (3) _____ an old cat, will not make
　　　　　　　　　　　　　　　　　　　Ⓐ it is　Ⓑ which is

the kind of noise that a barking dog would make. So, things where our neighbors are concerned look good. Do you remember (4) _____ really noisy
　　　　　　　　　　　　　　　　　　　　Ⓐ when we had　Ⓑ what we had
neighbors?

Grammar Up

Time Limit: 6 min, _____ / 18

어법상 빈 칸에 들어갈 알맞은 표현을 고르시오.

1   Some mountains, _____ are volcanoes, are still being made.
   (A)   which
   (B)   who
   (C)   what
   (D)   but

2   The singer has a beautiful wife _____ he made many songs.
   (A)   who
   (B)   whom she
   (C)   for whom
   (D)   with her

3   Animals _____ webbed feet are good swimmers.
   (A)   and have
   (B)   that have
   (C)   that they have
   (D)   to have that

4   Tornadoes are very strong storms _____ perhaps the strongest on Earth.
   (A)   are the winds
   (B)   the winds are
   (C)   that the winds are
   (D)   whose winds are

5   There are many famous portraits in the world, _____ was painted by Leonardo da Vinci.
   (A)   which of
   (B)   the one
   (C)   one of which
   (D)   one of them

6   My stepmother likes to work in the yard _____ shining.
   (A)   the sun is
   (B)   and the sun is
   (C)   when the sun
   (D)   whenever the sun is

7 Joe's dog, _____ Joe everywhere, had been given to him by his aunt.
  (A) which followed
  (B) it followed
  (C) followed
  (D) what followed

어법상 잘못된 부분을 고르시오.

8 Christmas which is the day not only for God but also for children.
  　　　　　　(A)　　　　　　(B)　　　(C)　　　　(D)

9 The mountain is green, what top is always white with snow.
  (A)　　　　　　　　(B)　　　(C)　　　　(D)

10 A witness should say that he or she has seen or heard.
  　　　　　(A)　　　(B)　　　　　(C)　　(D)

11 Have you ever been to New York, which you can make friends from all countries?
  　　　(A) (B)　　　　　　　(C)　　　　　　　　　(D)

12 Henry David Thoreau was a writer and naturalist whom lived in the nineteenth century.
  　　　　　　　　　　　(A)　　　　　　　　(B)　　(C)　　(D)

13 This book contains many interesting stories who can interest children.
  (A)　　　　　(B)　　　　　　(C)　　　　(D)

14 The bases in a baseball game that are the four stations, and the players must go around them.
  　　　　　　　　　　(A)　　　　(B)　　　　　　　　　(C)
  (D)

15 We have electrical machines can wash and dry clothes automatically.
  　　　(A)　　　(B)　　　　　　　(C)　　(D)

16 My brother is in this picture which it was taken in L.A. last year.
  　　　(A) (B)　　　　(C)　　(D)

17 The man became Buddha was the son of a king in the mountains of India.
  　　　(A)　　　　　　　　(B)　　　　　(C)　　(D)

18 Some animals take their food and energy from other organisms on that they live.
  (A)　　　　　　　　　(B)　　　　　　(C)　(D)

Grammar in Context

A teacher who changed my life

Is there a teacher who really changed your life? I had a teacher who was like that. In college, when I took a course in French literature, I met Dr. White. Her lectures, which really made the subject interesting, pointed out all _____ can be learned from authors who wrote in French. Two of the authors _____ she discussed were Stendhal and Camus. One thing _____ she pointed out was how much modern bestsellers owe to Stendahl, who wrote about people who lived in exciting times when the world was changing greatly. Camus, who was a very different writer, also wrote in a different age from Stendahl's. Stendahl wrote stories _____ were set in the 19th century. Camus, who wrote in the 20th century, when dictators like Hitler and Stalin ruled, saw the world changed in very ugly ways by the tyranny and warfare which that century produced. These were just a few things that I learned in Dr. White's course, which gave me a whole new view of literature.

170 words, Reading Time: _____

1 빈 칸에 공통으로 들어갈 관계사를 쓰시오.

2 뒤에서 세 번째 관계사를 찾아 쓰시오.

3 다음 문장이 참이면 T를 쓰고, 거짓이면 F를 쓰시오.
  _____ (1) Dr. White was a teacher who lectured on French literature in college.
  _____ (2) Stendahl and Camus are French novelists who have a very similar style of writing.
  _____ (3) It is inferred that Camus was pessimistic about the human condition.

4 **Chain of Thought:** 다음 문장을 논리적 흐름에 따라 앞에서부터 이해해 봅시다.
  (1) I had / a teacher / who really changed / my life.
  → 나는 있다 [누가? 무엇이?] _____ [어떤 선생님이냐 하면] _____ [누구를?/무엇을?] _____
  (2) Stendahl wrote / about people / who lived / in exciting times / when the world was changing / greatly.
  → _____ _____ _____ _____ _____ _____

규칙 1: 문장을 생각의 흐름에 따른 사고단위(Thought Unit)로 나누어 이해한다.
규칙 2: 명사 뒤에는 그 명사를 설명하는 형용사(구, 절)가 따라나올 것을 예상한다. 다른 뜻(부사구, 절)을 가진 어구가 나오면 전체 문장에 적합하도록 해석한다.
규칙 3: 문장을 뒤에서부터 해석하려고 하면 Chain of Thought에 따른 문장 이해에 혼란이 생길 수 있으므로 각별히 주의해야 한다. 뒷부분은 모두 가리고 앞에서부터 해당 부분만을 보면서 이해하도록 한다.

CHAPTER 18

전치사구
_Prepositional Phrases

18-1 전치사와 끊어 읽기, 이어 읽기

'전치사구(전치사+전치사의 목적어)'는 두 개 이상의 단어가 모여 하나의 단어와 같은 의미와 역할을 갖는다. 따라서, 전치사와 전치사의 목적어를 끊어 읽어서는 안 되며, 붙여(이어) 읽어야 한다. 또한 전치사 앞에서는 끊어 읽어야 명확한 의미를 상대방에게 전달할 수 있다. 이는 "아버지가 방에 들어가신다"를 "아버지 가방에 들어가신다"로 읽을 때 생기는 혼동과 비슷하다. 한편 끊어 읽기와 이어 읽기 연습은 문법과 독해 학습에도 매우 효과적이지만, Speaking과 Listening 학습을 위해서도 핵심적인 기초 학습에 속한다.

1 전치사구의 해부도

Are you interested in what he said to a person by the name of Brian on Saturday?

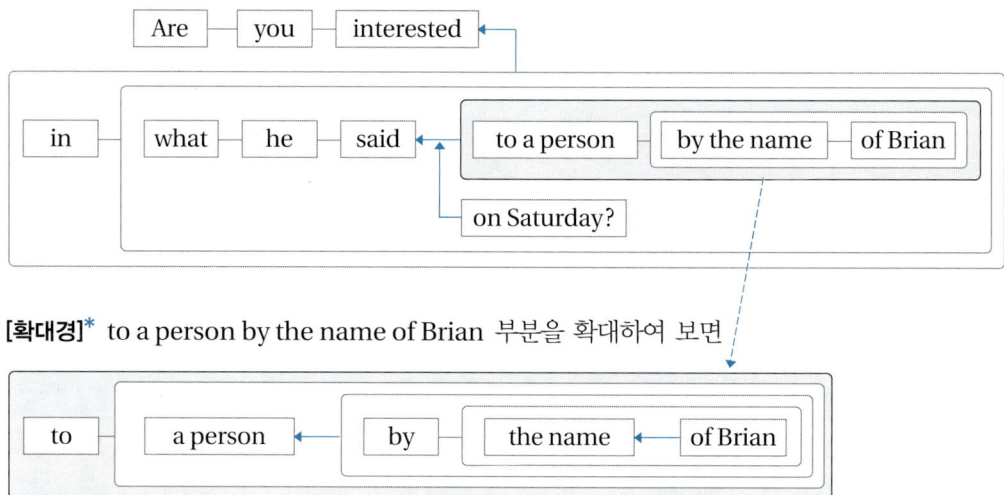

[확대경]* to a person by the name of Brian 부분을 확대하여 보면

- 끊어 읽어야 하는 부분이 고정되어 있는 것은 아니다. 사람에 따라서 길게 붙여 읽기도 하고 짧게 끊어 읽기도 한다. 또한, 강조하고 싶은 부분은 별도로 끊어 읽기도 한다.

- 아래의 문장을 '/'로 표시된 부분에서 끊어 읽고 그 사이의 단어들을 이어서 읽을 때, 전치사와 관사가 자연스럽게 약세 발음됨을 느낄 수 있으면 올바르게 읽은 것이다.
Are you interested / in what he said / to a person / by the name of Brian / on Saturday?

> 대화하는 실제 상황에서는 읽을 때와 달리 무슨 말을 할까 생각하는 과정에서 끊고 이어지는 부분에 관한 기본 원칙이 다양하게 변화한다. TOEFL iBT 청취에서는 이와 같은 다양한 실제 상황이 포함되어 있다.

2 전치사와 전치사구 [Prepositional Phrases]

- 전치사는 명사와 명사 상당어구*를 목적어로 취하여 구를 형성한다.
- 전치사구는 형용사 또는 부사와 같은 역할을 한다.

Sally's gone / **without** saying good-bye / **to** her ex-boyfriend.
My grandmother died / **from** sadness / **after** a couple of days / **from** the day / her hamster died.

▶ 위의 예문에서 (when) her hamster died는 day를 수식하는 형용사절이다.

Maria is proud / *of* being a member / of Lemon University Press.　(O)
Maria is proud *of* to be a member of Lemon University Press.　(×)
Maria is proud *of* that she is a member of Lemon University Press.　(×)

- to-부정사구와 that절은 전치사와 함께 사용하지 않는다. (Ch.16-2 참고)
따라서, to-부정사구와 that절을 사용하는 경우에는 전치사를 생략한다.

Maria is proud / **to be** a member / of Lemon University Press.　(O)
Maria is proud / **that** she is a member / of Lemon University Press.　(O)

- 동사-부사가 결합된 Phrasal Verbs의 경우 동사와 부사를 이어 읽어야 한다.

Before the 17th century, / people **found out** / the way **of** making fire / **with** a magnifying* glass.

Check Up

1 〔Speak-out〕 전치사를 찾아 동그라미를 하고 그 목적어(명사 및 그 상당어구)에 밑줄을 그으시오. 그리고, 끊어 읽기와 이어 읽기에 유의하여 큰 소리로 세 번씩 말하시오.

(1) Robbie was happy about his new job.
(2) People in this village are very kind and generous.
(3) Letters written long ago are important to historians.
(4) Try on shoes to make sure they fit*.
(5) The answer to a question depends on how the question is asked.

(6) Make the sauce by boiling the cream and sugar for 15 minutes.
(7) The original story that the film is based on has a happy ending.
(8) Around the mid-20th century, technology put machines in charge* of many jobs that humans had done before.

2 **Speak-out** 밑줄 친 전치사구의 역할(형용사, 부사)을 쓰고, 끊어 읽기와 이어 읽기에 유의하여 큰 소리로 세 번씩 말하시오.

_____ (1) I was in the bank when you called me.
_____ (2) My grandmother, who is 80 years old, is in good health.
_____ (3) We want young people of ability, confidence, and ambition.
_____ (4) In better times, he would have led a better life.
_____ (5) Please make yourself at home and help yourself to the food.
_____ (6) Have you seen the movie *"Woman in Red"*?
_____ (7) Jessica arrived earlier by two hours.
_____ (8) The water in the bath is so hot that I cannot step into it.

3 **Speak-out** 앞에서 열 번째 전치사구를 찾아 그 역할(형용사, 부사)을 쓰고, 끊어 읽기와 이어 읽기에 유의하여 지문 전체를 큰 소리로 읽으시오.

> This restaurant / has been in business / since 1990. On Monday through Friday, / it opens at 8 a.m. / and stays open until 10 p.m. It is open from 8 a.m. / to 10 p.m. each Saturday. On Sunday, / it is closed. The bill for lunch / is never above five dollars. Some sandwiches / are below two dollars. With meals, / customers get free cups / of coffee. During summer, / you can eat inside the restaurant / or at tables outside it. Above the doorway / hangs a big kite. Beside the door / is an old gas pump. There is no other / place like it. Try going there / on your lunch break!

comments

- **[확대경] to a person by the name of Brian** Of Brian은 the name을 수식하는 형용사 역할을 하고, by the name of Brian은 a person을 수식하는 형용사 역할을 한다. 한편 to a person by the name of Brian은 talked를 수식하는 부사의 역할을 한다.
- **명사 상당어구** 명사, 대명사, 동명사구, 부정사구, 명사절
- **magnify** [mǽgnəfài] v. 확대하다, 과장하다
- **fit** [fit] v. ~에 (알)맞다, 적합하다
- **charge** [tʃɑːrdʒ] n. 책임, 의무, 관리, 담당 / in charge (of) ~을 맡고 있는, 담당의

18-2 주요 전치사: in, on, at

원어민들은 in, on, at과 같은 단어들의 차이점에 대하여 특별히 학습할 필요가 없다. 그러나, 우리는 전치사의 용법에 대해 부분적으로만 알 뿐이고, 일상회화의 다양한 상황에서 어떤 전치사를 사용하는 것이 옳은지 몰라 당황할 때가 많다. 따라서, 원어민들과는 달리 외국어로 영어를 학습하는 우리에게는 단어의 근본적 개념 연구로부터 시작하여 자연스러운 언어 학습으로 이어질 수 있는 학습법이 필요하다.

1 in, on, at의 근본 개념

In (~안에)	On (~에 붙어 있는)	At (~에)
제한된 범위, 기간 (within some kind of definite limits)	범위의 제한, 세부적인 개념, 정확한 개념	세부적인 개념, 특정한 시간, 목적 의식
In과 on은 제한된 범위를 벗어나지 못하므로 한계성이 강함		부근(next to, beside*)의 개념 포함
3차원적 개념 (on, at보다 큰 감각)	2차원적 개념 (on보다 작은, at보다 정확한 개념)	
도시, 국가, 산맥, 계절 등	거리, 요일, 날짜	시각, 주소, 전화번호

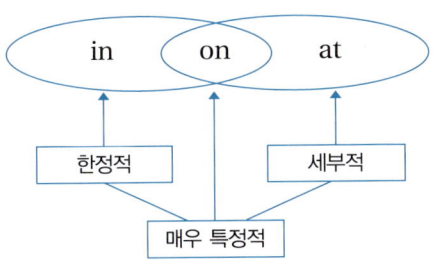

▶ On은 한계성이 강한 in과 세부적 개념이 강한 at의 특징을 동시에 갖는다. 따라서, 세부적인 사항을 나타낼 때 일반적으로 at을 사용하지만, 강한 정확성을 표현할 때에는 세부적인 개념과 한계성을 동시에 갖는 on을 사용한다.
ex. on time vs. in time*

▶ In과 on은 제한된 범위를 벗어나지 못한다.
ex. in 2006 (2006년 1월 1일 새벽 0시부터 2006년 12월 31일 밤 12시까지 / 2006년 12월 31일 밤 12시를 1초라도 넘기면 2007년이 된다.)

▶ At은 제한된 범위를 말할 수 없거나 범위의 한계를 불분명하게 표현할 때 사용한다. 또한 목적 의식을 갖고 방문한 장소를 표현한다.
ex. at 7 (6시 59분 48초라고 말하는 사람은 없다. 그냥 7시라고 말한다.)
in the building (건물 안) vs. at the building (건물 부근도 포함)

2 in, on, at의 다양한 사용 예

1) Time

They got married **in** July, 2005.

I'll be with you **in** a minute. (금방 (돌아) 올게요/잠시만 기다리세요)

All work should be done **within** 24 hours.

▶ '~을 넘지 않는(not beyond in time)'의 의미를 강조할 때에는 within을 쓴다.

on a particular day / **on** the 3rd of May / **on** Easter* 특정한 날, 요일, 날짜

▸ On은 in과 마찬가지로 제한된 범위를 표현하지만, 2차원적 개념으로 in보다는 작은 범위를 가리키는 느낌이 있다.

They are moving **on** July 16th.

We'll have our meeting **on** a morning* next week, but I'm not yet sure which one.

Steve emigrated to New Zealand with his family **at** 13. (= at the age of thirteen)

They were **at** lunch when I saw them yesterday.

at two o'clock / **at** lunch / **at** that time / **at** the moment / **at** dinner / **at** Easter*

▸ In은 제한된 기간을 표현하지만, at은 세부적인 특정한 시각, 날짜를 표현하며 부근을 포함하는 의미도 갖는다.
  ex. I'll finish it **in** 10 minutes. / I'll see you **at** 10 o'clock.

at times (경우에 따라서는, 때로는) / **at** all times (= always) / **at** the same time

▸ It is not easy for old persons to keep up **with** the times*.

2) Place

- In은 3차원적 개념이 있는 공간, 지역을 가리키므로 at에 비해 크고 넓은 곳을 가리키는 느낌이 있다. 그러나, 단순히 넓은 장소는 in, 좁은 장소는 at으로 학습하면 안 된다. At은 세부적이거나 부근을 포함하는 장소 및 목적을 갖고 방문한 장소를 표현하며, in은 단지 제한된 범위의 장소를 표현한다.

- In은 어느 정도의 기간을 포함하는 반면 at은 특정한 시간에 한정된다. 따라서, in the hospital은 '입원 중' 이라는 표현이 되며, at the hospital은 '진찰을 받는 중' 또는 '단순한 방문 중' 이라는 표현이 가능해 진다. In/At the hospital이 장소를 표현하는 것은 기본이다.

He is a three year junior **in** my high school.   (그는 나의 고등학교 3년 후배이다)

I'm waiting for you **in / at** the hospital.   단순한 장소 표현

I always keep everything **in** the safe **on** the second floor of the building.

He stayed **in the hospital** for several days after his operation.

We were **in the same college**, which was female-only **at** that time.

We usually sit **on** the armless chair, but **in** an armchair today.

Ken has lived **in** Venice for two years.

They like to go camping **in** the Rocky Mountains.   산맥

on the street   도로와 보도 포함–American English
in the street   도로와 보도 포함–British English / 도로만–American English

The bank is **at** 40 Wall Street.   특정한 장소, 세부적 주소

I met him by chance **at** the bus stop.   특정한 장소/부근

I cannot receive a phone call when I'm **at** work.   목적 의식

He threw a radio **at** me.   목적 의식

The Tower of London is **on** the Thames.   템즈 강변에 (붙어 있음)

There are a lot of banks **on** Teheran Street.   테헤란로 옆에 (붙어 있음)

The painting is **on** the wall **at** the cafe **on** the third floor **in** the hospital.

Read the article **on** page 19 and write your name **at** the top of the page.

Check Up

1 밑줄 친 전치사구의 의미를 비교하여 토론하시오.

(1) ⓐ I'll see you <u>in the morning</u>.
   ⓑ I'll see you <u>on Friday morning</u>.

(2) ⓐ David is <u>in the hospital</u>.
   ⓑ David is <u>at the hospital</u>.

(3) ⓐ He only sees her <u>on Christmas day</u>.
   ⓑ He only sees her <u>at Christmas</u>.

(4) ⓐ She gave a detailed account of what happened <u>on the fateful night</u>.
   ⓑ It happened <u>at night</u>.

2 둘 중 알맞은 표현을 고르고, 전치사의 의미에 유의하여 해석하시오.

(1) I keep stamps (in, on, at) the top drawer.

(2) My boyfriend's house is (in, on, at) the coast.

(3) Look! All the trees (in, on, at) the garden are covered with snow.

(4) When young, I was never accustomed to being the only child (in, on, at) a table full of adults.

(5) His office is (in, on, at) the 4th floor (in, on, at) the opposite building.

(6) It was (in, on, at) age 11 that Brian emigrated to Australia with his family.

(7) The car broke down (in, on, at) the day that they were supposed to leave.

(8) (In, On, At) 1762, (in, on, at) the age of six, Mozart traveled throughout Europe with his father and performed for kings and queens.

3 🔊 Speak-out 다음 우리말을 영어로 옮겨 큰 소리로 세 번씩 말하시오.

(1) 콘서트는 7시에 시작한다.
→ _____

(2) 주 회의는 금요일 10시에 열린다.
→ _____

(3) 나무는 겨울보다 여름에 더 빨리 자란다.
→ _____

(4) 미니 스커트는 1960년대에 대유행(all the rage)이었다.
→ _____

(5) 답안지(answer sheet)에 답을 표시하시오.
→ _____

(6) Charlie는 알프스 산맥의 작은 마을에 산다.
→ _____

(7) 서울은 한강 변에 있다.
→ _____

(8) 그가 앞에 서 있었기 때문에 Sue는 그를 잘 볼 수 있었다.
→ _____

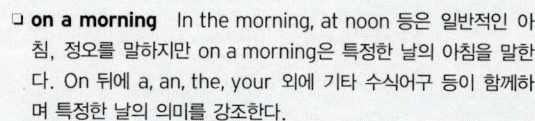

❏ **beside** [bisáid] *prep.* ~의 곁에(서) / **besides** [bisáiz] *prep.* ~외에(도) —*adv.* 게다가, 그 밖에

❏ **on time vs. in time** On time은 '정각에, 정해진 시간에 딱 맞추어'라는 의미를 강조하는 반면 in time은 '정해진 시간 내에'라는 표현으로써 on time 보다는 정확성이 떨어진다.
ex. I'll be there **on time**. / I'll be there **in time**.

❏ **on Easter** 부활절에 (부활절 당일에)

❏ **at Easter** 부활절 기간에 (부활절과 부활절 전후의 연휴 기간을 포함)

❏ **on a morning** In the morning, at noon 등은 일반적인 아침, 정오를 말하지만 on a morning은 특정한 날의 아침을 말한다. On 뒤에 a, an, the, your 외에 기타 수식어구 등이 함께하며 특정한 날의 의미를 강조한다.

❏ **the times** 현재 또는 현재의 유행을 말한다. *The Times*라는 신문 이름도 있다.

18-3 기타 전치사

어려운 단어는 의미나 사용법이 폭넓지 않으므로 단어 자체가 어려워 보여도 한 번 알고 나면 일상회화에서 사용하는 것은 무척 단순하다. 문제는 일반적인 단어들이다. 더구나 형태상 너무 쉬워 보이는 전치사는 정복하기가 매우 어렵다. 암기할 것이 많은 항목일수록 필요한 부분만을 암기하고, 다양한 예문을 통해 전치사에 대한 감각을 익히고 이해하는 것이 전치사를 정복하는 실질적인 방법이다.

1 장소(place)를 나타내는 전치사

1) above, over, below, under

She looked at herself in the mirror **above/over** the table. ~보다 위에
She looked at herself in the mirror **below/under** the clock. ~보다 아래에
The cloud flew low **over** the houses.
We decide to take a path running **under** the trees.
Once upon a time a small town lay **over/under** the hill.

▸ 수평적 이동(horizontal movement), 지역(area), 표면(surface)을 가리킬 때에는 above, below를 사용하지 않는다.

2) through, across, along, throughout

A chill wind blew in the room **through** the open window. ~을 통하여
Bob drove **through** the Sahara and visited Egypt. ~을 지나서

▸ Through는 3차원적 개념을 갖는다.

My old house is just **across** the bridge. ~의 건너편에
We now can get **across** the English Channel* by train-ferry. ~을 가로질러

▸ Across는 2차원적 개념을 갖는다.

There is a variety of beautiful flowers all **along** the roads. ~을 따라서
Flu virus spreads **throughout** the country. ~의 도처에/구석구석에

3) for, to, toward, from

Is this the bus **for** Hollywood? ~을 향하여
Finn went **to** Africa and never returned. ~쪽으로/~에게

▸ For는 단순히 방향을 나타내는 반면 to는 방향 또는 목적지에 닿았음을 의미한다.

When I looked **toward*** her, she smiled a sweet smile. ~을 향하여
Clementine is an art dealer coming **from** France. ~로부터/~에서

▸ 이동의 시작점, 기원, 출신을 나타낸다.

4) before, in front, behind, after

A crowd of people had assembled* **in front of** / **before** City Hall. ~앞에

▶ Before는 in front of와 같은 의미를 갖지만, 현대 영어에서는 in front of를 더 선호한다.

The car **behind** us is a new model made by COCO. ~뒤에
Why don't you go **after** him? ~을 따라/좇아

5) near, close to, by, beside, next to

Robbie moved to a house **near** / **close to** his girlfriend's. ~의 가까이에
Now he lives **closer to** his girlfriend's than to his parents'.
A toy soldier is **by a bowl of goldfish** on the table. ~의 가까이에
Put the cake **beside** / **next to** the candle. ~의 바로 옆에

Pop Quiz 1 둘 중 알맞은 표현을 고르고, 전치사의 의미에 유의하여 해석하시오.

(1) He found his pajamas (under, below) the blanket.
(2) Visitors enter (through, across) the green door on the right.
(3) You can have groceries delivered (to, for) your home.
(4) Captain Jim and his crew are sailing (for, from) the new continent.
(5) A car was parked (before, in front) of the house.
(6) My desk was (near, close) the door but now is (near, close) to Chris's.

---

2 시간(time)을 나타내는 전치사

1) for, since, during, through, over

Are you going away **for** a few days next week? ~동안
Charlie **has worked** at a toy company **for** a couple of years.

▶ For는 'how long ~?'에 대한 대답으로 사용되며 행동이 지속된 기간을 의미한다. 특정한 기간이 숫자로 표시되는 경우가 많다.

Long time no see. I guess I **haven't seen** you **since** last year. ~이후에/~부터
Tickets **have been** on sale **since** last Monday.

▶ Since는 행동이 시작된 과거의 특정 시점에서 현재까지를 의미하므로 반드시 완료 시제와 함께 쓴다.
▶ 완료 시제가 아닌 다른 시제와 함께 쓸 때에는 from을 사용한다.
  ex. Tickets **will be** on sale **from** next Monday.

It rained all day, but it stopped **during** the night. ~내에

▶ 'When ~?'에 대한 대답으로 사용된다.

Lucy kept quiet all **through** breakfast. ~내내

▶ 'How long ~?' 에 대한 대답으로 사용된다. 행동이 지속된 기간의 처음부터 끝까지를 의미한다.

Over breakfast the Browns discussed plans for the summer holidays.
~하는 동안 / ~기간에 걸쳐서

2) until / till, by

I have to be in Spain **until / till** Friday. ~전에 / ~까지

You'll never know how strong you are **until** you get tested. 접속사인 경우

You had better finish it **by** next Monday. ~까지

▶ Until / Till은 정해진 시간까지 지속됨을 나타내는 반면 by는 정해진 시간 안에 발생하거나 완료가 가능함을 나타낸다.

3) to, from, between

A daily lunch special is available **to** 4 p.m. ~까지

I arrived at a quarter **to** five. (5시까지 30분 = 4시 30분)

From childhood, he was a great reader. ~부터

She lived in Tokyo **from** 1997 to / until / till 2005.

The Panama Canal, built **between** 1904 and 1914 by the U.S., connects the Caribbean Sea with the Pacific Ocean. ~사이에

4) before, after, past

We broke up a few days **before** Valentine's Day. ~이전에 / ~이전까지

However, we met again a few weeks **after** Valentine's Day. ~이후에 / ~이후까지

It's **past** your bedtime ~이 지나서

It's a quarter **past** nine. (9시를 지나서 15분 = 9시 15분)

Pop Quiz 2   둘 중 알맞은 표현을 고르고, 전치사의 의미에 유의하여 해석하시오.

(1) I just want to sit down **(for, since)** five minutes.
(2) Carol has been waiting for her turn to speak **(for, since)** twelve o'clock.
(3) **(During, Over)** the tea break, you'll be served lemonade and cookies.
(4) He would sit in the cafe **(until, by)** closing time.
(5) The highway will be open **(from, since)** April 5th.
(6) The dog was standing **(from, between)** the tree and the bench.

3 그 밖의 쓰임을 갖는 전치사

1) by

Love can be felt **by** everyone.	~에 의해
Why don't you send it **by** mail?	~로/~에 의해(수단)
Learn **by** doing.	~함으로써(방법)

1) with

She walked **with** him to the front door without saying a word.	~와 함께
We bought a desk **with** secret drawers at the flea market.	~을 가지고/~을 지니고
It's fun to see the night sky **with** a telescope.	~을 사용하여/~을 써서
The artist works **with** his hands, **with** his brains, and **with** his heart.	

3) for

She's going to buy a bed with a mosquito net **for** her baby.	~을 위해(대상)
Tell me three essentials **for** happiness.	~을 위해(목적)
They had nothing all day and cannot sleep **for** hunger.	~때문에(이유)
I'm looking for a chair suitable **for** use in the living room.	~에 적합한/좋은

4) of

Anna is the leader **of** an orchestra.	~의(소유·관계)
Cheese is made **of** milk.	~로 만들어진/~로(재료·원료)
Sadly, my mother died **of** cancer.	~때문에(이유)

5) between, among*

There are two trees. He's standing **between** them.	~사이에
There are a lot of flowers. A bee is flying **among** them.	~사이에

6) about

Sally rarely spoke **about** her boyfriend, Mark.	~에 대해
He has made several short films **about** love and life.	~와 관련하여

7) on

Everything in that store is **on** sale at 40 percent off.	과정에 있는
Don't give up and keep **on** trying.	지속 중인
Charlie's comments **on** my decision were relatively harsh.	~에 관한

Check Up

1 둘 중 알맞은 표현을 고르고, 전치사의 의미에 유의하여 해석하시오.

(1) A chef at the restaurant recommended ribs (with, for) red chili sauce.
(2) Ms. Brown, a friend (with, of) my mother's, brought a bottle of white wine.
(3) Houses (of, for) wood and straw were blown away by a big bad wolf.
(4) They are (about, on) strike* for better working conditions.
(5) He provided a link (between, among) America's past and its future.
(6) Her early work included illustrations (for, of) children's magazines.
(7) (With, By) that tiny vocabulary, he wrote the famous book, *Green Eggs and Ham*.
(8) Where two different languages are spoken (by, on) large numbers of people, some mixing is bound* to occur.

2 **Speak-out** 빈 칸에 들어갈 알맞은 전치사를 보기에서 골라 쓰고, 끊어 읽기와 이어 읽기에 유의하여 지문 전체를 큰 소리로 읽으시오.

보기 | through   across   along   toward

To get to our office / from Harristown, / drive south (1) _____ Route 5. Turn left at State Street / in Stanville. Drive east on State Street / over the bridge / (2) _____ the creek*, / past the shopping center, / and (3) _____ the tunnel / under North Hill. After that, / you will be near an intersection* / with a stoplight. Look for a sign / beside the intersection. An arrow on the sign / points (4) _____ our office. Turn right and look / for a building / with a fountain* / in front of it. Our office is / in that building. Park behind the building / and walk into it / through the door / on the left.

3 빈 칸에 공통으로 들어갈 전치사를 보기에서 골라 쓰시오.

보기 | on   for   between

(1) _____ ⓐ The children set off* _____ school.
              ⓑ What are you going to have _____ lunch?
              ⓒ Sprinters must run very fast, but only _____ a short time.

(2) _____ ⓐ My girlfriend is away _____ a business trip.
ⓑ They're looking for a book _____ rabbits.
ⓒ The North and South Poles are the coldest places _____ Earth.

(3) _____ ⓐ She gets up _____ 6 and 7 o'clock in the morning.
ⓑ The ship sails _____ the icebergs to the Poiuy Island.
ⓒ The final match will present a contrast in play style _____ the two players.

4 Speak-out 다음 우리말을 영어로 옮겨 큰 소리로 세 번씩 말하시오.

(1) John은 2003년 이후로 런던에 살고 있다.
⇒ _____

(2) John은 3년 동안 런던에 살고 있다.
⇒ _____

(3) John은 2003년부터 2005년까지 런던에 살았다.
⇒ _____

(4) 그녀는 창문을 통해 별똥별(shooting star)을 보고 있다.
⇒ _____

(5) 길 건너편에는 ABC은행이 있다.
⇒ _____

(6) 모든 길은 로마로 통한다.
⇒ _____

(7) 우리는 다음 수요일에 시카고를 향해 떠날 것이다.
⇒ _____

(8) 그들은 어제 그 일에 적합한 사람을 뽑았다.
⇒ _____

comments

❏ **the English Channel** 영국해협 (영국과 프랑스 사이에 있는 해협으로, 정기 항로와 해저 터널이 뚫려 있어 영국과 유럽 대륙을 연결하는 통로 역할을 한다.) / channel [tʃǽnl] *n*. 해협, 수로, 운하

❏ **to, toward** To는 정확한 방향 또는 행동이 끝나는 지점에 달했음을 가리키는 반면 toward는 방향만을 나타낼 뿐 목적지에 도착했는지의 여부는 알 수 없다. 한편, 일상회화에서는 toward 대신 towards를 사용하는 경우가 종종 있지만 표준 영어라고는 할 수 없다.

❏ **assemble** [əsémbəl] *v*. 모이다, 집합하다, 회합하다

❏ **between, among** 일반적으로 between은 둘 사이를 뜻하고 among은 셋 이상의 사이를 뜻한다. 그러나, 현대 영어에서는 소수의 정해진 수를 나타낼 경우 between을 쓰기도 한다.
ex. You can choose **between** French, Spanish, and Chinese as your second foreign language.

❏ **strike** [straik] *n*. (동맹) 파업

❏ **bound** [baund] *adj*. 꼭 ~하게 되어 있는 (주로 to-부정사와 결합한 형태로 사용된다.)

❏ **set off** 출발하다, 시작하다 (off는 부사)

❏ **creek** [kri:k] *n*. 지류, 샛강, 하구

❏ **intersection** [ìntərsékʃən] *n*. 횡단, 교차, 교차로

❏ **fountain** [fáuntən] *n*. 샘, 분수

18-4 주의해야 할 전치사 표현

어떤 전치사는 부사 또는 접속사로 쓰이는 경우가 있다. 이에 대한 확실한 구분 학습이 필요하다. 또한 명사+전치사, 형용사+전치사, 구 형태의 전치사 등의 관용적 표현을 암기하는 것이 필요할 수 있다. 물론, 그 관용적 표현이라는 것도 전치사의 의미가 명사, 형용사, 동사의 의미와 조합이 잘 이루어지는 것이므로 암기만 하려 하지 말고 이해가 병행되어야 한다.

1 전치사와 관용어구

1) 형용사+전치사

This book is **full of** good information.
Who is **responsible for** this terrible mess?
The picture is a lot **different from** any other pictures in the room.

famous FOR	ready FOR	tired OF	different FROM	crowded WITH
prepared FOR	afraid OF	proud OF	absent FROM	good AT
responsible FOR	fond OF	full OF	interested IN	bad AT

2) 명사+전치사

Acid rain has done great **damage to** the forest.
His life is probably a good **example of** a successful businessman's.

example OF	result OF	damage TO	reason FOR
cause OF	solution TO	attention TO	increase/decrease IN

3) 구 형태의 전치사

Henry made his compass point north **instead of** south.
Hey, come **along with** me!

because OF	as a result OF	in front OF	according TO
instead OF	in spite OF	along WITH	thanks TO

2 전치사의 생략

- last, next, this, that, 수량형용사+시간을 나타내는 명사
- tomorrow, yesterday, the day before yesterday, the day after tomorrow 등

See you **next Friday** / **this Friday**.
A strange man visited us **one Thursday** in April.
The final test is **the day after tomorrow**, so I'll be at the library **tomorrow**.

▶ 단순한 시간 표현 이외의 추가적 의미를 전달하려면 적절한 의미의 전치사가 필요하다.
ex. It has been raining **since** last week. / The rain will end **by** tomorrow.

3 전치사와 접속사, 부사의 혼동

■ 일부 전치사는 전치사 뿐만 아니라 접속사 또는 부사의 역할을 하기도 한다.

The chocolate on the table is only **for** you.	전치사
I've not been able to eat anything, **for** I had a stomachache.	접속사
Death sees everyone **as** an equal.	전치사
He crushed the glasses in his back pocket **as** he flopped on the sofa.	접속사
Is there a man who is good at cooking **as well as*** cleaning?	전치사, 접속사
Friendship is **like** wine; the older it gets, the better it is.	전치사
Hold **on**, please.	부사 (hold 수식, 지속의 의미)
I've worked at a small company in Hawaii **since** 2005.	전치사
Despite/In spite of having a headache, Robbie enjoyed the film.	전치사

Check Up

1 빈 칸에 알맞은 전치사를 넣어 문장을 완성하시오. 필요 없는 곳에는 ×표를 하시오.

(1) I'm very good _____ directions.
(2) I'm tired _____ being single. Where is my sweetie?
(3) You can see a sharp increase _____ the number of the unemployed.
(4) According _____ the record, the building was built more than 600 years ago.
(5) The cause _____ the explosion is still being investigated.
(6) What is the reason _____ being late?
(7) How are you feeling _____ today?
(8) I'm sorry, but I totally forgot to call you _____ the day before yesterday.

2 밑줄 친 표현의 쓰임을 고르시오.

전치사☐ 부사☐ 접속사☐ (1) Soon their religion could not last <u>as</u> a social order.
전치사☐ 부사☐ 접속사☐ (2) She couldn't read the sign, <u>for</u> her eyesight was not good.
전치사☐ 부사☐ 접속사☐ (3) They talked <u>on</u> in the dark for a while.

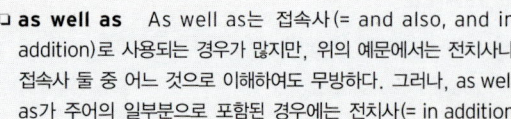

❏ **as well as** As well as는 접속사(= and also, and in addition)로 사용되는 경우가 많지만, 위의 예문에서는 전치사나 접속사 둘 중 어느 것으로 이해하여도 무방하다. 그러나, as well as가 주어의 일부분으로 포함된 경우에는 전치사(= in addition to)로 보는 것이 옳으며, 이 때 주어와 동사의 일치에 주의해야 한다.
ex. He, **as well as** his girlfriend, <u>is</u> coming to the party next Friday.

Grammar Review

1 밑줄 친 전치사가 바르게 쓰였으면 ○표를 하고, 잘못 쓰였으면 ×표를 하시오.

_____ (1) Late in night, two men and a woman meet at an all-night coffee shop.

_____ (2) He and his men died of cold, murder, bad food, and starvation.

_____ (3) Another essayist, Joan Didion, wrote about her time at New York City.

_____ (4) Despite of a careful search, no trace of the lost car has been found.

_____ (5) I worked on a cattle ranch of the Kevin brothers a few years ago.

_____ (6) She became famous with making serious art out of ordinary things like cans of soup.

_____ (7) Cartoons, a single drawing on the newspaper, were often comments on events of the day.

_____ (8) Ken has been studying Russian during three years, but he still doesn't understand it very well.

2 다음 글을 읽고, 빈 칸에 들어갈 알맞은 표현을 고르시오.

Are you a visitor in town? Welcome! Our community has something for everyone, from restaurants to bookstores. (1) _____ is packed with historic
　　　　　　Ⓐ In our town　Ⓑ Out town

attractions, too. As you walk down Main Street, look around you. The scene has not changed much since 1850! Unlike many other towns, our town has preserved many of its oldest buildings (2) _____ wars, fires, and floods. During a walk
　　　　　　　　　　　Ⓐ despite　Ⓑ though

along Main Street, you will think you are walking back (3) _____ ! Stroll
　　　　　　　　　　　　　　　Ⓐ over time　Ⓑ though time

toward City Hall, built around 1880 and expanded after World War I. Inside City Hall is a museum about local history. Outside the building is a monument to our first mayor, who was born in 1776 on a farm near the bridge over historic Wilson Creek. Enjoy your visit (4) _____ our town! You are looking across time at
　　　　　　　　　　　Ⓐ to　Ⓑ for

centuries of history!

Grammar Up

Time Limit: 3 min, _____ / 10

어법상 빈 칸에 들어갈 알맞은 표현을 고르시오.

1. _____ the spring break we went to Cape Cod.
   - (A) During
   - (B) When
   - (C) With
   - (D) By

2. This machine will work _____ electricity.
   - (A) unless
   - (B) if
   - (C) without
   - (D) as

3. _____ their old age, my grandparents succeeded in climbing up Mt. Halla.
   - (A) Because
   - (B) Despite
   - (C) By
   - (D) Though

어법상 잘못된 부분을 고르시오.

4. The song she sang for <u>us</u> is different <u>of</u> <u>what</u> she sang <u>on stage</u> last night.
                           (A)   (B) (C)   (D)

5. <u>Land</u> is more <u>expensive</u> <u>at</u> <u>heavily</u> populated zones.
     (A)   (B)   (C) (D)

6. <u>It</u> is hard <u>to decide</u> <u>between</u> chicken and fish <u>of</u> dinner.
   (A)   (B)   (C)   (D)

7. <u>All my</u> ancestors <u>were born</u>, <u>lived</u>, died, and were buried <u>this town</u>.
     (A)   (B)   (C)   (D)

8. <u>In spite</u> his physical handicap, Beethoven <u>composed</u> <u>many</u> great <u>symphonies</u>.
     (A)   (B)   (C)   (D)

9. <u>The</u> Smiths called <u>off</u> <u>their</u> fishing plan <u>because</u> rain.
     (A)   (B) (C)   (D)

10. <u>When</u> Mary was <u>sixteen</u>, she <u>published of</u> her first <u>novel</u>.
      (A)   (B)   (C)   (D)

CHAPTER 19

구와 절
_Phrases and Clauses

19-1 구와 절 형태 종합

언어학자들은 하나의 단어를 구로 취급하기도 하고, 구를 절로 취급하기도 한다. 그러나, 본 교재에서 구는 전치사구와 준동사구에 한정하며 절은 명사절, 형용사절, 부사절에 한정하기로 한다. 구와 절은 끊어 읽는 것이 기본이다. 본 Chapter를 학습하면서 '/' 된 부분은 끊어 읽는 연습을 병행해야 하며, '/' 표시가 없다고 하더라도 Chapter 10을 참고하여 끊고* 이어 읽는 연습을 하도록 한다.

1 구[Phrases] 종합

분 류	형 태		역 할		
전치사구	전치사+명사(상당어구)		·	형용사	부사
준동사구	to+동사원형+α*	부정사구	명사	형용사	부사
	동사원형-ing+α	동명사구, (현재)분사구	명사	형용사	(부사)
	동사원형-ed+α	(과거)분사구	·	형용사	(부사)

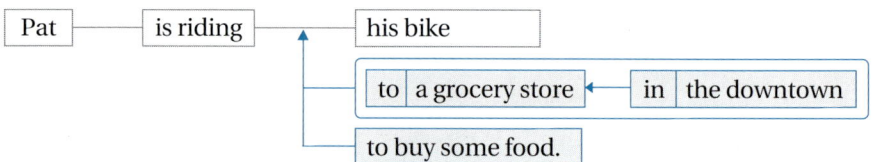

Pat is riding / his bike/ to a grocery store / in the downtown / to buy some food.

▶ 술어전체 is riding에 목적어 his bike와 수식어 to a grocery store, to buy some food가 연결되어 있다. In the downtown은 a grocery store를 꾸며주는 수식어이다.

2 절[Clauses] 종합

■ 절은 주절, 동등한 절, 종속된 절로 구분하며, 종속된 절은 다시 명사절, 형용사절, 부사절로 나누어진다.

1) 동등한 절

2) 종속된 절

Check Up

1 밑줄 친 구 또는 절의 역할(명사/형용사/부사)을 쓰고, 끊어 읽기와 이어 읽기에 유의하여 큰 소리로 세 번씩 말하시오.

   _____ (1) It needs dusting.
   _____ (2) The beans want picking.
   _____ (3) I saw him looking at me.
   _____ (4) I miss you, but I believe that we'll be together soon.
   _____ (5) There was no hope that she would recover her health.
   _____ (6) Christine forgot returning the video tape.
   _____ (7) Ted forgot to return the book to the library before he went on vacation to Puerto Rico.
   _____ (8) You are silly to miss such a good opportunity as that.
   _____ (9) Brian stopped to ask directions to the Hyatt Regency* Hotel.
   _____ (10) We had to work throughout the night to get the shipment ready.
   _____ (11) I deliberately didn't read the book before going to see the film.
   _____ (12) Julia is the person responsible for graphics.
   _____ (13) He's been successful in spite of all the difficulties that he's encountered in the business world.

2 **Speak-out** 다음 우리말을 영어로 옮겨 큰 소리로 세 번씩 말하시오.

(1) 그녀가 살고 있는 그 집은 바다 위로 멋진 전망을 가지고 있다.
   ➪ _____

(2) 우리는 페이지의 제일 위에 주어진 지시사항을 따랐다.
   ➪ _____

(3) 감기에 걸렸을 때에는 밖에서 노는 것보다 집에서 쉬는 것이 더 좋다.
   ➪ _____

(4) 창문 바깥에 서 있는 큰 나무는 오후에 벽 위로 사랑스러운 그림자를 던진다.
   ➪ _____

 comments

- **끊어 읽기** 끊어 읽는 부분은 정해져 있는 것은 아니다. 영어를 잘 읽을 수 있는 속도, 호흡의 짧고 김, 강조하고자 하는 단위 등의 조건에 따라 사람마다 다를 수 있다.
- **α** 동사 뒤에 나오는 목적어, 보어 등을 가리킨다.
- **sack** [sæk] *n.* 부대, 자루, 봉지

- **regency** [ríːdʒənsi] *n.* 섭정 정치, 섭정 기간 (섭정(攝政)이란 왕이 직접 통치할 수 없는 때에 다른 사람이 권력을 위임 받아 대신 통치를 하는 정치 형태를 말한다. Regency는 19세기 초 영국 섭정기에 유행했던 건축, 가구 등의 양식을 말하기도 한다.)

19-2 절의 축약 (1): 생략

주절과 종속절(명사절, 형용사절, 부사절)의 주어가 같은 경우에는 종속절에 있는 ①종속접속사, 주어, 또는 be동사를 '생략'하거나 ②술어를 준동사로 '형태를 바꾸어' 구의 형태로 '축약'시킬 수 있다. 언어의 전달은 명확성을 유지하면서도 간략할 수 있으면 가장 좋다. 물론 그것 때문에 의미 전달에 혼동이 발생하면 간략한 것은 의미가 없다. 같은 말을 반복해서 하는 사람과 만나는 것이 얼마나 지겨운 일이겠는가. 하지만, 사랑한다는 말은 반복해야 오해가 없다!

1 부사절에서의 생략

Nick had an accident while (he was) driving to work this morning.
Even though (he is) not disabled, he used to park in "handicapped only" parking spaces.
(Whether it is) Good or bad, the decision we made is the only solution we can find.

▶ 부사절의 주어가 주절의 주어와 같을 때, 부사절의 '(접속사+)주어+be동사'를 생략할 수 있다.
▶ be동사는 의미가 없는 연결동사(Linking Verbs)에 불과하므로 생략할 수 있지만, 동작동사(Action Verbs)는 생략할 수 없으므로 준동사의 형태로 변환시킨다. (Ch.19-3 참고)

If you **stay** at the office, please answer the phone.   부사절
→ **Staying** at the office, please answer the phone.
Jake slowly approached the beggar who **looked** at him with his eyes full of tears.   형용사절
→ Jake slowly approached the beggar **looking** at him with his eyes full of tears.

2 형용사절에서의 생략

1) 동등한 절

- 생략된 형태가 준동사 또는 형용사의 형태로 남는 예

    She has a garden (which is) planted with a variety of trees.
    There is a garden, (which is) planted with flowers, at the end of the street.
    Julie is the person (who is) responsible for internet marketing.
    Julie, (who is) responsible for internet marketing, is the only person I trust.

    ▶ 형용사절이 주어와 동사의 사이에 있을 때 '주격관계대명사+be동사'를 생략한 채 말(Speaking)을 하면 의미 전달에 명확성이 떨어진다. 그러나, 글(Reading, Writing)에서는 반복하여 읽을 수도 있고 comma(,)를 사용하는 등 보완이 가능하므로 의미에 혼동이 없다.

- 생략된 형태가 명사만 남아 동격(Appositives)의 형태가 되는 예

    Seattle, (which is) her native city, is well known for its peaceful scenery.
    They're looking at paintings by Martini, (who is) a famous Italian painter.

    ▶ 형용사절이 축약된 형태로 부가적인 정보를 전달한다.

2) '선행사' 또는 '관계사'의 생략

The man (whom/who/that) Austin talked to is my teacher.　　목적격 관계사 생략

Today is the day when/on which I get paid.

→ Today is the day I get paid.　　관계부사 생략

→ Today is when I get paid.　　선행사 생략

▶ 선행사가 생략되는 경우 형용사절(관계부사절)이 명사절의 역할을 하게 된다.

Check Up

1 생략할 수 있는 부분을 찾아 ( )를 하고, 생략된 문장을 끊어 읽기와 이어 읽기에 유의하여 큰 소리로 세 번씩 말하시오.

(1) Since she is a new student, Carla feels shy and insecure*.
(2) After he was bitten by the parrot, Robbie's finger was sore* for a week.
(3) Though she was mournful over her dog's death, Susan held back the tears.
(4) When she was a teenager, Rita collected pictures of her favorite rock stars.
(5) Raul lives in the small city which is located near Seoul.
(6) Olga is writing a picture book which is on American language and culture.
(7) Do you know the girl with dark brown hair who is walking along the street?
(8) Would you believe it if I told you there was a turtle which is faster than a rabbit?

2 동격을 사용하여 다음 두 문장을 한 문장으로 고쳐 쓰시오.

(1) Mercury* has the symbol Hg. It is the only liquid metal.
　➡ _____
(2) Have you ever visited the Cheongwadae? It is the home of the President.
　➡ _____
(3) Sinclair Lewis won a Nobel Prize. He was a famous novelist.
　➡ _____

- **insecure** [ìnsikjúər]　adj. 불안한, 걱정스러운, 위태로운
- **sore** [sɔːr]　adj. (염증·상처 등이) 아픈, 쓰린, 쑤시는
- **mercury** [məːrkjuri]　n. 수은 (은백색의 금속 광택이 나는 무거운 액체이며, 상온에서 액체인 유일한 금속이다.)

19-3 절의 축약 (2): 분사구

● 절을 축약하는 방법에는 ① 단순히 생략해도 되는 경우와 ② 변형이 필요한 경우가 있다. 본 Unit에서는 형용사절, 부사절이 현재 또는 과거 분사구로 변형되어 축약되는 경우에 대해 학습한다. 생략 및 축약은 주로 글에서 사용한다. 일상회화에서는 생략 및 축약이 의미 전달의 명확성을 떨어뜨릴 수 있으므로 주의해야 한다. 따라서, 글이나 회화에서 무조건 모든 문장을 생략하거나 축약하는 것은 위험하다.

1 형용사절의 축약

■ 동작동사(Action Verbs)의 경우 be동사(Linking Verbs)와 달리 단순한 생략이 불가능하므로 준동사의 형태로 변환시킨다.

The book is one of the best English grammar books (that was) ever written for ESL/EFL* students. The book, **consisting** of 20 chapters with an appendix and answer key, has about 400 pages. Anyone **wanting** to improve his or her English can study with it.*

2 부사절의 축약

1) 종속절과 주절의 주어와 시제가 같을 때

기본문장	After Nick registered for college, he applied for a room in a dormitory.
1단계	After registered for college, he applied for a room in a dormitory. **주어 생략**: 종속절의 주어가 주절의 주어와 같을 때 삭제한다.
2단계	After registering for college, he applied for a room in a dormitory. **동사의 형태 변화**: -ing 형태(부사구)로 바꾼다.
3단계	Registering for college, he applied for a room in a dormitory. **접속사 생략***: 단, 접속사가 문맥의 의미를 이해하는데 반드시 필요한 경우에는 생략하지 않는다. (Because는 항상 생략한다.)

Before they had come to New York, they had been farm workers.
→ **Before coming** to New York, they had been farm workers.
→ **Coming** to New York, they had been farm workers.

Because Chan was lazy, he was poor throughout his life.
→ **(Being) Lazy**, he was poor throughout his life.

▶ Being을 생략할 수 있지만, 축약된 형태가 너무 간단하면 말을 할 때 딱딱한 느낌이 들 수 있으므로 being을 생략하지 않기도 한다.

2) 종속절과 주절의 시제가 다를 때: 완료 시제 사용

Since I **was born** in April, I **like** April very much.
→ (**Having been**) **Born** in April, I **like** April very much.
When Carol **had taken** a shower, she **went** to bed.
→ **Having taken** a shower, Carol **went** to bed.

3 주절과 종속절의 주어가 다른 경우*

When <u>the teacher</u> came in, <u>all students</u> stood up.
→ <u>The teacher</u> coming in, all students stood up.
Since <u>it</u> grew dark, <u>I</u> went home in haste.
→ <u>It</u> growing dark, I went home in haste.

Strictly speaking, this gallery is not a place worth visiting.   (엄밀히 말하자면)
Considering your age, you did a good job.   (~을 고려하면)
Judging from her experience, she could do the job well.   (~으로 판단하자면)

▶ 주절의 주어와도 관계없고, 그 자체적으로도 주어가 없다. 독립적으로 삽입구의 역할을 한다. (무인칭독립분사구문)
▶ generally speaking, taking into consideration ~ 등

4 분사구의 부정

Because I didn't want to hurt her feelings, I kept silent about the news.
→ **Not** wanting to hurt her feelings, I kept silent about the news.
While Joe didn't care, things got all messed up.
→ Joe **never** caring, things got all messed up.

Check Up

1   **Speak-out**   다음 문장을 축약하여 큰 소리로 세 번씩 말하시오.

(1) We live in the house which overlooks the park.
(2) The fence which surrounds our house is made of wood.
(3) Anyone who wants to learn English with us is welcome.
(4) Our solar system is in a galaxy that is called the Milky Way.
(5) Two out of three people who are injured in crashes survived.

2 🔊 Speak-out 주어진 문장과 같은 의미가 되도록 빈 칸에 알맞은 표현을 쓰고, 큰 소리로 세 번씩 말하시오.

(1) While Kate was chopping potatoes, she cut her finger.
→ _____ _____ potatoes, Kate cut her finger.
→ _____ _____, Kate cut her finger.

(2) As I had no one to go to the concert with, I went alone.
→ _____ _____ no one to go to the concert with, I went alone.
→ _____ _____ _____ to go to the concert with, I went alone.

(3) Before he or she writes novels, plays, or any other things, the writer always collects enough material.
→ _____ _____ novels, plays, or any other things, the writer always collects enough material.
→ _____ novels, plays, or any other things, the writer always collects enough material.

(4) If she had learned French, she would not have difficulty reading the book.
→ _____ _____ _____ French, she would not have difficulty reading the book.
→ _____ _____ _____, she would not have difficulty reading the book.

(5) Though he was injured in a car accident, he's not reluctant to ride in a car at all.
→ _____ _____ in a car accident, he's not reluctant to ride in a car at all.
→ _____ in a car accident, he's not reluctant to ride in a car at all.

(6) When they had eaten their fill, they looked for somewhere to sleep.
→ _____ _____ _____ their fill, they looked for somewhere to sleep.
→ _____ _____ _____ _____, they looked for somewhere to sleep.

3 🔊 Speak-out 다음 문장을 축약 형태를 활용하여 큰 소리로 세 번씩 말하시오.

(1) Because a fly kept on buzzing in my ear, I couldn't concentrate on my work.
→ _____

(2) When the waiter came to our table, we ordered spaghetti and pizza.
→ _____

(3) Though the road was frozen hard, he hurriedly set off toward the village.
→ _____

(4) While Sam was reading a book last night, the light was turned off all of a sudden.
→ _____

4 밑줄 친 표현에 유의하여, 다음 문장을 해석하시오.

(1) <u>Frankly speaking</u>, he was a picky creature.
(2) <u>Generally speaking</u>, women use text messages* more often than men.
(3) The rate of single parenthood, <u>considering the survey</u>, will continuously increase.
(4) <u>Strictly speaking</u>, the sentence is not grammatical.

5 **Speak-out** 다음 문장을 축약 형태를 활용하여 큰 소리로 세 번씩 말하시오.

(1) When she was not in New York, Robin missed her.
⇢ _____

(2) Since I was not interested, I didn't apply for the job.
⇢ _____

(3) Because I didn't feel like being with them, I stayed out for a while.
⇢ _____

(4) Though he wasn't as healthy as before, my grandfather could run ten kilometers without stopping.
⇢ _____

- **ESL/EFL** English as a Second/Foreign Language의 줄임말 (ESL은 미국에 가서 영어를 공부하는 것과 같이 영어가 일상적으로 통용되는 환경에서 배우는 제2외국어로서의 영어를 말하고, EFL은 한국과 같이 영어가 일상적으로 통용되지 않는 환경에서 배우는 외국어로서의 영어를 말한다.)
- **지문 연구1** 첫 번째 축약형은 종속절과 주절의 주어가 같을 때 단순히 '접속사+be동사'를 생략한 경우이고, 두 번째와 세 번째 축약형은 (현재)분사구로 축약한 경우이다.
  ex. Anyone <u>who wants</u> to improve ~
  → Anyone <u>wanting</u> to improve ~
- **지문 연구2** 두 번째 축약형은 형용사구 또는 부사구로 해석할 수 있는데, 어느 쪽으로 해석을 해도 의미적인 차이는 없다.
  ex. The book, <u>consisting of 20 chapters</u> ~
     (형용사구: 20 챕터로 구성된 그 책은)

<u>Consisting of 20 chapters</u> ~, the book ~
  (부사구: 그 책은 20 챕터로 구성되어 있어서)
- **접속사 생략** 부사절을 축약하는 과정에서 접속사를 생략한다는 것은 해당 문장을 이해하는데 접속사의 정확한 의미가 중요하지 않음을 뜻한다. 또한, 접속사가 생략되어 Having a headache가 되면 부사구라고 생각할 수도 있지만, I를 수식하는 형용사구로 보아도 전체 의미에 차이점이 별로 없다. 일반적으로 부사절이 분사구로 축약되면 형용사구로 취급하는 문법학자가 많다. 하지만, 문장의 뒤에 나오는 분사구는 의미적으로 부사구의 역할로 취급되는 경우가 많다. 따라서, 부사절을 분사구로 축약하는 연습은 필요하지만 분사구를 부사절로 되돌리는 연습에는 신중함이 요구된다.
- **주절과 종속절의 주어가 다른 경우** 국내문법책에서는 '독립분사구문'이라고 부른다.
- **text message** 이동전화의 문자 메시지

19-4 절의 축약 (3): 전치사구와 부정사구

부사절, 형용사절, 명사절이 전치사구 또는 부정사구로 표현되어도 의미 차이가 없는 경우도 있다. 그러나, 축약으로 전달하려는 의미에 차이가 생길 수도 있다. 특히, 순간적으로 의미가 교환되는 Speaking에 있어서는 축약된 형태가 어색할 수도 있고 의미 전달에 혼란이 발생할 수도 있다. 따라서, 축약된 문장을 사용할 때에는 적절한 경우인지에 대한 주의가 필요하다.

1 부사절의 축약: 전치사구

- 부사절을 이끄는 종속접속사와 같은 뜻을 가진 전치사를 사용하여 부사절을 전치사구로 축약한다.

Though/Although he protects them, the flowers are all withered.
→ **In spite of/Despite** his protection, the flowers are all withered.

The traffic was tied up in many places **because** it had been snowing all night.
→ The traffic was tied up in many places **because of** the snow.
▸ Because of 대신에 **due to**, **owing to**를 사용할 수 있다. (의미가 비슷하기는 하지만 똑같지는 않음)

When they reached the island, they found a sandy beach all along the sea.
→ **Upon/On reaching** the island, they found a sandy beach all along the sea.

Tell me whatever you'd like to do **while** you visit Washington, D.C.
→ Tell me whatever you'd like to do **during** a visit to Washington, D.C.

As most of us do, you value your ability to see and hear, but you completely ignore your sense of smell.
→ **Like** most of us, you value your ability to see and hear, but you ~

2 형용사절의 축약: 부정사구

- 종속절의 주어가 주절의 주어와 같은 경우 형용사절을 부정사구로 축약할 수 있다.

She's looking for a house. + She lives in the house.
→ She's looking for a house **in which she lives**.
→ She's looking for a house (**that**) **she lives in**.
→ She's looking for a house **to live in**.   (better)

3 명사절의 축약: 부정사구

1) 간접의문문의 축약

No one in the room told me <u>when we should meet</u>.
→ No one in the room told me **when to meet**.

Do you have any idea <u>how we should open the box</u>?
→ Do you have any idea **how to open the box**?

2) 형용사+that절의 축약

Lucy is still *afraid* <u>that she must sleep in her own room</u>.
→ Lucy is still *afraid* **to sleep in her own room**.

It is *necessary* <u>that you should look after plants carefully during bad weather</u>.
→ It is *necessary* **(for you) to look after plants carefully during bad weather**.

▶ 의미상 주어가 일반인이거나 서로가 누구에 대하여 말하고 있는지 이미 알고 있는 경우에는 생략할 수 있다.

Check Up

1 다음 문장이 바르게 쓰였으면 ○표를 하고, 잘못 쓰였으면 ×표를 하시오.

_____ (1) It is true that children tend to act like their parents do.

_____ (2) The situation has improved because their hidden efforts.

_____ (3) Bill was late again despite she warned him to be on time.

_____ (4) On take off, the plane would gain altitude* and fly high above the sea.

_____ (5) He has bright blue eyes as his grandmother who passed away last year.

_____ (6) The problem of child abuse* continues to grow due to the indifference of the general public.

2 🔊 **Speak-out** 다음 문장을 축약 형태를 활용하여 큰 소리로 세 번씩 말하시오.

(1) When he arrived home, he discovered a letter waiting for him. (on -ing)
⇢ _____

(2) We plan to stay at grandmother's in Canada while we are on the Christmas holidays. (during)
⇢ _____

(3) Peter was the brother of a painter and went to study art as his brother did in New York. (like)
⇢ _____

3 🔊 **Speak-out** 다음 문장을 축약 형태를 활용하여 큰 소리로 세 번씩 말하시오.

(1) She couldn't make up her mind what she should wear on an interview.
⇢ _____

(2) If you're worrying where you should start your research, you will find this book helpful.
⇢ _____

(3) Neither Harry nor I decided how many people we should invite to the Halloween party.
⇢ _____

4 🔊 **Speak-out** 다음 우리말을 영어로 옮겨 큰 소리로 세 번씩 말하시오. (부정사구 사용)

(1) 힘든 일 뒤에는 충분히 잘 쉬어주는 것이 중요하다.
⇢ _____

(2) 어디에서 등록을 하는지 말해 주시겠어요?
⇢ _____

(3) 나는 많은 장난감이 든 상자를 받고 매우 기뻤다.
⇢ _____

□ **형용사+that절** That절은 전치사의 목적어가 될 수 없으므로 전치사가 탈락되는 현상이다. 'Sorry for that ~'의 형태에서는 that절이 명사절로 for의 목적어이지만, for가 생략된 형태에서는 that 명사절이 for that의 의미를 지니므로 의미적으로는 부사절이 된다.

□ **altitude** [ǽltətjùːd] n. 높이, 고도, 해발
□ **abuse** [əbjúːz] n. 학대, 혹사, 남용, 오용

Grammar Review

1 다음 문장에서 종속된 절을 찾아 밑줄을 긋고, 그 역할을 보기에서 골라 쓰시오.

보기 | 명사   형용사   부사

_____ (1) The town that the college is in is very small.
_____ (2) The MVP award will be given to the player who performed best.
_____ (3) He sat nervously in the dental clinic while he was waiting to have his wisdom tooth pulled.
_____ (4) Do you know the fact that a typical house cat may weigh from 3 to 6 kilograms?

2 다음 문장이 바르게 쓰였으면 ○표를 하고, 잘못 쓰였으면 ×표를 하시오.

_____ (1) Be tired, she went to bed early.
_____ (2) When didn't producing art of his own, he was busy weeding and planting.
_____ (3) You washing that wool sweater, you should have looked at the label.
_____ (4) Never afraid of controversy, she was known for her irony and sharp wit.

3 다음 글을 읽고, 빈 칸에 들어갈 알맞은 표현을 고르시오.

　　Living downtown, we live near the commuter train station that is next to City Hall. When (1) _____ at the train station every day, we see hundreds
　　　　　　　　　　　Ⓐ we looking   Ⓑ looking
of people waiting to ride the trains. Though able to travel just as fast by car, many people waiting there simply like the trains (2) _____ every hour or so.
　　　　　　　　　　　　　　　　　　　　　　　　Ⓐ leaving   Ⓑ left
Although old in some cases, the trains still have many riders (3) _____ of
　　　　　　　　　　　　　　　　　　　　　　　　　　　　　Ⓐ fond   Ⓑ being fond
them. Riders like the old-fashioned look and sounds that a train has.
When you are riding on the train, you can even have a doughnut and coffee (4) _____. You cannot do that when you are driving a car! Planning
　　　Ⓐ traveling   Ⓑ while traveling
your next trip, why not plan to go by train?

Grammar Up

Time Limit: 6 min, _____ / 18

어법상 빈 칸에 들어갈 알맞은 표현을 고르시오.

1 In Legoland, _____, the houses are much smaller than the real ones.
(A) is a model town in Denmark
(B) a model town in Denmark
(C) where a model town in Denmark
(D) and a model town in Denmark

2 _____ with her family, Elizabeth studied English Literature at the Oxford University.
(A) While in England
(B) England where she is
(C) Her being in England
(D) In England, while she

3 His English teacher recommends _____ he begin an easier program.
(A) why
(B) what
(C) that
(D) it is

4 _____ acorns in fall, it hides them in the ground.
(A) When does the squirrel find
(B) The squirrel which finds
(C) When the squirrel is found
(D) When the squirrel finds

5 The Mona Lisa was painted by an Italian painter, _____.
(A) who Leonardo da Vinci
(B) was Leonardo da Vinci
(C) Leonardo da Vinci
(D) Leonardo da Vinci had

6 The people _____ in the rain are getting wet.
(A) waiting for the bus
(B) waited for the bus
(C) to wait for the bus
(D) who waiting for the bus

7 _____ the director shouted "Action," she started the camera.
  (A) During
  (B) Because of
  (C) In spite of
  (D) As soon as

어법상 잘못된 부분을 고르시오.

8 Though be poor and miserable in his thirties, Bill is happy now.
  　(A)　(B)　　　　　　(C)　　(D)

9 After got out of high school, I spent a year traveling.
  (A)　(B)　　　　　　　(C)　　(D)

10 Either of them don't know which road they should take.
  　　　(A)　(B)　　(C)　　　(D)

11 Because not wanting to die of lung cancer, he decided to stop smoking.
  (A)　(B)　　　　(C)　　　　　　　　　　　(D)

12 Beans taste very good cooking with fat meat.
  (A)　　　(B)　(C)　　　　(D)

13 Animals must eat living things, included plants and animals.
  (A)　　　(B)　(C)　　　(D)

14 I having visited before, I don't really want to go to San Diego.
  (A)　(B)　(C)　　　(D)

15 Sally put on her sunglasses despite it was a cloudy day.
  　　(A)　　(B)　　　(C) (D)

16 The most important thing you have to learn is where draw the line.
  　　(A)　　　　　　　(B)　　(C)　　　(D)

17 The city is very old and has a hotel building in the early 18th century.
  　　　　(A)　　　　(B)　　　(C)　(D)

18 Because of he had read it several times, he learned the whole story by heart.
  (A)　　　(B)　　　　(C)　　　　　　　　　　　(D)

Grammar in Context

A Commuter Train Accident

A slight accident delayed commuter train service this morning. A commuter train, _____ of five cars and an engine, had an accident while it was approaching the city. The train struck a limb falling from a tree during a storm that was accompanied by strong winds. A public relations officer said, "The train moving at high speed, the limb just made a loud noise. But no one riding on the train was in danger." Though it is not serious, the accident forced the train to slow down for the rest of its journey, in case it met other limbs falling from trees. That was the incident that was responsible for the slight delay in train service this morning. Being always concerned about safety, the railroad wants to reassure passengers that there was no danger. And the railroad sent out a crew immediately to remove the limb from the tracks.

147 words, Reading Time: _____

1 빈 칸에 들어갈 알맞은 표현을 고르시오.

Ⓐ consists   Ⓑ consisting   Ⓒ which consisting   Ⓓ consisted

2 밑줄 친 부분을 분사구로 축약하여 다시 쓰시오.

3 문맥상 limb 의 의미와 가장 가까운 것을 고르시오.

Ⓐ arm   Ⓑ leg   Ⓒ branch   Ⓓ leaf

4 **Chain of Thought:** 다음 문장을 논리적 흐름에 따라 앞에서부터 이해해 봅시다.

(1) A slight accident delayed / commuter train service / this morning.
⇨ 가벼운 사고가 지연시켰다 [무엇을?] _____ [언제?/왜?/어떻게?] _____

(2) The railroad sent out / a crew / immediately / to remove / the limb / from the tracks.
⇨ _____ _____ _____ _____ _____ _____

규칙 1: 문장을 생각의 흐름에 따른 사고단위(Thought Unit)로 나누어 이해한다.
규칙 2: 명사 뒤에는 그 명사를 설명하는 형용사(구, 절)가 따라나올 것을 예상한다. 다른 뜻(부사구, 절)을 가진 어구가 나오면 전체 문장에 적합하도록 해석한다.
규칙 3: 문장을 뒤에서부터 해석하려고 하면 Chain of Thought에 따른 문장 이해에 혼란이 생길 수 있으므로 각별히 주의해야 한다. 뒷부분은 모두 가리고 앞에서부터 해당 부분만을 보면서 이해하도록 한다.

CHAPTER **20**

일치, 삽입, 생략, 강조
_Agreement, Parenthesis, Ellipsis, and Emphasis

20-1 일치

주어가 3인칭 단수이고 동사가 현재형인 경우에 주어와 동사의 일치 문제가 주로 발생한다. 명사 및 명사 상당어구가 주어의 역할을 한다. 따라서, 어떤 명사 및 명사 상당어구가 단수로 취급되는지 또는 복수로 취급되는지에 대한 학습이 중요하다. 필요하다면 Chapter 2 명사 편을 복습하는 것도 좋은 방법이다. 본 Unit에서는 구와 절을 포함한 다양한 주어의 예를 간략하게 정리해 보기로 한다.

1 주어와 동사의 일치 [Agreement]

■ 주어를 정확하게 찾고, 그 주어가 단수인지 복수인지를 확인하는 것이 관건이다.

1) 단/복수가 혼동되는 명사들 (Ch.2 참고)

Mathematics is Susan's major subject.

The lastest news was very shocking to us.

All the information is given to the applicants verbally* and in writing.

▶ 셀 수 없는 명사는 단/복수의 개념이 없지만, 문법적 필요에 의해 단수로 취급한다.

2) 주부에 수식어구가 포함된 경우

Something strange happens to us.

Robbie, one of my classmates, is good at making model rockets.

Someone whom you can share a secret with is a good friend.

▶ 주어와 동사 사이에 형용사절이 포함된 경우 주부는 **두 번째 동사(술어, 술어전체) 바로 앞**까지다.
   ex. Someone whom you can share a secret with / is a good friend.

3) 구 또는 절이 주어

Painting pictures requires much preparation.

To know all is to forgive all.

How people interact with each other is the basis of sociology.

▶ 구, 절은 수(number) 개념 자체가 없지만, 문법적 필요에 의해 단수로 취급한다.

4) or 및 상관접속사로 연결된 주어

Not only the windows but also the door was broken.

Either you or she needs to give advice to him.

Neither he nor we have permission to do it.

A seal* or two dolphins are in the show.

▶ 주어가 or 및 위의 상관접속사로 연결되어 있을 때 동사와 가까운 주어에 동사를 일치시킨다.

Green *as well as* yellow **is** my favorite.

▸ As well as yellow는 전치사구이므로, 주어-동사의 수 일치에 영향을 미치지 않는다.

She *and* my girlfriend **love** to ride bikes along the Han River on sunny days.

▸ Bread *and* butter **is** very easy to make.　　(버터 바른 빵)

5) 기타

Here **is** another bowl of popcorn to eat when watching movies.

Here* **comes** the summer.

There **are** a few obstacles* for you to overcome to improve the situation.

*Most of** the book **was** a lot of boring talk.　　(그 책의 내용 대부분)

Most of the books **were** a lot of boring talk.　　(대부분의 책들)

▸ most of, any of, some of, all of, none of은 단수와 복수에 모두 사용될 수 있으며, 결합하는 명사의 수에 따라 동사의 수가 결정된다.

Either of the two players **was** quite successful.

▸ either, neither, each, every는 단수로 취급한다.

A *number of* rules **govern** a baseball game.　　(많은 규칙들)
The *number of* cat species **is** about forty.　　(고양이 종(種)의 수)

▸ A number of는 수량을 나타내는 형용사이며, the number (of)는 '~의 수'의 뜻을 갖는 명사이다.

2 명사와 인칭 및 지시대명사의 일치

Ann's sister is concerned about **her** own grades.　　성

Beavers* use twigs* and other plant materials to build **their** nests.　　수, 인칭

Having read the magazine, I put **it** back on the shelf.

The area of my room is larger than **that** of yours.

The pets of your neighbor are as cute as **those** of mine.

Check Up

1 둘 중 알맞은 표현을 고르고, 큰 소리로 세 번씩 읽으시오.

(1) A: I think physics (is, are) as interesting as chemistry.
B: No. Chemistry is much more interesting than physics.

(2) A: Here (is, are) the receipt and change.
B: Thanks a lot.

(3) There (is, are) several pairs of shoes. Which shoes (is, are) yours?

(4) A: I wonder where my glasses (is, are).
B: You are already wearing them.

(5) The style of clothes that my roommate wears (is, are) terrible.

(6) To my surprise, few people (has, have) tried to cook this.

(7) There (is, are) several reasons why I decided to take the course.

(8) The boys and girls who were sitting on the bench (is, are) from our neighborhood.

(9) Even two dollars (was, were) too much for me to pay for a meal in those days.

(10) There (is, are) one thing you should consider before accepting the proposal.

(11) For most people, finishing their work (means, mean) going home to rest.

(12) Bob now believes that drinking and driving* (is, are) wrong and (has, have) acknowledged that what he did that night (was, were) a mistake.

2 둘 중 알맞은 문장을 고르시오.

(1) _____ ⓐ None of the movies was much fun.
ⓑ None of the movies were much fun.

(2) _____ ⓐ I think some of what he has said is true.
ⓑ I think some of what he has said are true.

(3) _____ ⓐ Before all of five minutes was over, the city lay in ruins.
ⓑ Before all of five minutes were over, the city lay in ruins.

(4) _____ ⓐ The number of people who want to go to the concert goes on increasing.
ⓑ The number of people who want to go to the concert go on increasing.

3 빈 칸에 알맞은 대명사를 넣어 문장을 완성하시오.

(1) The college of human sciences changed _____ entrance requirements.
(2) Ken attended a meeting while _____ wife Mary shopped at a mall.
(3) Bears are often regarded as mild animals, but _____ are sometimes fierce*.
(4) Sam and his wife will visit us tomorrow, and we will have dinner with _____.
(5) Like the wolf, the coyote is known for _____ distinctive cry.
(6) The legs of the table are as thick as _____ of the elephants.
(7) On this point, views of mine differed entirely from _____ of yours.
(8) The size of South Korea is smaller than _____ of North Korea; however, the population of South Korea is larger than _____ of North Korea.

4 Speak-out 다음 우리말을 영어로 옮겨 큰 소리로 세 번씩 말하시오.

(1) 당신과 나 둘 중 하나가 잘못이다. (either ~ or)
→ _____

(2) 당신 뿐만 아니라 그녀 또한 잘못이다. (not only ~ but also)
→ _____

(3) 일요일이기 때문에 대부분의 가게가 문을 닫았다. (most of)
→ _____

(4) 파티에는 많은 사람들이 있었다. (a number of)
→ _____

---

comments

Charlie did **most of** the work.

- **verbally** [və́ːrbəli]   adv. 말로, 말에 관하여, 구두로
- **seal** [siːl]   n. 바다표범, 물개
- **here** 현재 일어나고 있는 사건 및 상황
- **obstacle** [ábstəkl]   n. 장애(물), 지장, 장해(물)
- **most of vs. majority of**   Most of와 비슷한 뜻을 가진 표현으로 majority of가 있다. 그러나, majority of는 주로 수(number) 개념이 있는 명사의 복수형, 집합명사와 함께 사용한다.
  ex. Most/The majority of <u>people</u> voted for him.
- **beaver** [bíːvər]   n. 비버(크고 넓적한 꼬리와 큰 이빨을 가지고 있으며 털이 나 있는 동물로서, 자신의 이빨로 나무를 베어 강에 둑을 짓고 산다.)
- **twig** [twig]   n. 작은 가지, 가는 가지
- **drinking and driving** 음주운전 (접속사 and로 연결되어 있지만 관용적인 표현으로서 하나의 단수 명사처럼 취급한다.)
- **fierce** [fiərs]   adj. 사나운, 거친, 무시무시한

20-2 삽입

○ 삽입(Parenthesis)은 문장에 추가적인 정보(additional information)를 더하기 위해 단어, 구, 절을 첨가하는 것을 말한다. (Ch.19-2 동격, Ch.17-4 쉼표와 관계사절 참고)

1 삽입의 다양한 예

Today I visited Hilda Cooper, **a friend who is in the hospital**.
You know, 10 days sounds like an awful long time to them.
This is the book which **I think** is very interseting.
One of the matters which **I believe** are important is the ability to bring out the best in others.
▸ One thing that **I believe** is that honesty is a short cut to success. (관계대명사 뒤에 나오는 I believe가 삽입이 아닌 경우)

As the 21st century opened, **then**, "progress" **– which Americans once thought would make their future brighter –** had become a seemingly uncontrollable threat.
Paleontologists (**scientists who study ancient life**) used to have a problem **– that is, how could they study fossils without destroying them**?

| 삽입과 Punctuation |

구분	의미	예
괄호(brackets)	덜 중요한 사항 (less important)	Alfred Nobel (born in 1833) was the inventor of dynamite.
쉼표(commas)	중립적인 사항(neutral)	Alfred Nobel, born in 1833, was the inventor of dynamite.
대시(dashes)	강조하는 사항(emphasized)	Alfred Nobel - born in 1833 - was the inventor of dynamite.

Check Up

1 삽입된 부분을 찾아 밑줄을 그으시오.

(1) This country, so to speak, needs better gun control laws.
(2) We set a record that I think is pretty good in this season.
(3) She is a girl who I know speaks five languages.
(4) After a few months in Spain, he hoped to become bilingual (speaking two languages).
(5) The West's traditional industries – mining, ranching, and logging – are clear losers in the new order.

20-3 생략

같은 단어가 반복되어 사용될 때 그 단어가 없어도 문맥을 이해하는데 문제가 없다면 해당 단어를 생략할 수 있다. 이로써 간결하고 명료한 문장을 만들 수 있다.

1 술부의 생략

- 문맥상 의미가 분명할 때 조동사만 남기고 술부를 생략할 수 있다.

  Your husband is getting fat. – Yes, I'm afraid he **is** (getting fat).
  Robbie hadn't done his assignment today. He was pleased to see that Tom **had** (done his homework instead).
  Steve doesn't enjoy pork as much as Chris **does** (enjoy pork).

2 부정사구의 생략

- 부정사구가 반복이 될 때 to만 남기고 나머지 부분을 생략할 수 있다. 이러한 용법으로 쓰이는 to를 대(代)부정사라고 한다.

  Can you come to my wedding ceremony on October 27th? – Yes, I'd love **to**.
  After a few days off, Bob felt refreshed, though he didn't expect **to**.
  I didn't tell you to use proper punctuation, grammar, and tenses, but you're expected **to**.

3 so/neither, so/not을 사용한 생략

1) so / neither + 동사 + 주어

  I like chocolate. – **So do I**.
  Harry grew a little prouder of himself day by day, and **so did I**.
  Nuts for the most part can be eaten raw, and **so can seeds**.
  The computer doesn't work. **Neither does the DVD* player**.
  The hot dogs didn't taste very nice. **Neither did the potatoes**.

  ▶ '~도 역시'(= also)라고 해석하며, 주어와 동사의 어순 변화(Inversion)에 주의한다.
  ▶ 상대방의 말에 대한 동의(agreement)를 나타내는 'So/Neither + 주어 + 동사'와 구별해서 사용하도록 한다.
    ex. You've missed writing your name here. – Oh, **so I have**. Thanks.

2) so / not

  I'm not sure if there are enough tickets left, but I think **so**. (충분한 표가 남았을 거라고 생각해)
  Can my car be repaired? – I hope **so**. (당신 차가 수리될 수 있기를 바라요)
  Are you sure he didn't call? – I'm afraid **not**. (그는 전화를 하지 않았을 거야)

Check Up

1 생략할 수 있는 부분을 찾아 ( )로 묶으시오.

(1) Who's a taxi driver? – I am a taxi driver.
(2) Ms. Kate will come and see you when she can come and see you.
(3) Let's go for a walk along the bank. – I'd love to go for a walk along the bank.
(4) Charlie was supposed to clean the room before the children arrive, but he hasn't cleaned the room.
(5) If we continue to pollute the environment as we have polluted the environment in the past, we may live to regret it.

2 Speak-out A에 대한 적절한 답을 B에 쓰고, 큰 소리로 세 번씩 말하시오.

(1) A: I'm thirsty.   B: So _____
(2) A: My husband gets paid every month.   B: _____ my husband.
(3) A: Steve is late again this morning.   B: _____ Robbie.
(4) A: I've never seen a ghost.   B: Neither _____
(5) A: Olga can't swim well enough.   B: _____ her brother.

3 밑줄 친 표현의 쓰임이 나머지와 다른 하나를 고르시오.

(1) _____ ⓐ Cats like fish, but dogs <u>don't</u>.
            ⓑ Never has Tom met Santa Claus, but he really wishes <u>to</u>.
            ⓒ The rabbit runs <u>so</u> fast that Sally can't follow it.

(2) _____ ⓐ Ms. Helen is driving a car to the kindergarten <u>to</u> pick up children.
            ⓑ He isn't tall enough to be a volleyball player, and <u>neither</u> am I.
            ⓒ "I can't call you today, but I <u>can</u> tomorrow," he said.

(3) _____ ⓐ I wouldn't be alone on the Easter holidays, and <u>neither</u> would he.
            ⓑ At that time, he was <u>not</u> in Seoul.
            ⓒ Sometimes people forget things, and <u>so</u> do I.

□ **DVD** 영상과 음성을 디지털화 하여 저장할 수 있도록 만든 12cm 가량의 광디스크를 말하며, 고화질의 영화를 담는 영상 매체로서 뿐만 아니라 컴퓨터 기억 장치로도 사용된다. DVD는 Digital Video Disc의 줄임말이다.

20-4 강조

- Speaking에서의 강조는 강세발음을 활용하는 것이 자주 사용되고, Writing과 Reading에서는 적절한 단어의 첨가 및 활용이 적합해 보인다. 기본적인 표현을 의미가 강조되는 다른 표현으로 바꾸어도 가능해 진다. 강조하는 방법은 매우 다양하지만, 본 Unit에서는 기본적인 몇 가지만을 다루도록 한다.

1 Speaking에서의 강조: 강세발음

- Speaking에서는 강세발음을 통해 특정한 표현을 강조할 수 있다.

  I see a little polar bear in my dream on Thursdays.
  The company has launched* a new type of sugar-free candy.
  Your story reminds me of a terrible memory about apples.
  The beast climbed up a huge building with the beauty seated on its shoulder.

2 동사의 강조

I **do** believe that there's good* in everybody.
Ms. Potter **did** do her best to keep the promise to her son.
Do make yourself at home and have some biscuits.

3 it ~ that, what을 사용한 강조

The detective found the letter under the carpet.
→ **It** was the detective **that**/**who** found the letter under the carpet.
→ **It** was the letter **that**/**which** the detective found under the carpet.
→ **It** was under the carpet **that**/**where** the detective found the letter.

The guests played mini-golf after tea.

→ **What** the guests played after tea was mini-golf.
→ **What** the guests did after tea was (to) play mini-golf.
→ **What** happened after tea was (that) the guests played mini-golf.

4 기타 강조 표현

How anxiously she awaited my answer!
What a beautiful song (it is)!

▶ 감탄문: how + 형용사/부사(+주어+동사) vs. what(+a/an+부사+형용사)+명사(+주어+동사)

How **on earth/in the world** did such a miserable thing happen to the little boy?

▸ On earth/In the world는 wh-의문사를 강조하여 '세상에, 도대체 왜'의 의미를 나타낸다.

My father used to tell us life **itself** is a learning process.

▸ 재귀대명사의 삽입을 통한 강조 용법

Santa Claus I saw last night.　　　　　　　　　　Inversion (목적어)
Rarely had I met such a handsome guy in my life.　Inversion (부정어구)
After a few months, the mouse became friends with the cat.　Fronting (전치사구)

Check Up

1　조동사 do의 역할(A항)과 그 예(B항)를 알맞게 연결하시오.

　　　A　　　　　　　　　　　B
(1) 강조　　•　　　•　ⓐ Did you see the flag was moving?
(2) 의문문　•　　　•　ⓑ It does not matter if you are a millionaire or not.
(3) 부정문　•　　　•　ⓒ She says she doesn't care, but she does.
(4) 생략　　•　　　•　ⓓ A teaspoon of salt does make it delicious.

2　 밑줄 친 부분을 강조하는 문장을 만들어 큰 소리로 세 번씩 말하시오.

(1) it ~ that　ⓐ Mr. Carry keeps fresh herbs in the kitchen.
　　　　　　　ⓑ Mr. Carry keeps fresh herbs in the kitchen.
　　　　　　　ⓒ Mr. Carry keeps fresh herbs in the kitchen.

(2) what　　　ⓐ I took a warm bath before going to bed.
　　　　　　　ⓑ I took a warm bath before going to bed.
　　　　　　　ⓒ I took a warm bath before going to bed.

 comments

❑ **launch** [lɔːntʃ]　v. (배 등을) 진수시키다, (로켓 등을) 발사하다, (계획 등을) 시작하다　❑ **good** [gud]　n. 장점, 아름다운 점, 효용, 값어치

Grammar Review

1 다음 문장이 바르게 쓰였으면 ○표를 하고, 잘못 쓰였으면 ×표를 하시오.

_____ (1) The cheese have less fat than the ordinary one.
_____ (2) The health resort which is for the old people are across the road.
_____ (3) A number of books was missing from the shelf.
_____ (4) The number of books were indeed large.
_____ (5) It is Robert that reveals the secret.
_____ (6) What I did first, more than anything, was called the police.
_____ (7) Sorry I bothered you, but I didn't mean to.
_____ (8) Tomatoes are not fruit, and so are pumpkins.

2 A와 B를 알맞게 연결하여 대화문을 완성하시오.

A
(1) Did they get to Banana Island safely?
(2) My wife and I enjoy cooking.
(3) Do you want a drink?
(4) I cannot describe it.

B
ⓐ So I do.
ⓑ I'm afraid not.
ⓒ Neither can I.
ⓓ So do we.

3 주어진 표현이 들어갈 알맞은 위치를 고르시오.

(1) When he does ∧ a part in a play, he ∧ turn ∧ into ∧ the character. (do)
　　　　　　　(A)　　　　　　　　　(B)　　　(C)　　　(D)

(2) Why ∧ would ∧ she ∧ want to go to ∧ such a place? (on earth)
　　　(A)　　　(B)　　(C)　　　　　　(D)

(3) What ∧ horrible ∧ thing ∧ it ∧ was! (a)
　　　 (A)　　　　(B)　　　(C)　(D)

(4) It is ∧ her courage and ∧ beauty ∧ everyone ∧ admires. (that)
　　　　(A)　　　　　　　　(B)　　　(C)　　　　(D)

(5) How ∧ I was ∧ to see ∧ them ∧ all go! (glad)
　　　 (A)　　　(B)　　　(C)　　　(D)

4 다음 우리말을 영어로 옮겨 큰 소리로 세 번씩 말하시오. (밑줄 친 부분을 강조할 것)

(1) 2005년에 이 책을 쓴 사람이 바로 <u>그녀</u>이다. (it ~ that)
→ _____

(2) 2005년에 그녀가 쓴 것이 바로 <u>이 책</u>이다. (it ~ that)
→ _____

(3) 그녀가 이 책을 쓴 것은 바로 <u>2005년</u>이었다. (it ~ that)
→ _____

(4) Thomas가 내게 준 것은 바로 <u>그의 전화번호</u>였다. (what)
→ _____

(5) 집에 도착한 후 내가 한 일은 바로 <u>즉시 Thomas에게 전화한 것</u>이었다. (what)
→ _____

(6) 집에 도착한 후 있었던 일은 바로 <u>내가 즉시 Thomas에게 전화한 것</u>이었다. (what)
→ _____

5 다음 글을 읽고, 빈 칸에 들어갈 알맞은 표현을 고르시오.

Something strange happened on North America's Lake Superior on November 21, 1902. A ship, (1) _____, simply disappeared! Twenty men
Ⓐ the *Bannockburn*   Ⓑ it's the *Bannockburn*

were lost. No one survived. Was there a storm at the time? No, there was not. The weather was slightly hazy, (2) _____ hardly bad. Moreover, the ship
Ⓐ but   Ⓑ but it

disappeared just after passing another ship, the *Algonquin*. Its captain – the *Algonquin's* – thought Bannockburn was lost from sight very fast. Was there anything else unusual? Apparently, there was not. One moment, *Bannockburn* was there. Then it was gone! We can find no explanation, though we have tried to. A ship (3) _____ wreckage on the lake later, but not where *Bannockburn* was
Ⓐ do find   Ⓑ did find

thought to have been. Did *Bannockburn* blow up? We do not think so. No one on *Algonquin* heard an explosion. What happened is a mystery which (4) _____
Ⓐ we believe   Ⓑ we believe it

no one has ever solved. But people do keep trying to do so!

Grammar Up

Time Limit: 6 min, _____ / 18

어법상 빈 칸에 들어갈 알맞은 표현을 고르시오.

1 _____ cause not only heavy traffic, but also air pollution.
- (A) Too many car
- (B) Too many car is
- (C) Too many cars
- (D) Too many cars were

2 _____ the Amazon River that is the second longest river after the Nile.
- (A) It
- (B) It is
- (C) There is
- (D) Although

3 Penguins use their wings not in flying, but in helping _____.
- (A) them swim
- (B) they swim
- (C) they to swim
- (D) they are swimming

4 Once the company did a play about Sherlock Holmes, _____.
- (A) he is the detective
- (B) and the detective
- (C) the detective is
- (D) the detective

5 Gospel music is the kind of intense, joyful music _____ makes the spirit sing.
- (A) however
- (B) what I think
- (C) that I think
- (D) I think

6 He's the one _____ is interested in ecology.
- (A) who I believe
- (B) whom I believe
- (C) which I believe
- (D) whose

7 Four main directions, east, west, north, and south, _____ where things are.
   (A) it tells
   (B) they tell
   (C) tells you
   (D) tell you

8 In the old days painters made portraits, _____, like photos today.
   (A) pictures of people
   (B) people who in pictures
   (C) pictures and people
   (D) pictures of people which

어법상 잘못된 부분을 고르시오.

9 <u>The</u> tallest animal <u>in</u> the world <u>are</u> the <u>giraffe</u>.
   (A)   (B)   (C)   (D)

10 It was <u>ten minutes</u> that <u>they</u> <u>changed</u> his whole life <u>forever</u>.
         (A)   (B)   (C)   (D)

11 It is <u>the tiger</u> <u>that</u> I'd like to see <u>it</u> when <u>going</u> to the zoo.
         (A)   (B)   (C)   (D)

12 <u>That</u> she possesses <u>is</u> the ability <u>to remember</u> <u>whatever</u> she reads in books.
      (A)   (B)   (C)   (D)

13 Driving a car <u>through</u> the heavy rain <u>are</u> <u>exciting</u> but <u>dangerous</u>.
                    (A)   (B)   (C)   (D)

14 Vincent <u>couldn't</u> remember <u>when or where</u> he met <u>her</u>, but he thought he did <u>knew</u> her.
              (A)   (B)   (C)   (D)

15 <u>Doing</u> something over <u>and</u> over <u>make</u> you good <u>at</u> it.
       (A)   (B)   (C)   (D)

16 <u>Never</u> in her life <u>have</u> she been <u>so</u> free of <u>worry</u>.
       (A)   (B)   (C)   (D)

17 Chewing gum <u>comes</u> from <u>a kind</u> of juice of the tree, which <u>grow</u> in hot <u>countries</u>.
                  (A)   (B)   (C)   (D)

18 Hummingbirds are <u>such</u> tiny and <u>light</u> that <u>they</u> can sit on <u>a flower</u>.
                        (A)   (B)   (C)   (D)

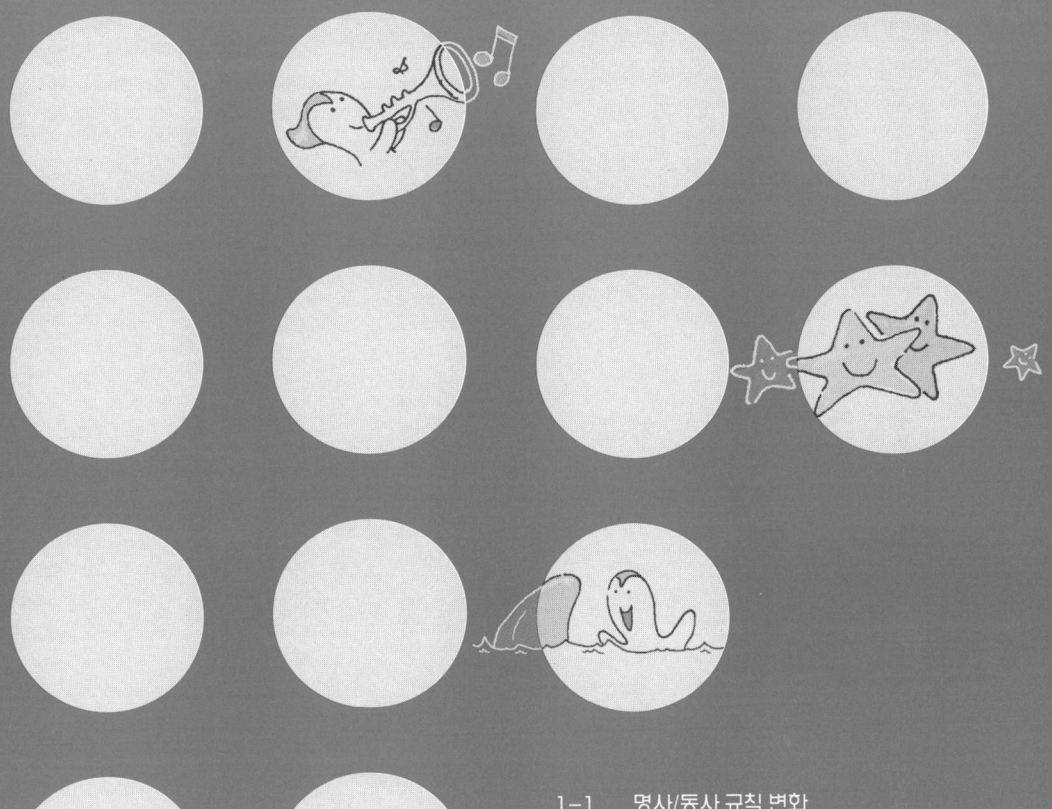

Appendix

1-1. 명사/동사 규칙 변화
1-2. 발음
2. 명사의 복수형 불규칙 변화
3-1. 동사의 현재형 불규칙 변화
3-2. be/do/have 동사의 과거/과거분사형
3-3. 동사의 과거/과거분사형 불규칙 변화
4-1. 형용사, 부사의 비교급/최상급
4-2. 비교급 형태가 들어간 문장 만들기
4-3. -ly로 끝나는 부사 만들기
5-1. 인칭대명사의 종류와 변형
5-2. 재귀대명사의 종류
6. 축약형
7-1. 기수와 서수
7-2. 숫자 읽는 법
8. 동명사를 목적어로 취하는 동사의 예
9. to 부정사를 목적어로 취하는 동사의 예
10. 동사 + 목적어 + to 부정사

1-1. 명사/동사 규칙 변화

명사의 복수형	동사의 3인칭 단수 현재형	동사의 과거/과거분사형	동사의 진행형
① 기본적으로 명사 어미에 -s를 붙인다. bana**s**, bee**s**, book**s**, month**s**, lip**s**, shop**s**, stove**s**	① 동사원형에 -s를 붙인다. answer**s**, eat**s**, happen**s**, hope**s**, make**s**, speak**s**, visit**s**, write**s**	① 동사원형의 어미에 -(e)d를 붙인다. live – live**d**, start – start**ed**, stay – stay**ed**, call – call**ed**	① 동사원형에 -ing를 붙인다. ask**ing**, do**ing**, go**ing**, hold**ing**, read**ing**, spend**ing**, wear**ing**
② -ch, -sh, -s, -x, -z → -es를 붙인다. beach**es**, dish**es**, bus**es**, dress**es**	② -ch, -sh, -s, -x, -z → -es를 붙인다. catch**es**, finish**es**, miss**es**, fix**es**, buzz**es**		② -e를 없애고 -ing를 붙인다. hope – hop**ing**, take – tak**ing** *주의: -ee로 끝나면 -ing만 붙인다. agree – agree**ing**
③ '자음+y' → y를 i로 고치고 -es를 붙인다. baby → bab**ies**, city → cit**ies** • '모음+y'로 끝나면 -s를 붙인다. boy**s**, day**s**, key**s**, monkey**s**	③ '자음+y' → y를 i로 고치고 -es를 붙인다. carry → carr**ies**, fly → fl**ies**, study → stud**ies**, worry → worr**ies** • '모음+y'로 끝나면 -s를 붙인다. buy**s**, enjoy**s**, obey**s**, play**s**, say**s**	② '자음+y' → y를 i로 고치고 -ed를 붙인다. carry – carr**ied**, try – tr**ied** • '모음+y'로 끝나면 -ed를 붙인다. destroy – destroy**ed**, play – play**ed**, stay – stay**ed**	③ -ie → ie를 y로 바꾸고 -ing를 붙인다. die – d**ying**, lie – l**ying**, tie – t**ying**
④ -o로 끝나면 주로 -es를 붙인다. hero**es**, tomato**es**, zero**es** • -s만 붙이는 경우 piano**s**, radio**s**, video**s**, zoo**s**		〈'자모자'는 '자모자자'〉 ③ '자음+모음+자음'으로 끝나는 단음절 또는 2음절 동사 중 마지막 자음에 강세가 있는 동사는 자음을 한 번 더 쓰고 -ed를 붙인다. permit – permit**ted**, plan – plan**ned**, plug – plug**ged**, stop – stop**ped** (예외) fix – fix**ed**, sew – sew**ed**	〈'자모자'는 '자모자자'〉 ④ '자음+모음+자음'으로 끝나는 단음절 또는 2음절 동사 중 마지막 자음에 강세가 있는 동사는 자음을 한 번 더 쓰고 -ing를 붙인다. jog – jog**ging**, get – get**ting**, run – run**ning**, sit – sit**ting** *형용사, 부사의 비교급에도 적용
⑤ -f(e)를 v로 고치고 -es를 붙인다. half → hal**ves**, knife → kni**ves** • -s만 붙이는 경우 belief**s**, chef**s**, cliff**s**, proof**s**			

*〈'자모자'는 '자모자자' 라〉의 공식은 ① 동사의 과거형 ② 동사의 진행형 ③ 비교급에만 적용된다. 가장 기본적인 변화 형태인 명사의 복수형과 동사의 3인칭 단수 현재형에는 적용되지 않는다.

1-2. 발음

명사의 복수형	동사의 3인칭 단수 현재형	동사의 과거/과거분사형
① /z/ – 유성음 [b, d, g 등과 모든 모음]으로 끝나는 명사 뒤에 -s verb**s**, card**s**, dog**s**, bee**s**	① /z/ – 유성음 [b, d, g, v 등과 모든 모음]으로 끝나는 동사 뒤에 -s buy**s**, carrie**s**, love**s**, pay**s**, read**s**, see**s**	① /d/ – 유성음과 모음으로 끝나는 동사 뒤에 -(e)d bath**ed**, call**ed**, charg**ed**, di**ed**, learn**ed**, lov**ed**, nam**ed**, us**ed**
② /ɪz/ – [s, x, ʃ, tʃ 등]의 발음으로 끝나는 명사 뒤에 -es bus**es**, box**es**, dish**es**, bench**es**, kiss**es**	② /ɪz/ – [s, x, ʃ, tʃ 등]의 발음으로 끝나는 동사 뒤에 -es catch**es**, fix**es**, miss**es**, punish**es**, teach**es**, wash**es**	② /ɪd/ – [d, t]의 발음으로 끝나는 동사 뒤에 -ed add**ed**, decid**ed**, end**ed**, hat**ed**, need**ed**, wait**ed**, want**ed**
③ /s/ – 무성음 [p, k, t, f, θ 등]으로 끝나는 명사 뒤에 -s cat**s**, desk**s**, roof**s**, month**s**	③ /s/ – 무성음 [p, k, t, f 등]으로 끝나는 동사 뒤에 -s eat**s**, hope**s**, laugh**s**, pick**s**	③ /t/ – 무성음 [p, k, t, f 등]으로 끝나는 동사 뒤에 -(e)d cook**ed**, help**ed**, jump**ed**, kiss**ed**, lik**ed**, wash**ed**, watch**ed**

* 무성음에는 **p, k, t, f, θ**, s, ʃ, tʃ, h의 9개가 있다. 그 중에서 **p, k, t, f, θ** 발음 다음의 -s만 /s/ 발음한다.

2. 명사의 복수형 불규칙 변화

① 끝부분이 첨가되는 명사	child → child**ren**, ox → ox**en**
② 모음 또는 자음이 변화하는 명사	foot → f**ee**t, goose → g**ee**se, man → m**e**n, mouse → m**ice**, tooth → t**ee**th, woman → wom**e**n
③ 단복수형이 같은 명사	sheep, series, deer, fish(*or* fishes)
④ 형태가 다른 명사	person → people(*or* persons)
⑤ 복수형태로만 쓰이는 명사	belongings, clothes, glasses, goods, groceries, jeans, pajamas, pants, scissors, shorts

3-1. 동사의 현재형 불규칙 변화

주어	be	do	have
I	am	do	have
You	are	do	have
He / She / It	is	does	has
We	are	do	have
You	are	do	have
They	are	do	have

3-2. be/do/have 동사의 과거/과거분사형

원형	과거형		과거분사형
be	주어가 I / He / She / It 일 때	was	been
	주어가 You / We / They 일 때	were	
do	did		done
have	had		had

3-3. 동사의 과거/과거분사형 불규칙 변화

원형	과거	과거분사	원형	과거	과거분사
[유형 1] A – B – C			dig	dug	dug
bear	bore	borne/born	dream	dreamt/dreamed	dreamt/dreamed
begin	began	begun	feed	fed	fed
bite	bit	bitten	feel	felt	felt
blow	blew	blown	find	found	found
break	broke	broken	fight	fought	fought
choose	chose	chosen	get	got	got/gotten
draw	drew	drown	hear	heard	heard
drink	**drank**	**drunk**	hold	held	held
drive	drove	driven	keep	kept	kept
eat	ate	eaten	**lay**	**laid**	**laid**
fall	fell	fallen	lead	led	led
fly	flew	flown	leave	left	left
forget	forgot	forgotten	lend	lent	lent
freeze	froze	frozen	**light**	**lit/lighted**	**lit/lighted**
give	gave	given	lose	lost	lost
go	went	gone	make	made	made
grow	grew	grown	mean	meant	meant
hide	**hid**	**hidden**	meet	met	met
know	knew	known	pay	paid	paid
lie	**lay**	**lain**	say	said	said
ride	rode	ridden	sell	sold	sold
ring	rang	rung	shine	shone/shined	shone/shined
rise	rose	risen	shoot	shot	shot
see	saw	seen	sit	sat	sat
shake	shook	shaken	sleep	slept	slept
show	**showed**	**shown/showed**	spend	spent	spent
sing	sang	sung	stick	stuck	stuck
sink	sank	sunk	teach	taught	taught
sow	sowed	sown/sowed	win	won	won
spring	sprang	sprung	[유형 3] A – A – A		
sew	sewed	sewn/sewed	cast	cast	cast
steal	stole	stolen	cost	cost	cost
swear	**swore**	**sworn**	fit	fit/fitted	fit/fitted
swim	swam	swum	hurt	hurt	hurt
take	took	taken	let	let	let
tear	tore	torn	put	put	put
throw	threw	thrown	quit	quit	quit
wake	**woke**	**woken**	read	read	read
wear	**wore**	**worn**	set	set	set
write	wrote	written	shut	shut	shut
[유형 2] A – B – B			[유형 4] A – B – A		
bring	brought	brought	become	became	become
build	built	built	come	came	come
buy	bought	bought	run	ran	run
catch	caught	caught	[유형 5] A – A – B		
deal	dealt	dealt	beat	beat	beaten

4-1. 형용사, 부사의 비교급/최상급

1음절과 일부 2음절의 형용사, 부사	대부분의 2음절과 3음절 이상의 형용사와 부사
① 형용사, 부사에 -(e)r, -(e)st를 붙인다. fast – fast**er** – fast**est**, late – lat**er** – lat**est**, near – near**er** – near**est**, nice – nic**er** – nic**est**	④ 형용사, 부사 앞에 more, most를 쓴다. active – **more** active – **most** active, difficult – **more** difficult – **most** difficult, frequent – **more** frequent – **most** frequent, important – **more** important – **most** important
〈'자모자'는 '자모자자'라〉 ② '단자음+단모음+단자음'으로 끝나면 자음을 한번 더 쓰고 –er, –est를 붙인다. big – big**ger** – big**gest**, flat – flat**ter** – flat**test**, wet – wet**ter** – wet**test**	⑤ -ed, -ing로 끝나는 단어는 앞에 more, most를 쓴다. tired – **more** tired – **most** tired, relaxed – **more** relaxed – **most** relaxed, boring – **more** boring – **most** boring, charming – **more** charming – **most** charming
③ '자음+y'로 끝나면 y를 i로 바꾸고 –er, –est를 붙인다. dirty – dirt**ier** – dirt**iest**, funny – funn**ier** – funn**iest**, happy – happ**ier** – happ**iest**, lonely – lonel**ier** – lonel**iest**, lucky – luck**ier** – luck**iest**, pretty – prett**ier** – prett**iest**	⑥ '형용사+ly'로 끝나는 부사는 앞에 more, most를 쓴다. brightly – **more** brightly – **most** brightly, cheaply – **more** cheaply – **most** cheaply, quickly – **more** quickly – **most** quickly, slowly – **more** slowly – **most** slowly

- 2음절 단어 중 -er, -ow, -le, -some으로 끝나는 대부분의 형용사는 –(e)r, –(e)st 또는 more, most 겸용
  clever, narrow, noble, idle, simple, subtle, handsome 등
- -(e)r, -(e)st를 붙여야 하는지 more, most를 써야 하는지 확신이 없는 경우에는 more, most를 사용하는 편이 낫다: angry, common, friendly, gentle, handsome, narrow, quiet, simple 등
- '단자음+단모음+단자음'으로 끝나는 단어의 마지막이 –w로 끝나는 경우는 –er, –est만 붙인다.
  slow – slower – slowest, low – lower – lowest 등

4-2. 비교급 형태가 들어간 문장 만들기

① 형용사, 부사의 비교급+than+비교 대상: ~보다 더 …한

The blue jacket is cheap. → The blue jacket is **cheaper than** the white one (is).
She arrived late. → She arrived **later than** the other students (did).
His illness was serious. → His illness was **more serious than** we first thought.

He finished the work more quickly than <u>I did</u>.　　문법적으로 맞고, 회화에서도 자주 사용
He finished the work more quickly than <u>I</u>.　　　　문법적으로 맞지만, 회화에서 자주 사용 안 함
He finished the work more quickly than <u>me</u>.　　　문법적으로 틀리지만, 회화에서 자주 사용

② 비교 대상을 나타내지 않아도 의미가 통하는 경우

Can you please speak **more loudly**?
Please be **more polite** next time.
It's getting **harder** (and harder) to find a job. (강조를 하는 경우에는 and harder를 첨가)
These days **more** (and more) people are learning a foreign language.

4-3. -ly로 끝나는 부사 만들기

형용사의 마지막 철자	바꾸기	더하기	예
대부분의 형용사		+ly	slow**ly**, late**ly**, bright**ly**, honest**ly**, hopeful**ly**, polite**ly**
-y	-y → -i		eas**y** → eas**ily**, luck**y** → luck**ily**, happ**y** → happ**ily**
-le	-le →		terrib**le** → terrib**ly**, comforab**le** → comfortab**ly**
-ue	-ue → -u		tr**ue** → tr**uly**
-ic		+ally	magi**c** → magi**cally**, ironi**c** → ironi**cally**

• -ly로 끝난다고 해서 반드시 부사는 아니다. ly로 끝나는 형용사: friendly, lovely, costly, orderly, lively, lonely, silly, ugly 등

5-1. 인칭대명사의 종류와 변형

구분		단수(Singular)				복수(Plural)			
		주격	목적격	소유격	소유대명사	주격	목적격	소유격	소유대명사
1인칭(First Person)		I	me	my	mine	we	us	our	ours
2인칭(Second Person)		you	you	your	yours	you	you	your	yours
3인칭	남성(male)	he	him	his	his	they	them	their	theirs
	여성(female)	she	her	her	hers				
	중성(neuter)	it	it	its					

5-2. 재귀대명사의 종류

I	–	myself	it	–	itself
you	–	yourself	we	–	ourselves
he	–	himself	you	–	yourselves
she	→	herself	they	→	themselves

<X7

6. 축약형

축약	발음	축약 전	축약	발음	축약 전
I'm	[aim]	I am	they're	[ðɛəR]	they are
I've	[aiv]	I have	they've	[ðeiv]	they have
I'll	[ail]	I will	they'll	[ðeil]	they will
I'd	[aid]	I had/would	they'd	[ðeid]	they had/would
you're	[juəR]	you are	there's	[ðɛəRz]	there is/has
you've	[ju:v]	you have	there'll	[ðɛəRl]	there will
you'll	[ju:l]	you will	there'd	[ðɛəRd]	there had/would
you'd	[ju:d]	you had/would			
			aren't	[ɑ:Rnt]	are not
he's	[hi:z]	he is/has	can't	[kænt]	cannot
he'll	[hi:l]	he will	couldn't	[kudnt]	could not
he'd	[hi:d]	he had/would	didn't	[didnt]	did not
			doesn't	[dʌznt]	does not
she's	[ʃi:z]	she is/has	don't	[dount]	do not
she'll	[ʃi:l]	she will	hadn't	[hædnt]	had not
she'd	[ʃi:d]	she had/would	hasn't	[hæznt]	has not
			haven't	[hævnt]	have not
it's	[its]	it is/has	isn't	[iznt]	is not
it'll	[itl]	it will	mustn't	[mʌsnt]	must not
it'd	[itəd]	it had/would	shouldn't	[ʃudnt]	should not
			wasn't	[wʌznt]	was not
we're	[wiəR]	we are	weren't	[wə:Rnt]	were not
we've	[wi:v]	we have	won't	[wount]	will not
we'll	[wi:l]	we will	wouldn't	[wudnt]	would not
we'd	[wi:d]	we had/would			

*She was~, He was~를 She's~ 또는 He's~로 축약하면 안 된다. She's, He's는 She is/has~, He is/has의 축약형에 한 한다.

7-1. 기수와 서수

	기수	서수		기수	서수
1	one	first (1st)	21	twenty-one	twenty-first (21st)
2	two	second (2nd)	30	thirty	thirtieth (30th)
3	three	third (3rd)	40	**forty**	**fortieth (40th)**
4	four	fourth (4th)	50	fifty	fiftieth (50th)
5	five	**fifth** (5th)	60	sixty	sixtieth (60th)
6	six	sixth (6th)	70	seventy	seventieth (70th)
7	seven	seventh (7th)	80	eighty	eightieth (80th)
8	eight	eighth (8th)	90	ninety	ninetieth (90th)
9	nine	**ninth** (9th)	100	one hundred	one hundredth (100th)
10	ten	tenth (10th)	200	two hundred	two hundredth (200th)
11	eleven	eleventh (11th)	1,000	one thousand	one thousandth (1,000th)
12	twelve	**twelfth** (12th)	10,000	ten thousand	ten thousandth (10,000th)
13	thirteen	thirteenth (13th)	백 만	million	millionth
14	fourteen	fourteenth (14th)	십 억	billion	billionth
15	fifteen	fifteenth (15th)			
16	sixteen	sixteenth (16th)			
17	seventeen	seventeenth (17th)			
18	eighteen	eighteenth (18th)			
19	nineteen	nineteenth (19th)			
20	twenty	twentieth (20th)			

7-2. 숫자 읽는 법

숫자 hundred 뒤에는 and를 넣어 읽는다. 1,000: thousand 1,000,000: million 1,000,000,000: billion	777: seven hundred (and) seventy-seven 3,152,000 three million one hundred (and) fifty-two thousand
연도 두 자리씩 끊어 읽는다.	1979: nineteen seventy-nine *cf.* 2005: two thousand (and) five
날짜 서수로 읽는다.	5월 25일: May 25th *or* the 25th of May
시간 시간과 분을 나누어 읽는다.	1시 17분: one seventeen, seventeen past one (분 past 시: -시 -분)
전화번호 한 자리씩 읽는다.	759-7120: seven five nine seven one two zero *or* seven fifty-nine seventy-one twenty
소수 소수점은 point라 읽고, 소수점 뒤는 한 자리씩 읽는다.	38.64: thirty-eight point six four
분수 분자는 기수로, 분모는 서수로 읽는다. 분자가 2 이상일 때는 분모에 -s를 붙인다.	$\frac{1}{3}$: one third, $\frac{1}{4}$: a (one) fourth = a quarter $3\frac{1}{8}$: three and one eighth, $\frac{2}{3}$: two third**s**
연산기호 + addition ex) 3+7=10 → − subtraction ex) 8−2=6 → × multiplication ex) 2×6=12 → ÷ division ex) 9÷3=3 →	three **plus/and** seven **equals/is** ten eight **minus** two **equals/is** six two **times/multiplied by** six **equals/is** twelve nine **divided by** three **equals/is** three

8. 동명사를 목적어로 취하는 동사의 예

1. abandon — Old friends do not **abandon loving** friendship.
2. admit — She never **admits making** any mistake.
3. adore — I **adore spending** time with my family.
4. advise — He **advised keeping** your eyes wide open before marriage.
5. allow — They don't **allow speaking** in any language other than English.
6. anticipate — We didn't **anticipate making** any drastic changes within a year.
7. appreciate — I really appreciate **having** met you.
8. avoid — **Avoid forcing** your child to eat if she or he is not hungry.
9. burst out — I told him a joke, but he **burst out crying**.
10. can't help — I **cannot help thinking** of you.
11. commence — We'll **commence looking** for a new manager.
12. complete — They finally **completed rebuilding** the destroyed house.
13. confess to — The man **confessed to having** taken part in the crime.
14. consider — Have you **considered moving** instead of **remodeling**?
15. contemplate — I **contemplated flying** to England to see my friend.
16. defer — The troops **deferred going** until the storm was over.
17. delay — We **delayed planning** for a workshop.
18. deny — He **denied telling** me anything about himself.
19. describe — The woman **described having seen** the accident.
20. detest — I **detest doing** any evil things.
21. discuss — We **discussed doing** business in China.
22. dislike — I **dislike doing** the same thing over and over again.
23. dread* — I'm **dreading going** back to school tomorrow.
24. endure — He couldn't **endure being** insulted any longer.
25. enjoy — A lot of people **enjoy sunbathing** at the beach.
26. escape — You can't **escape working** on the project.
27. evade — They intentionally **evaded paying** taxes.
28. face — She couldn't have **faced being** alone.
29. fancy — He doesn't **fancy going** shopping.
30. feel like — I don't **feel like going** out today.
31. finish — You should have **finished fixing** it a week ago.
32. give up — I **gave up calling** because the phone lines were always busy.
33. imagine — She **imagined waking** up from a nightmare.
34. involve — The job **involves supporting and working** closely with customers.
35. justify — Nothing can **justify doing** wrong to achieve a goal.
36. keep (on) — He **kept on eating** in the buffet restaurant.
37. leave off — They had to **leave off digging** because of rain. (= stop doing something)

38.	mention	The newspaper **mentioned raising** taxes in the country.
39.	mind	I don't **mind eating** leftovers as long as they retain their taste.
40.	miss	I will **miss seeing** your smiling face and **hearing** your cheerful voice.
41.	postpone	They had to **postpone going** on the trip.
42.	practice	I have **practiced riding** a bike every day.
43.	prevent	It will help you (to) **prevent missing** important messages.
44.	put off	He always **put off doing** laundry for as long as possible.
45.	quit	My computer **quit working**.
46.	recall	He didn't **recall having** been there before.
47.	recollect	Kate **recollected meeting** Lewis two years ago.
48.	recommend	The doctor **recommended doing** more exercise.
49.	regret	I **regretted quitting** the job.
50.	report	The company **reported eliminating** 20 positions.
51.	resent	They **resent having** to work overtime.
52.	resist	He still **resists talking** with you.
53.	risk	Don't **risk damaging** your health by smoking.
54.	stop	We want to **stop repeating** the tragedy.
55.	suggest	Mr. Wager **suggested revising** the policy.
56.	tolerate	She is so sensitive that she cannot **tolerate being** around perfume.
57.	understand	I can't **understand falling** in love with someone you've never seen.

*dread to think는 관용적으로 쓰임. I **dread to think** that anything horrible might happen.

9. to 부정사를 목적어로 취하는 동사의 예

1.	afford	How can you **afford to travel** so often?
2.	agree	The two companies **agreed to merge** and signed the contract.
3.	aim	We are **aiming to reach** the goal in the near future.
4.	arrange	We can **arrange to have** your wedding performed anywhere.
5.	ask	The Prime Minister **asked to address** the legislature.
6.	attempt	More and more people have **attempted to stop** smoking over years.
7.	beg	The people were **begging to get** out of the burning building.
8.	choose	William will **choose to cover** up his bald head with a hat.
9.	claim	He falsely **claimed to own** the motorcycle involved in the accident.
10.	consent	The defendant finally **consented to go** the police.
11.	decide	I **decided to give** back the ring to him.
12.	demand	I would have **demanded to see** the items before purchasing.
13.	deserve	I don't think I **deserve to have** such a wonderful woman as you.

14.	expect	She **seems to have** expected to see him again.
15.	fail	The government is **failing to confront** the problem.
16.	help	This tip will **help (to) find** the stolen goods.
17.	hesitate	Don't **hesitate to visit** me.
18.	hope	She **hopes to be** a kindergarten teacher after graduation.
19.	learn	I **learned to look** up the words in the dictionary.
20.	manage	He could hardly **manage to keep** his mouth shut.
21.	mean	I didn't **mean to hurt** your feelings.
22.	neglect	We **have neglected to protect** our children from violence.
23.	offer	The government **offered to create** more jobs this year.
24.	prepare	You should **prepare to live** on a special diet.
25.	pretend	He took out his cell phone and **pretended to get** a phone call from his boss.
26.	propose	The project **proposed to widen** the channel to 400 meters from 345 meters.
27.	promise	They **promised to make** him a star overnight.
28.	refuse	The court **refused to get** involved in the case.
29.	swear	I **swear not to disseminate** this information.
30.	trouble	He has never **troubled to learn** the language.
31.	want	Children always **want to run and play** wherever they are.
32.	wish	I **wish to have** a grand piano.
33.	would like	Some people **would like to donate** their bodies to medical science.

10. 동사 + 목적어 + to 부정사

1.	advise	The doctor **advised <u>me</u> to drink** green tea.
2.	allow	The lease **allows <u>us</u> to keep** a pet.
3.	ask	We **asked <u>John</u> to meet** us at the coffee shop.
4.	beg	The committee **begged <u>the chairman</u> to change** his mind.
5.	cause	Bad weather **caused <u>us</u> to postpone** our trip.
6.	challenge	Our team **challenged <u>their team</u> to play** a game.
7.	command	The king **commanded <u>his people</u> to store** grain.
8.	compel	The law **compels <u>me</u> to stop** at red lights.
9.	convince	Your arguments **convinced <u>me</u> to support** the petition.
10.	encourage	The city **encourages <u>people</u> to give** to charity.
11.	expect	Did you really **expect <u>anyone</u> to believe** your excuse?
12.	forbid	Regulations **forbid <u>me</u> to interfere** in this situation.
13.	force	Dry weather **forced <u>everyone</u> to conserve** water.
14.	get	Pain in his legs **got <u>Andrew</u> to see** a doctor.

15.	help	Her classmates **helped <u>Sylvia</u> to prepare** for the exam.
16.	hire	They **hired <u>a workman</u> to repair** the road.
17.	instruct	The manual **instructs <u>us</u> to install** a new motor.
18.	intend	The president **intends <u>him</u> to serve** as ambassador.
19.	invite	Friends **invited <u>us</u> to have** dinner at a restaurant.
20.	like	We **like <u>him</u> to make** music.
21.	love	We **love <u>her</u> to sing**.
22.	mean	He **meant <u>his words</u> to comfort** her.
23.	need	The company **needs <u>us</u> to do** this job.
24.	oblige	Filial respect **obliges <u>me</u> to listen** to my parents.
25.	order	The captain **ordered <u>the officer</u> to change** the ship's course.
26.	permit	The rules **permit <u>you</u> to carry** a certain amount of luggage.
27.	persuade	Did they **persuade <u>you</u> to join** their campaign?
28.	prefer	We **prefer <u>him</u> to work** on another project.
29.	recommend	The professor **recommended <u>me</u> to take** this job.
30.	remind	His son **reminded <u>him</u> to take** his medication.
31.	request	This letter **requests <u>us</u> to make** a donation.
32.	require	Icy roads **require <u>motorists</u> to drive** with care.
33.	teach	Schools **teach <u>children</u> to follow** the rules of society.
34.	tell	The directions **told <u>us</u> to turn** right at Main Street.
35.	tempt	The sight of chocolate **tempted <u>me</u> to buy** some.
36.	trouble	I'm sorry I must **trouble <u>you</u> to do** this.
37.	urge	The police **urged <u>everyone</u> to stay** calm.
38.	want	Do you **want <u>me</u> to open** the window?
39.	warn	Big signs **warned <u>people</u> to stop** at the gate.

중학영어 X-Series!

"영어공부, 어렵다구요?
X-시리즈로 쉽게 하세요!"

WORD AX1, AX2, AX3
중학 영단어

암기력의 극대화!

과학적으로 입증된 5감을 활용한
7차례 자연 반복 학습으로 발음+청취+단어 암기를 한번에!

193 pages / 12,000원
CD 2장 포함

231 pages / 12,500원
CD 2장 포함

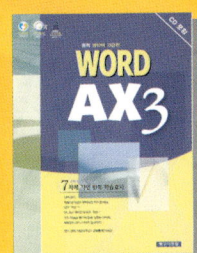
248 pages / 13,000원
CD 2장 포함

Grammar CX1, CX2, CX3

정말 다른 문법책!

기존 문법의 새로운 범위 제시!
시각적 효과를 이용하여 자세하고 쉽게
원리를 파헤친 영문법 교재

259 pages / 9,000원

296 pages / 10,000원

404 pages / 16,000원

Reading RX1, RX2, RX3

활용 100%
효과 200%!

총체적인 영어실력 향상! 쉽고 흥미로운
독해지문을 통해 Reading Skill을
체계적으로 학습한다!

Book One
135 pages
7,000원
Book Two
184 pages / 10,000원
CD 1장 포함

Book One
135 pages
7,000원
Book Two
188 pages / 10,000원
CD 1장 포함

Book One
144 pages
7,000원
Book Two
180 pages / 10,000원
CD 1장 포함

LinguaForum TOEFL® iBT Core Topic Guide

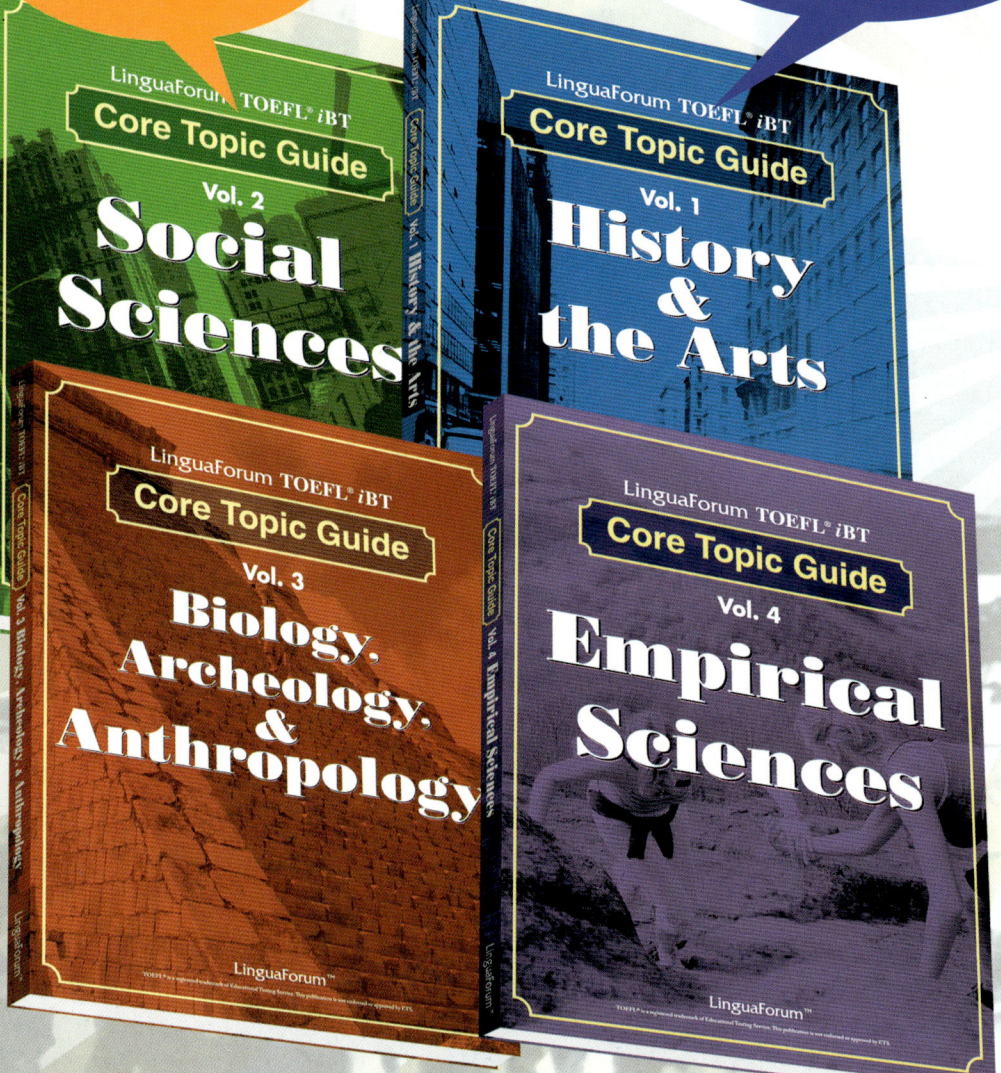

LinguaForum
TOEFL® iBT

Part B

ANSWER KEY

링구아포럼™

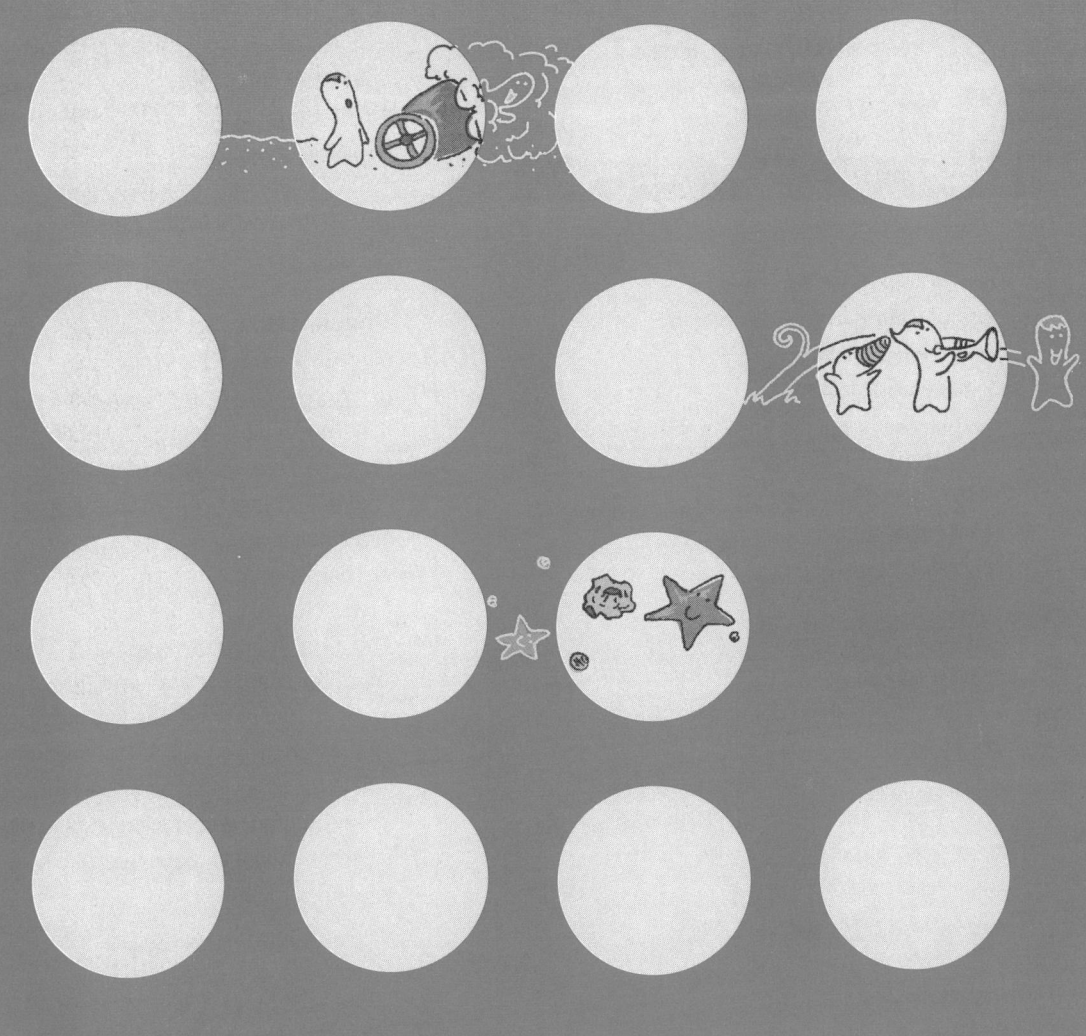

정답 및 해설
_Answer Key

CHAPTER 11
어순의 기본과 도치 / Word Order and Inversion

 11-1 꼬리에 꼬리를 무는 어순과 Speaking

🐢 Pop Quiz 1　　　　　　　　　　p.173

(1) Lucy offered an apple to me.
Lucy는 권했다 　무엇을?
사과를 (권했는데) 　누구에게?
나에게 (사과를 권했다.)

(2) The baby-sitter put the baby on the bed.
보모는 놓았다 　누구를?/무엇을?
아기를 (놓았는데) 　어디에?
침대에 (아기를 놓았다.)

(3) This rug is made of cotton and wool in India.
이 양탄자는 만들어진다 　무엇으로?
면과 양모로 (만들어지는데) 　어디에서?
인도에서 (면과 양모로 만들어진다.)

(4) A smell in the yellow room makes them nervous little by little.
노란 방의 냄새는 ~이/가 ~상태가 되게 한다
　누가?/무엇이?
그들이 　어떤 상태가 되게 하느냐 하면
초조한 상태가 되게 한다 　어떻게?
조금씩 (그들이 초조한 상태가 되게 한다.)

🐢 Pop Quiz 2　　　　　　　　　　p.173

(1) 많은 이유 　어떤 이유이냐 하면
  – 운동을 해야 할 많은 이유
   (many reasons to exercise)
  – 일기를 써야 할 많은 이유
   (many reasons for keeping a diary)
  – 내가 대학을 가기로 결정한 이유 (many reasons why I decided to go to college)

(2) 벽 　어떤 벽이냐 하면
  – 빨간 벽돌로 만들어진 벽 (a wall of red bricks all around their property)
  – 겨우 12 인치 높이의 벽
   (a wall only 12 inches high)

(3) 발표 　어떤 발표이냐 하면
  – 3분기 판매량에 관한 발표 (an announcement on the third quarter sales next week)
  – 그녀가 자신의 지위에서 은퇴할 것이라는 발표 (an announcement that she is to resign her position)

(4) 사람 　어떤 사람이냐 하면
  – 올바른 취침 습관을 가진 사람 (A person with good sleeping habits)
  – 아침에 일찍 일어나는 사람
   (A person who gets up early)

🐢 Check Up　　　　　　　　　　p.174

1.

(1) Living in a big city is ↳ Living in a big city is more convenient than living in a small town.

(2) I want ↳ I want to live in a small town.

(3) I have ↳ I have two reasons for wanting to live in a small town.
   Or There are ↳ There are two reasons why I want to live in a small town.

(4) The most important reason is ↳ The most important reason is that small towns are free from the heavy traffic of a big city.

(5) The second reason is ↳ The second reason is that I can enjoy fresh air in the morning, a blue sky in autumn, and shining stars at night.

(6) I want ↳ I want to leave the big city and move to a small town.

2.

(1) 그녀의 남편에 대해 (불평을 하지 않는데), 다른 사람들에게 (그녀의 남편에 대해 불평을 하지 않는다.)

(2) 나는 받았다 　무엇을?
수신자 부담 전화를 (받았는데) 　누구로부터 받았느냐 하면
나의 형으로부터 (수신자 부담 전화를 받았는데)
　어떤 형이냐 하면
하와이에 살고 있는 (나의 형으로부터 수신자 부담 전화를 받았다.)

(3) 그 칠리는 어떠하다 　어떠하냐 하면
너무 쓰고 맛이 없는데 　그래서 어떻게 되었느냐 하면
우리는 그것을 먹을 수 없었는데 　어떻게 먹을 수 없었
느냐 하면
더 이상 (그것을 먹을 수 없었다.)

(4) 우리는 흥분해 있다 　왜?
필리핀에 가게 되어서 (흥분해 있는데) 　언제?/누구와 함께?/왜?

여름 휴가 동안에 (필리핀에 가게 되어서 흥분해 있다.)
(5) 당신은 기억해야 한다 무엇을?
앞치마를 가지고 올 것을 (기억해야 하는데) 왜?
당신의 옷을 보호하기 위해 (앞치마를 가지고 올 것을 기억해야 한다.)

3.
(1) ① Maria ② doesn't like
③ washing dishes ④ very much.
(2) ① When he was in prison,
② he ③ learned
④ a lot of things ⑤ from books.
(3) ① You ② can send
③ him ④ an email
⑤ with a click ⑥ of your mouse.
(4) ① Bill ② checked
③ his answers ④ with the key
⑤ after he did all exercises.

11-2 어순의 도치

Pop Quiz   p.177

(1) Along the street came a strange man.
(2) Into the water splashed the swimmer.
(3) Under the tree were lying a rabbit and a turtle.
(4) In the library should we be quiet.
(5) Only in an emergency should you use the exit.
(6) Rarely does it rain.
(7) Rarely does it rain in Egypt.
(8) Nothing did they say about my hairdo.
(9) Hardly ever does she break a promise, as far as I know.
(10) Seldom would they visit their family.
(11) Never have I seen such a beautiful sunset.
(12) Under no circumstances can he make an excuse for telling a lie.

해설
(5) 원래 "You can see a row of van Goghs on the long wall."이 있었지만 이 문장을 도치하면 (On the long wall can you see a row of van Goghs.) 어색해지므로 수정함.
(8) nothing = not + anything
(9) Ever는 hardly와 의미적으로 연결되어 있으므로 (hardly를 수식, 강조) hardly와 함께 이동한다.

(12) no = not + any

Check Up   p.179

1.
(1) The Asian leaders sit along the walls.
아시아의 지도자들이 벽을 따라 앉아 있다.
Along the walls / sit / the Asian leaders.
(2) A pile of small boxes was under the Christmas tree.
작은 상자 더미가 크리스마스 트리 아래에 있었다.
Under the Christmas tree / was a pile / of small boxes.
(3) Ten minutes had never gone by so slowly.
십 분이 그렇게 천천히 지나간 적이 없었다.
Never / had ten minutes / gone by / so slowly.
(4) He had no sooner left Korea than he missed kimchi.
그는 한국을 떠나자마자 김치가 그리워졌다.
No sooner / had he left Korea / than he missed kimchi.
(5) Joel could rarely write a letter because he was so busy.
Joel은 너무 바빴기 때문에 좀처럼 편지를 쓸 수 없었다.
Rarely could Joel / write a letter / because he was / so busy.

2.
(1) How old do you think I am?
(2) What do you imagine Mark is doing?
(3) Why do you think they call her Snow White?
(4) Where do you believe you will go when you pass away?

11-3 동사 – 목적어의 어순

Check Up   p.181

1.
(1) it away ↳ Don't throw it away / until we've finished cooking.
(2) to it ↳ I'm sure that / a lot of people / will object / to it.
(3) it up ↳ If you give me your cup, / I'll fill it up / for

you.
(4) in him ↳ You couldn't succeed / if you didn't believe / in him.
(5) on it ↳ Because I've not seen the report, / I can hardly comment / on it.
(6) it down ↳ After due consideration, / we decided / to turn it down.

2.
(1) adv. ↳ Helen thanked me / for fixing up / her old bike.
(2) prep. ↳ She will never succeed / in keeping the peace / between her pet dogs.
(3) adv. ↳ Bill is trying on / the clothing and shoes / which his girlfriend gave him.
(4) prep., prep. ↳ Did her parents approve / of her decision / to marry a foreigner / who came from Canada?
(5) prep. ↳ The company consists / of more than 50 researchers / who are all smart and competent.

3.
(1) ⓑ ↳ 우리 아버지는 우리에게 밤에 잠이 들도록 노래를 불러주곤 하셨다.
(2) ⓑ ↳ Anderson 부인은 남편을 위해 스웨터를 만들어 주었다.
(3) ⓐ ↳ 그 책은 우리에게 20 달러의 값을 치르게 했다.
(4) ⓑ ↳ 그는 네가 높은 점수를 받은 것을 부러워한다.

4.
(1) The Galaxy consists ↳ The Galaxy consists / of a lot of stars.
(2) Mr. and Ms. Grant are ↳ Mr. and Ms. Grant are busy / looking after their baby.
(3) Neil described ↳ Neil described / his girlfriend / to me.

Grammar Review
p.183

1.
(1) ○
(2) × ↳ Charlie may hate her, but his survival depends on her.

(3) × ↳ Nowhere was it more dramatic than at sea.
(4) × ↳ What do you think he is trying to do with them?
(5) ○
(6) × ↳ She recommended to me a doctor who is good with children.

2.
(1) Some banks charge us a fixed fee for every transaction.
(2) Never did the little girl see the wolf again.
(3) What do you imagine happens between Kate and Daniel after the book ends?

해설 (1) transaction [trænsǽkʃən] n. (업무·교섭 따위의) 처리, 취급

3.
(1) Ⓐ (2) Ⓑ
(3) Ⓐ (4) Ⓑ

해설 vendor [véndər] n. 노점 상인, 행상인
(4) 연결동사는 보어와 밀접한 관계에 있으므로 보어가 이동할 때 함께 이동한다.

해석 그렇게 이상한 사람이 마을에 나타난 적은 없었다! 시장 길을 통해 문짝을 등에 진 남자가 걸어왔다! "당신은 왜 문짝을 가지고 다니나요?"라고 한 상인이 그에게 물었다. "우리 집을 도둑들로부터 지키기 위해서입니다!"라고 그가 말했다. "그게 당신의 집에 있던 문을 대신할 건가요?"라고 상인이 물었다. 남자는 "아니요."라고 대답했다. 상인은 물었다. "당신이 그걸 등에 지고 다니면 어떻게 그것이 당신 집을 지킬 수 있나요?" 그 남자는 상인에게 설명했다. "우리 집에 들어가려면 도둑은 문을 열어야 하지요! 내가 그 문을 가지고 다니면, 도둑은 그걸 열 수가 없답니다! 그러면 그는 들어올 수가 없고, 그래서 우리 집은 안전하지요!" 그의 생각은 정말 논리적이었지만... 동시에 정말 잘못 되었다!

Grammar Up
p.184

1. (B) 2. (C) 3. (A) 4. (C) 5. (D) 6. (C)
7. (A) 8. (A) 9. (A) 10. (D) 11. (A) 12. (C)
13. (D) 14. (A) 15. (B) 16. (B) 17. (B) 18. (D)

해설
2. liver [lívər] n. 간장 (肝腸: 간과 창자)
3. substance [sʌ́bstəns] n. 물질, 재질, 재료
   carbon [káːrbən] n. 탄소 (Carbon 14는 탄소의 동위원소로서, 무게가 다른 탄소의 한 종류이다. 양성자 6개와 중

성자 8개로 이루어진 핵으로 되어 있다.)
12. haunt [hɔ:nt]   *v.* 출몰하다, 자주 나타나다
14. retire [ritáiər]   *v.* 퇴직하다, 은퇴하다

Grammar in Context   p.186

1. laughed at him

2. Such methods will never succeed in getting rice!

3. ⓒ

4.
(1) 쥐 부부가 채워 놓았음을 (알았는데), 그들의 집을 (채워 놓 았는데), 쌀로 (채워 놓았는데), 온 겨울을 대비하기 위해 (그들의 집을 쌀로 채워 놓았음을 알고 있었다.)
(2) 쥐 부부는 매우 감명을 받았다 왜?
    그의 공손함에 (감명을 받아서)
    그 결과 어떻게 되었느냐하면
    그들은 까치에게 주었다 무엇을?
    큰 가방을 (주었는데) 어떤 큰 가방이냐 하면
    쌀이 든 큰 가방을 (까치에게 주었다.)

해설 courteous [kə́:rtiəs] *adj.* 예의 바른, 정중한 /
      courtesy [kə́:rtəsi] *n.* 예의, 공손, 친절
      magpie [mǽgpài] *n.* 까치
      pheasant [féznt] *n.* 꿩

해설 **예의 바른 까치**
    한국에는 꿩, 비둘기, 까치에 관한 우화가 전해진다. 어느 겨울, 식량이 거의 없었다. 이전에는 한 번도 새들이 그렇게 배가 고파 본 적이 없었다! 그들은 약간의 쌀이라도 바랐다. 그들은 쥐와 그의 아내가 온 겨울을 대비하기 위해 그들의 집을 쌀로 가득 채워 놓았음을 알고 있었다. 새들은 쥐 부부를 부러워했다. 비둘기가 무례하게 소리쳤다, "우리와 함께 나눠!" 쥐 부부가 말했다, "저리 가!" 꿩이 소리쳤다, "쌀을 좀 주세요, 그렇지 않으면 빼앗아 갈 거예요!" 그러나 쥐 부부는 그를 비웃었다. "이건 우리 것이야!" 하고 그들이 대답했다. 까치는 생각했다, "저런 방법으로는 절대 쌀을 얻는 데 성공할 수 없어!" 그래서, 그는 쥐 부부에게 설명했다, "착한 이웃님들, 쌀을 약간 나눠 주신다면 정말 감사할 거예요." 쥐 부부는 까치의 예의 바른 행동을 인정했다. 누구도 그처럼 정중한 부탁을 거절할 수 없을 것이다! 쥐 부부는 까치의 공손함에 감동을 받아서 그에게 쌀이 든 큰 가방을 주었다. 그 후, 예의 바른 까치는 한국의 명예로운 상징이 되었다.

CHAPTER 12
시제 / Tenses

12-1 기본시제: 현재, 과거, 미래

🐢 **Check Up**   p.190

1.
(1) comes   (2) had
(3) is   (4) took, wasn't
(5) are, spend

2.
(1) will   (2) am going, are going
(3) will   (4) is going
(5) won't, will

3.
(1) ⓐ   (2) ⓒ
(3) ⓑ

4.
(1) 미래 ↳ 기말 시험이 5월 말에 있을 예정이다.
(2) 미래 ↳ 기차는 11시에 출발할 예정이며, 곧이어 매시간의 서비스가 시작될 겁니다.
(3) 미래 ↳ 비행기는 10~15분 내에 서울에 도착할 예정이다.
(4) 미래 ↳ 영화 『바람과 함께 사라지다』가 3월 3일 한국에서 개봉될 것이다.

5.
(1) A: Kate usually <u>sits</u> in the front row during class.
    B: But today she <u>is sitting</u> in the last row.
(2) A: Watch the following picture carefully. What <u>is</u> the chef <u>doing</u> now?
    B: The chef <u>is tasting</u> the soup.
(3) A: Close your eyes and listen carefully. What <u>am</u> I <u>doing</u> now?
    B: You <u>are clapping</u> your hands.

해설 Taste가 '~맛이 나다' 라는 뜻의 상태를 나타낼 때는 진행형을 쓸 수 없지만, '~의 맛을 보다' 라는 의도적인 동작을 나타낼 때에는 진행형이 가능하다. (Ch.12-3 참고)

6.
(1) I will/am going to send my father a card on his birthday next week.
(2) Mr. Smith usually leaves the office at 5 o'clock, but he will/is going to leave an hour earlier today.
(3) I am taking the 4 o'clock plane to New York.
(4) The gallery opens at ten tomorrow morning.

12-2 완료 시제

Check Up
p.194

1.
(1) ⓐ 그녀는 내게 "당신은 무슨 일을 했습니까?"라고 물었다.
ⓑ 그녀는 내게 "당신은 무슨 일을 해 왔습니까?"라고 물었다.
(2) ⓐ 지난 월요일에 그들은 대통령에게 상황을 보고했다.
ⓑ 매주 월요일마다 그들은 대통령에게 상황을 보고해 왔다.
(3) ⓐ 내가 집에 도착했을 때 그 TV 쇼가 시작했다.
ⓑ 내가 집에 도착했을 때 그 TV 쇼는 벌써 시작했다.
(4) ⓐ 더 좋은 점수를 받지 못해서 실망스러웠니?
ⓑ 더 좋은 점수를 받지 못했던 게 실망스러웠니?

2.
(1) have studied
(2) has known
(3) did you get, haven't seen
(4) were
(5) have ever visited
(6) has not been

3.
(1) had gone, arrived
(2) hadn't rained
(3) had been, became
(4) had been
(5) wore, had not been
(6) wondered, had left
(7) had already called, got
(8) told, had not taken

하게 하기 위해서 과거완료를 써야 하지만 일상회화에서는 과거 시제를 사용하기도 한다.
ex. Jill was a fire officer before she became a plumber.

4.
(1) A: Have you seen snow?
B: Last January, I saw it for the first time in my life.
(2) A: Where did you live three years ago?
B: I lived in London.
(3) A: How many times have you worn a new blue sweater since you bought it?
B: I wore it once at my brother's wedding last month.
(4) A: Since this morning, Charlie has called you four times.
B: When did he call?
A: He called at 9:10, 10:25, 11:30, and 1:50.

12-3 진행 시제

Check Up
p.197

1.
(1) is moving
(2) am not having
(3) answer, am taking
(4) is, are sleeping
(5) was eating, memorized
(6) ran, was getting
(7) was sleeping, was dreaming
(8) was harvesting, approached
(9) will be raining
(10) will be appearing

2.
(1) Something might happen to you.
(2) Something is happening behind the door.
(3) I became interested in architecture while I was traveling in Europe.
(4) I was talking to my wife when he heard someone come in.

해설 (3) Jill이 배관공이기 이전에 소방관이었다는 관계를 확실

12-4 시제의 일치

Check Up
p.199

1.
(1) found (2) saw
(3) was (4) hears
(5) was (6) stop
(7) doesn't change (8) get

2.
(1) ○
(2) × ↳ Tina put on sweaters because it <u>was</u> so cold yesterday.
(3) ○
(4) × ↳ Debbie swears by the moon that she <u>will be</u> always with him.
(5) × ↳ She learned from a biology class that frogs <u>sleep</u> in winter.
(6) ○
(7) × ↳ Sunlight <u>leaves</u> the sun's surface eight minutes before we see it.
(8) × ↳ Have you thought about whether you'll continue to study or get a job when you <u>graduate</u> from college?

Grammar Review
p.200

1.
(1) × ↳ It <u>is</u> not safe to talk on the phone when you are driving the car.
(2) × ↳ Since 1994, the winter Olympic games <u>has been held</u> every two years.
(3) ○
(4) × ↳ When Napoleon lost the war with Russia in 1812, he <u>was</u> sent to St. Helena.
(5) × ↳ After they <u>clear</u> the house, living conditions will begin to improve.

2.
(1) The football season will begin in Korea next month.
(2) Yes, I visited Cheju Island recently.
(3) I was watching the news when you called me last night.

3.
(1) Ⓐ (2) Ⓑ
(3) Ⓐ (4) Ⓑ

 광산은 사회에 필수적이다. 사람들이 금속 도구를 사용해오는 한 광산은 있어 왔으며, 앞으로도 역시 광산은 반드시 존속될 것이다. 그러나 광산이 필요한 만큼 그것들은 환경에 매우 위험하다. 매일 광산은 위험한 화학 물질을 환경에 방출하고 있다. 이러한 대부분의 오염은 더 이상 기능을 하지 않는 광산에서부터 비롯된다. 광산이 문을 닫게 되면 광산 회사들은 더 이상 광산에서 돈을 벌어들일 수 없다. 그 때까지 광산 회사들은 광산을 깨끗이 유지하기 위해 돈을 지출하는 반면, 그들은 아무런 이익이 없기 때문에 광산을 깨끗이 하기 위해 계속 돈을 지출하기는 원하지 않을 것이다. 광산을 깨끗이 유지할 사람이 없다면, 광산은 토양과 화학물질을 내보내기 시작할 것이다. 이와 같이 버려진 광산은 먼 미래에도 우리 환경을 오염시킬 것이다.

Grammar Up
p.201

1. (A) 2. (B) 3. (C) 4. (A) 5. (D) 6. (C)
7. (D) 8. (C) 9. (B) 10. (C) 11. (A) 12. (B)
13. (D) 14. (B) 15. (A) 16. (D) 17. (A) 18. (B)

해설
2. consume [kənsúːm] *v.* 소비하다, 써버리다
10. grocery [gróusəri] *n.* 식료품, 잡화 또는 그러한 것들을 파는 가게

CHAPTER 13
조동사 / Modal Verbs

13-1 조동사의 개념, 역할 및 종류

Check Up   p.205

1.
(1) may / 1군 조동사
(2) has / 2군 조동사
(3) should / 1군 조동사, be / 2군 조동사
(4) must / 1군 조동사, have / 2군 조동사

2.
(1) × ↳ It is cold outside, so we should <u>wear</u> jackets.
(2) × ↳ Everyone <u>can</u> enjoy this board game.
(3) × ↳ His theory <u>will be</u> proved wrong soon.
(4) × ↳ The documents <u>may not be</u> read without permission.
(5) ○
(6) × ↳ You'll <u>be able to</u> find out the answer at the end of this course.

3.
(1) Simon will buy a limousine.
(미래의 일에 대한 의지의 뜻이 첨가된다.)
(2) The man may be a gardener of the white house.
(추측의 뜻이 첨가된다.)
(3) Must the box be wrapped?
(강한 필요성, 의무의 뜻이 첨가된다.)
(4) You can see the mountains from here on a clear day. (능력의 뜻이 첨가된다.)

13-2 Degrees of Certainty

Check Up   p.207

1.
(1) daddy, mommy, Sue
(2) the garden hose, the rain, the sprinkler

2.
(1) the cat, the dog, the hamster
(2) Jake, Fred, Sam

13-3 필요, 조언, 의무, 책임

Check Up   p.209

1.
(1) must   (2) have
(3) must   (4) should
(5) ought   (6) had

2.
(1) You must / have to say something about his fence.
(2) You will have to pay the additional costs.
(3) You don't have to put on an overcoat.
(4) Hunters must not kill deer without permission.

3.
(1) shouldn't have listened
(2) should have been
(3) should have spent
(4) shouldn't have eaten

4.
(1) Cindy should / had better not sleep late.
(2) Alex should / had better be careful with his words.
(3) Parents should / had better make their children wear their seatbelts in the car.

13-4 능력, 허가, 부탁, 제안

Pop Quiz   p.211
(1) 현재 ↳ 아마도 나의 개는 행복할 것이다. ('행복할 수 있었다'라고 해석하는 것은 어색하다.)
(2) 과거 ↳ 그녀는 겨우 한 살에 혼자 설 수 있었다.
(3) 과거, 현재 ↳ 우리는 지(수)평선 너머로 태양을 볼 수 있었다. (보려면 볼 수도 있다. - 현재)
(4) 과거 ↳ 나의 옛 차는 여섯 명을 태울 수 없었다.
(5) 과거 ↳ 그의 발명품은 들을 수 없는 사람들에게 도움이

(6) 현재 ↳ Sam은 아마 배가 고프지 않을 것이다.
(7) 과거 ↳ Sam은 아마 배가 고프지 않았을 것이다.
(8) 과거 ↳ 그 회사는 품질의 경쟁력을 유지할 수 있다고 말했다.

Check Up
p.213

1.
(1) would (2) could have p.p.
(3) might (4) must have p.p.
(5) should have p.p.

2.
(1) had   (2) would
(3) would (4) had
(5) would (6) would
(7) had

3.
(1) Present ↳ 아마도 그녀는 오늘 밤 늦게까지 일을 하고 있을 것이다.
(2) Present ↳ 네 열쇠는 그 안에 있을 것이다.
(3) Past ↳ Bill은 무언가 아주 잘못되었음을 알 수 있었다.
(4) Present ↳ 그는 2년 전에 수감되었는데 다음달에 석방될 것이다.
(5) Past ↳ 아무도 Ellen이 혼자 있기 좋아하는 것을 이해할 수 없었다.
(6) Past ↳ 그 소년은 나이가 14살보다 더 많지 않았을 것이다.

4.
(1) S (허가 ↳ 저기 있는 하모니카를 연주해도 됩니까?)
(2) D
(3) S (제안 ↳ 밥 먹으러 나가요.)
해설 (2) ⓐ는 'Brown씨는 플로리다에 살았었다'(과거의 상황)는 의미를 나타낸다. 그러나 ⓑ의 would는 used to와 달리 과거의 상황을 표현할 수 없다. ⓑ는 가정법으로서 '(만약 플로리다에 직업을 갖게 된다면) Brown씨는 플로리다에 살 거다'(현재 또는 미래의 상황에 대한 가정)라는 뜻을 갖는다.

5.
(1) May / Can / Could I drink some water?
(2) Would you mind closing the window?

(3) He cannot / couldn't / must not be hungry.
(4) He cannot / couldn't / must not be rich.
(5) Adolescents are not allowed to / are not permitted to / may not buy cigarettes or alcohol.
(6) Why don't you invite them to the Thanksgiving party?

Grammar Review
p.215

1.
(1) S   (2) D
(3) S
해설 (3) commit [kəmít] *v.* 범하다, 저지르다
suicide [súːəsaid] *n.* 자살, 자해
commit suicide 자살하다

2.
(1) ✕ ↳ The store may or <u>may not</u> sell batteries.
(2) ✕ ↳ You <u>had better not</u> eat something between meals.
(3) ✕ ↳ Would you mind <u>proofreading</u> this report?
(4) ○
(5) ✕ ↳ We should <u>do</u> something for the environment right now.
해설 (3) proofread [prúːfriːd] *v.* 교정보다
(4) proceed [prəsíːd] *v.* 나아가다, 계속하다, 시작하다

3.
(1) ⓑ   (2) ⓑ
(3) ⓐ   (4) ⓑ
해설 convey [kənvéi] *v.* 나르다, 전달하다, 알리다
해석 표지판은 얼마 안 되는 말로 많은 정보를 전달한다. 예를 들어보자. 여기에 예전에는 개방되었었지만, 지금은 폐쇄된 도로가 있다. 도로의 끝에는 커다란 적색 표지판이 있다. 표지판에는 "정지, 진입 금지"라고 쓰여 있다. 이 세 마디의 간단한 말은 복잡한 의미를 전달한다. 그것은 "여기서 정지하십시오. 더 이상 진입할 수 없습니다. 허가를 받지 않았으므로 들어올 수 없습니다. 물론, 당신은 들어올 수도 있습니다. 그러나 당신이 들어오면 곤경에 빠지게 될 것입니다."라는 의미를 나타낸다. 이 표지판을 본 누군가는 "내가 여기에 들어가도 될까? 아니요, 돌아가는 것이 좋겠어. 분명히 그 곳에 표지판이 있는 이유가 있을 거야. 경고에 따라야 해."라고 생각할 것이다. 세 마디의 말이 얼마나 많은 의미를 전달하는지 알겠는가? 표지판의 색깔은 전달 내용을 더욱 강력하게 만든다. 적색은 위험을 뜻한다. 그래서, 적색 표지판은 당신

이 아마도 이 곳에 들어가서는 안 되고, 반드시 들어가서는 안 되고, 들어가지 말아야 하고, 들어가지 않는 것이 낫다는 이 모든 의미가 담긴 세 마디의 말을 분명하게 만든다.

Grammar Up p.216

1. (B) 2. (C) 3. (D) 4. (A) 5. (D) 6. (D)
7. (C) 8. (C) 9. (B) 10. (A) 11. (C) 12. (B)
13. (A) 14. (C) 15. (A) 16. (B) 17. (B) 18. (C)

해설
6. anticipate [æntísəpèit] v. 예상하다, 기대하다
9. refund [rí:fʌnd] v. 환불하다

Grammar in Context p.218

1. (must, may,) **should**

2. would call (, would want, attracted, were changed)

3. Ⓐ

4.
(1) 밝은 색으로 (만들어져야 하는데), 쉽게 눈에 띨 수 있는
   (밝은 색으로 만들어져야 한다.)
(2) 아무도 원하지 않을 것이다 [무엇을?]
   어떤 옷을 입기를 (원하지 않는데) [어떤 옷이냐 하면]
   상어를 유인하는 (옷을 입기를 원하지 않는다.)
   그래서
   구명 조끼는 바뀌었다 [어떻게?]
   주황색으로 (바뀌었다.)

해설 the air force 공군
navy [néivi] n. 해군

해석 **구명조끼와 구명보트의 색상**
　구명조끼나 구명보트와 같은 제품은 매우 신중하게 만들어져야 한다. (인명구조 시) 사람의 생명이 이러한 것들에 달려있기 때문에 가능한 한 최상의 재질로 만들어져야 한다. 구명조끼와 구명보트의 모든 부분들이 조심스럽게 고려되어야 한다. 예를 들어, 당신은 구명조끼가 거의 항상 주황색이라는 사실에 주목해 본 적이 있는가? 여기에는 중요한 이유가 있다.
　구명조끼와 구명보트는 쉽게 눈에 띨 수 있는 밝은 색으로 만들어져야 한다. 갈색이나 녹색처럼 어두운 색상은 바다 속 어두운 배경색에 비추어 잘 보이지 않을 수 있기 때문에 좋지 않다. 예전에는 구명조끼가 밝은 노랑색 재질로 만들어지기도 했다. 이 색은 바다 속에서 눈에 띄기가 쉬웠고, 그래서 공군과 해군은 조종사들을 위해 노랑색 구명조끼를 사용했다. 그러나 그들은 상어가 노란색에 유인된다는 사실을 알아차리기 시작했고, 조종사들은 이 색을 "냠냠 노란색"이라고 부르곤 했다. 분명히, 누구도 상어를 유인하는 옷을 입기를 원하지 않았을 것이며, 그래서 구명조끼는 주황색으로 바뀌게 되었다.

CHAPTER 14
법과 가정법 / Mood and Subjunctive Mood

14-1 법과 명령법

Check Up *p.221*

1.
(1) ✗ ↳ <u>Don't let</u> them lean out of the window.
(2) ✗ ↳ Wait here for a minute, <u>will/won't/can/can't/you</u>?
(3) ○
(4) ○

2.
(1) Enjoy your holiday.
(2) Let's be ourselves.
(3) Don't do that again, or you'll be in trouble.
(4) Please don't let the dogs bark loudly this late.

3.
⑥, ③, ①, ⑤, ④, ②

14-2 가정법의 기본

Pop Quiz 1 *p.223*

(1) I <u>will + had taken</u> a shower. → I **would have taken** a shower.
(2) She would have met my friend.
(3) We would have been able to buy a new suit.
   Or We could have bought a new suit.
(4) Robbie and Lucy would have cheered for our team.

Pop Quiz 2 *p.223*

(1) If I had had time yesterday, I would have called her.
(2) If we were/had been there, we might have been able to help.
(3) If Kevin bought new guitar stings, he would play for the class.
(4) If you didn't have a secretary, you would have to type the reports yourself.

Check Up *p.224*

1.
(1) ⓐ No   ⓑ Yes
(2) ⓐ No   ⓑ No
(3) ⓐ No   ⓑ No

2.
(1) ✗ ↳ Ted <u>could</u> change the tire if he had a spare one.
(2) ○
(3) ✗ ↳ If you <u>worked</u> overtime, you could make extra money.
(4) ○
(5) ✗ ↳ If she had tasted it, she <u>would have liked</u> it.
(6) ✗ ↳ If you <u>had</u> been at the party last night, you could have met Bob.

3.
(1) Sally always answers the phone if she is at home.
(2) Sally would answer the phone if she were at home.
(3) If I knew enough about the car, I could fix it myself.
(4) If a doctor were not there, the situation would be worse.
(5) If Tom apologized to her, she would forgive him.
(6) If Ellen had a million dollars, she could travel all over the world.
(7) Human beings would die within moments if there were no air.
(8) If you bought a small car, you might save money on gasoline.

4.
(1) UR   (2) R
(3) UR   (4) R
(5) UR   (6) UR

5.
(1) If the weather is nice tomorrow, we will go to the zoo.
(2) If the weather were nice today, we would go to the zoo.
(3) If the weather had been nice yesterday, we would have gone to the zoo.
(4) If I had had my own car, I would have sung loudly to the radio.
(5) If Sally had set her alarm, she wouldn't have been late for class.
(6) If you had put the milk in the refrigerator, it wouldn't have gone bad.
(7) If Marcie had applied for the job, would they have employed her?
(8) If they had invested in that stock, they might have been wealthy.

14-3 가정법의 다양한 표현법

Pop Quiz 1 p.227
(1) ⓐ ↳ 여동생이 있으면 좋을 텐데. (현재 여동생이 없어서 아쉬워하는 감정 전달)
(2) ⓐ ↳ 내가 좀 더 잘생겼으면 좋을 텐데.
(3) ⓐ ↳ 기적을 이룰 수 있다면 좋을 텐데.
(4) ⓐ ↳ 대통령이 되기를 바래?
(5) ⓐ ↳ 모든 마을 사람들이 그가 곧 돌아오기를 바란다.
(6) ⓑ ↳ 지금에서야 나는 그녀의 조언을 따랐었으면 하고 바란다. (과거에 그녀의 조언을 따르지 않은 것에 대해 현재 아쉬워하는 감정 전달)
(7) ⓑ ↳ 그녀는 자신이 조금 더 열정적이었으면 하고 바란다.
(8) ⓑ ↳ 그녀는 그가 한 것보다 더 많이 도와줄 수 있었기를 하고 바란다.

Pop Quiz 2 p.227
(1) I wish it were not true.
(2) I wish it had not been true.
(3) I wished it were not true.
(4) I wished it had not been true.

Check Up p.228
1.
(1) 가정법 (2) 직설법
(3) 가정법 (4) 가정법

2.
(1) I wish I could speak French.
(2) I wish Richard were a braver boy.
(3) Bill wished that he were at the concert yesterday.
(4) Mary wished that she had been born in spring.

3.
(1) Joel eats a lot as if / as though he were not on a diet.
(2) Ms. Brown behaved as if / as though she were my mother.
(3) She talks about London as if / as though she had lived there for a long time.
(4) Ann acted as if / as though she had seen a ghost last night.

4.
(1) ⓒ (2) ⓑ

5.
(1) Without / But for her care and concern, I would have no chance at all.
(2) She would have started earlier without / but for delays in receiving a visa.
(3) Without / But for your help, he'd not have finished the race.

6.
(1) If Ken had practiced hard, he would be a world-leading tennis player.
(2) If Paine hadn't gone to school in Florida, we could have a chat over tea.
(3) Mr. Brown would not be overweight if he had not had a lot of candies and chocolate.
(4) The flowers by Joanna's bed would not be withering if she had watered them.

14-4 주의해야 할 조건절

Check Up
p.231

1.
(1) 가정법 (2) 직설법
(3) 직설법 (4) 직설법

2.
(1) ⓐ She speaks Korean as if/as though it is not her mother tongue.
ⓑ She speaks Korean as if/as though it were not her mother tongue.
(2) ⓐ Tom's father gave orders as if/as though he was a general in the army.
ⓑ Tom's father gave orders as if/as though he had been a general in the army.

3.
(1) Were there a golf course, we could play golf.
(2) Were Sarah walking very fast, she couldn't notice the sigh which says "Stop."
(3) Had Charles been here, we would have finished it more quickly.
(4) Had the market sold beans, I would not have bought rice.

4.
(1) ⓑ (2) ⓐ
(3) ⓓ (4) ⓒ

Grammar Review
p.232

1.
(1) ✗ ↳ Were the movies worth watching, I <u>would watch</u> them.
(2) ○
(3) ✗ ↳ Had I known the road was closed, I <u>would</u> not have gone there.
(4) ○
(5) ✗ ↳ If New York <u>were</u> a country, it would be the ninth largest economy in the world.
(6) ✗ ↳ Harry <u>would</u> major engineering if he were certain he could get a job in the space industry.

2.
(1) Ⓐ (2) Ⓑ
(3) Ⓐ (4) Ⓐ

해설 외계인을 만나는 일은 재미있을 것이다! 만약 당신이 길에서 외계인을 만난다면, 무슨 말을 할 것인가? 상상해 보라!
여러분: 당신은 외계인인가요?
외계인: 저를 보세요! 제가 만약 지구인이라면, 피부가 녹색이겠어요?
여러분: 왜 이 곳에 있는 거죠?
외계인: 그건 실수였어요! 내가 무슨 일을 하는지 알았다면, 지구에 오지는 않았을 거예요!
여러분: 무슨 일이 있었던 건가요?
외계인: 잘못된 프로그램을 사용했어요! 저는 화성을 방문하면 좋을 거라 생각했었죠. 그런데 그만 지구로 가는 프로그램을 사용했어요! 제가 좀더 신중했더라면 지금 이곳에 있지는 않을 거예요!
여러분: 지구를 좋아하지 않으세요?
외계인: 예! 여기 너무 덥고 습해요! 공기도 아주 탁해요. 당신이 외계인이라면 이런 공기에서 숨을 쉴 수 있을 것 같아요? 마치 스팀욕조 안에 있는 것 같아요! 내가 화성에 있다면 좋을 텐데요! 날 여기서 나가게 해줘요!

Grammar Up
p.233

1. (D) 2. (A) 3. (B) 4. (D) 5. (B) 6. (C)
7. (B) 8. (D) 9. (C) 10. (C) 11. (A) 12. (B)
13. (A) 14. (B) 15. (A) 16. (C) 17. (D) 18. (A)

해설
14. when young 부사절 when he was young이 축약된 형태이다. (Ch. 19-2 참고)
16. be about to 지금 막 ~하려고 하다 (about은 형용사)

CHAPTER 15
수동태 / Passives

15-1 효과적인 수동태 문장의 사용

Check Up   p.237

1.
(1) ⓐ, ⓑ의 뜻은 서로 같지만 일상회화에서는 일반적으로 능동태인 ⓑ가 더 선호된다.
(2) ⓐ, ⓑ의 뜻은 서로 같지만 일상회화에서는 일반적으로 능동태인 ⓑ가 더 선호된다.
(3) ⓐ, ⓑ의 뜻은 서로 같지만 일반적으로 일상회화에서는 능동태인 ⓑ가 더 선호된다.
(4) ⓐ, ⓑ의 뜻은 서로 같지만 I가 좋은 인상을 받았다는 점을 강조할 때는 수동태인 ⓐ가 더 선호된다.

2.
(1) New ideas were suggested by the book.
(2) No evidence of the missing child has been found until now.
(3) How long will the seminar be continued?

3.
ⓐ, ⓑ, ⓓ, ⓔ, ⓗ, ⓘ

4.
(1) was born   (2) was formally educated
(3) married   (4) gave birth to
(5) was hospitalized (6) was released
(7) became   (8) left
(9) moved   (10) recovered
(11) went   (12) was published
(13) was diagnosed   (14) died

해석 19세기 후반에서 20세기 초반 동안 미국에서 가장 유명한 여성작가 중 한 사람인 Charlotte Perkins Gilman은 1860년에 출생했다. 그녀의 집안은 가난했고, 그래서 그녀는 정규 교육을 4년 밖에 받지 못했다. 그녀는 1884년에 결혼하여 딸을 낳았다. 그러나, Gilman은 출산 후에 심각한 우울증을 앓게 되었다. 이로 인해 그녀는 필라델피아에 있는 병원에 입원되었다. 한달 동안의 입원 후 Gilman은 퇴원하였지만 곧 우울증이 재발하였다. 이 시기에 그녀는 남편을 떠나 딸과 함께 캘리포니아로 거처를 옮겼다. 그 곳에서 그녀는 건강을 회복하였고, 많은 서적을 집필하기 시작했다. Gilman은 우울증에 걸린 여인을 다룬 그녀의 자전적 단편 소설인 "The Yellow Wallpaper (노란 벽지)"로잘 알려져 있다. 이 작품은 1982년 New England Magazine에 게재되었다. 1932년 Gilman은 유방암 진단을 받았고, 그로부터 3년 뒤인 75세에 숨을 거두었다.

15-2 주의해야 할 수동태

Check Up   p.241

1.
(1) × ↳ Suddenly the book <u>fell</u> from the shelf.
(2) ○
(3) × ↳ Nothing astonishing <u>occurred</u> at all.
(4) ○
(5) ○
(6) × ↳ Balloons <u>burst</u> here and there.
(7) × ↳ The import <u>have</u> sharply <u>risen</u> for the last five years.
(8) × ↳ Digital photography <u>has become</u> more and more popular.

2.
(1) We could be taught a lot about how to succeed.
    A lot about how to succeed could be taught to us.
(2) She was offered 200 dollars to be a model by the photographer.
    200 dollars was offered to her to be a model by the photographer.
(3) James was being told a mysterious story.
    A mysterious story was being told to James.
(4) Jill was asked several questions at the meeting by the president.
    Several questions were asked of Jill at the meeting by the president.

3.
(1) ⓐ jump
    ⓑ is made to jump
(2) ⓐ swell out
    ⓑ Its body could be seen to swell out in a minute.
(3) ⓐ reach

    ⓑ She was made to reach the top by her hard work.
(4) ⓐ tremble
    ⓑ A tiny thing was even felt to tremble in the breeze.
(5) ⓐ ring
    ⓑ The bell was heard to ring, wasn't it?

4.
(1) It is said that Ms. Hooper has visited many countries.
    Ms. Hooper is said to have visited many countries.
(2) It is thought that she has been to Russia and China.
    She is thought to have been to Russia and China.
(3) It is supposed that she went to the Arctic, too.
    She is supposed to have gone to the Arctic, too.
(4) It is felt that she should write about her travels.
(5) It is anticipated that her stories will be exciting.
    Her stories are anticipated to be exciting.

해설 (4) 일반적으로 that절을 포함하는 문장은 두 가지 형태의 수동태가 가능하지만 주절의 동사가 feel인 경우는 'It is felt that ~'으로의 변형만 가능하다. Feel은 'She is felt to be a nice girl.'에서와 같이 to be가 뒤따르는 경우가 아니면 의미상 수동태가 불가능하기 때문이다.

5.
(1) The book store opens at 10:00.
(2) The book store is open.
(3) The café closes at 5:00.
(4) The café is closed.
(5) Can I rent this room?
(6) This room was rented yesterday (by somebody).
(7) This room rents for $400 per month.

15-3 수동태와 기타 사항

Check Up   p.244
1.
(1) ○   (2) ○
(3) ×   (4) ○
(5) ○   (6) ×
(7) ○   (8) ×

2.
(1) Rice is grown in Korea.
(2) A good harvest is predicted this year.
(3) Is the computer connected to the power supply?
(4) The fire was soon extinguished by the brave firefighters.
(5) Has the prince finally been rescued from the wizard?
(6) *The Lord of the Rings* was written and published in 1954-55 by J. R. R. Tolkien, a towering figure in fantasy literature.

3.
(1) by   (2) with
(3) by   (4) with

4.
(1) The dog with long hair gets shaved a couple of times a year.
(2) Why do people get married?
(3) Fortunately, the girl didn't get lost and came back home safely.

Grammar Review   p.246
1.
(1) × ↳ Harry said he was not <u>told</u> about the report at all.
(2) × ↳ Kelly lives in Los Angeles, but she <u>was born</u> in Minnesota.
(3) × ↳ Thirty-nine reservations have already <u>been</u> confirmed.
(4) × ↳ Do you know how many stops are <u>planned</u> on our bus trip?
(5) × ↳ It <u>is believed</u> that Mr. Larson had a home in the Rocky Mountains.
(6) × ↳ The air that surrounds the earth can <u>be divided</u> into four main layers.
(7) ○
(8) × ↳ In the 18th century, the Native Americans' way of life had <u>been changed</u> by

Europeans.

해설 (3) confirm [kənfə́ːrm] v. 확인하다, 확증하다

2.
(1) is said
(2) is stopped
(2) was launched, knew
(4) had been caught
(5) is suspected, has not yet found
(6) was taken, grew
(7) was seen, photographed
(8) found, lacked
(9) belongs, are taught
(10) led, disappeared

해설
(6) beard [bíərd] n. 턱수염
(8) vital [vaitl] adj. 아주 중요한, 절대 필요한, 치명적인
(9) territory [térətɔ̀ːri] n. 영토, 영해, 지역, 영역

3.
(1) ⓐ binds
ⓑ His hands are bound with rope tightly.
(2) ⓐ use
ⓑ The form of "be + past participle" is used in the passive.
(3) ⓐ built
ⓑ The house was built last year by Bob and his friends.
(4) ⓐ divided
ⓑ The cake was divided into eight slices by Mom.

4.
(1) The new textbook will be published at the end of February.
(2) Yes, they has been welcomed by the mayor of the city.
(3) Yes, it has been prepared by the ETS.
(4) Jim was considered to be a great pilot.
(5) Marie Curie was awarded the first Nobel Prize.

5.
(1) Ⓐ   (2) Ⓐ
(3) Ⓑ   (4) Ⓐ

해설 eclipse [iklíps] n. (해·달의) 식(蝕)

해설 일식을 본 적이 있는가? 아주 오랫동안 사람들은 일식을 두려워했다. 왜냐하면, 대중들에게 잘 알려져 있지 않아서였다. 그러나 오늘날에는 과학자들이 일식의 원인과 결과에 대해 많은 것들을 밝혀냈으며 따라서 사람들도 일식 현상에 친숙해지게 되었다. 일식은 달이 태양과 지구 사이를 일직선으로 통과할 때 발생한다. 태양 전체가 달에 가려질 때, 우리는 이것을 개기식이라고 부른다. 때때로 태양의 일부분이 가려지기도 한다. 이것을 부분식이라고 한다. 일식 현상은 7분 30초 이상 지속되지 않는다. 이제 당신의 눈으로 직접 일식을 관찰해 보는 건 어떨까?

Grammar Up   p.248

1. (C) 2. (D) 3. (A) 4. (C) 5. (B) 6. (C)
7. (A) 8. (C) 9. (B) 10. (D) 11. (A) 12. (C)
13. (B) 14. (D) 15. (B) 16. (C) 17. (B) 18. (C)

해설
2. hydrogen [háidrədʒən] n. 수소
   flammable [flǽməbəl] adj. 가연성의, 타기 쉬운

Grammar in Context   p.250

1. (is required, has, is raised, is,) has

2. is kept (, is required, won, is returned)

3.
(1) T   (2) F
(3) T

4.
(1) 정부를 운영하기 위해 (돈이 요구되는데), 큰 도시의 (정부를 운영하기 위해 많은 돈이 요구된다.)
(2) 당첨자는 요구된다 무엇을?
    세금을 낼 것이 (요구되는데) 어떤 세금이냐 하면
    돈에 대한 (세금을 낼 것이 요구되는데) 어떤 돈에 대한 세금이냐 하면
    그들이 받은 (돈에 대한 세금을 낼 것이 요구되는데) 어디에서 받은 돈이냐 하면
    복권에서 (받은 돈에 대한 세금을 낼 것이 요구된다.)

해설 budget [bʌ́dʒit] n. 예산, 예산안, 경비
portion [pɔ́ːrʃən] n. 일부, 부분, 몫

해석 **정부예산**

대도시의 정부를 운영하기 위해서는 많은 돈이 요구된다. 예를 들어, 로스엔젤레스의 경우 한 해 예산이 몇 십억 원에 달한다. 이 돈은 몇 가지 방법으로 모아진다. 첫 번째 방법은 세금을 통한 것이다. 도시의 거의 모든 것에는 세금이 포함되어 있다. 개인의 소득에 세금이 부과된다. 자동차나 주택이 매매 시에도 세금이 부과된다. 두 사람 사이에 어떤 식으로든 돈이 교환되면 대개 세금이 포함된다.

도시들은 또한 복권을 통해서도 돈을 모은다. 으레 복권은 장당 몇 달러에 대중에게 판매된다. 복권당첨자는 어마어마한 액수의 돈을 받지만, 그들이 받는 돈은 당첨금 전액이 아니다. 당첨금액의 많은 부분이 도시 정부에 의해 보유된다. 게다가 당첨자는 복권 당첨금에 대한 세금을 지불해야 하며, 그래서 당첨금 중 훨씬 더 많은 비율이 도시정부로 되돌려진다.

CHAPTER 16
명사절, 부사절 /
Noun Clauses and Adverb Clauses

16-1 명사절 (1): 의문사절과 whether/if절

Check Up p.253

1.
(1) what   (2) whose
(3) why   (4) Where, what
(5) if   (6) whether
(7) whether   (8) if

해설
(6) 일반적으로 whether / if절이 보어로 쓰일 때에는 whether가 선호된다. 또한, if는 or not이 바로 뒤에 따라나올 수 없으므로 whether가 정답이다.
(7) 전치사의 목적어가 될 때에는 반드시 whether를 쓴다.

2.
(1) 주어 ↳ <u>What he does in his spare time</u> is not obvious.
(2) 목적어 ↳ Sometimes Mr. Cosby used to forget <u>where he put his keys</u>.
(3) 보어 ↳ This is <u>why all the plans have failed miserably in spite of their efforts</u>.
(4) 목적어 ↳ The bear is looking into the jar to see <u>if there is honey</u>.
(5) 보어 ↳ The only question is <u>whether there live fish in the pond or not</u>.
(6) 주어 ↳ <u>How serious the situation has become</u> is being shown on the live TV show.
(7) 목적어 ↳ The police finally discovered <u>whether the footprints left on the floor were the suspect's</u>.
(8) 전치사의 목적어 ↳ At first she worried about <u>who would like her poems</u>, but she became one of the most beloved poets in history.

3.
(1) QUESTION: When is Ted going to leave for Chicago?

NOUN CLAUSE: Tell me when Ted is going to leave for Chicago.
(2) QUESTION: Where has Dean been since last week?
NOUN CLAUSE: Do you know where Dean has been since last week.
(3) QUESTION: Who is good at dealing with the problem?
NOUN CLAUSE: Please tell me who is good at dealing with the problem.
(4) QUESTION: Why did the relationship break up?
NOUN CLAUSE: Nobody knows why the relationship broke up.

4.
(1) I wonder if he took the pictures.
(2) Let's ask Sam whether he lives with his parents.
(3) Do you remember whether/if you locked the door to your bedroom?
(4) Whether she ate my chocolate cake is still a mystery.
(5) Whether you like Steve is not important to me.

5.
(1) The teacher asked me what four twos make.
(2) We don't know whether/if he knows Seoul well.
(3) She forgot where she put the glasses, and it took two days for us to find them.

16-2 명사절 (2): that절

Check Up
p.256

1.
(1) 주어 ↳ It is clear that the myth had many different sources.
(2) 목적어 ↳ Her father suggests that she should not go far from the hotel.
(3) 보어 ↳ The fact was that I was always interested in the story of animals.
(4) 목적어 ↳ She explained that she was a sales manager from Qwerty Computer Corp.
(5) 주어 ↳ It was true that the boy was extremely embarrassed.

(6) 목적어 ↳ He claims that the committee would willingly accept the view.
(7) 보어 ↳ The answer is that the tree should be uprooted before the queen arrives.
(8) 목적어 ↳ People in town think it best that they wait until the investigation is complete before they jump to conclusions.

2.
(1) Jake was disappointed that he lost the race so near the finish.
(2) They're glad that they're a great success in Edinburgh.
(3) I'm sorry that I was late for the weekly meeting.
(4) Sally's happy that she received a bundle of flowers from her boyfriend.

3.
(1) ⓑ ↳ The thing is that it costs no money.
(2) ⓐ ↳ The point is that I can have dinner at a different restaurant every day.
(3) ⓓ ↳ I think that I can fish and swim in the river.
(4) ⓒ ↳ I think that I can collect shells and pebbles.

16-3 부사절 (1): 시간, 조건

Check Up
p.259

1.
(1) while   (2) After
(3) as long as   (4) If
(5) until

2.
(1) ⓐ   (2) ⓒ
(3) ⓑ

3.
(1) meets   (2) knock
(3) asks   (4) becomes
(5) ascertain   (6) are

4.
(1) There are many things to consider when we

decide our major.
(2) Since I graduated from the middle school, I haven't met the teacher.
(3) If he comes while I am out, ask him to wait for a while.
(4) If time permits, I'll visit my uncle in New York in August.

16-4 부사절 (2): 이유, 대조, 목적, 결과

Check Up   p.262

1.
(1) All my belongings fell onto the ground as the lock on my suitcase broke.
(2) Sue is willing to help other people because she is a kind girl.
(3) Since sharks eat sick fish and animals, they keep oceans clean.
(4) Jim quit his job because the work was not interesting any longer.

2.
(1) Though Tom is not tall, he is a good basketball player.
(2) Though it was very cold outside, Bob went out without a coat.
(3) Although some clothes are quite expensive, they sell out in a minute.
(4) Even though the company is famous for its strict hiring policies, he is going to apply for a job.

3.
(1) ⓑ   (2) ⓐ
(3) ⓓ   (4) ⓒ

4.
(1) He hurried so that he was not late.
(2) Sue opens the window so that she makes the air refreshed.
(3) The traffic is so heavy that they cannot arrive on time.
(4) The weather was so fine that we could not just stay in.

(5) It is such a small car that a few of them have to walk.
(6) He was such a man of few words that I hardly knew about him.

Grammar Review   p.264

1.
(1) whether   (2) if
(3) since

2.
(1) × ◆ Brian wants to show the article to her but can't remember where it is.
(2) ○
(3) × ◆ We all know that he has plenty of experience with them.
(4) × ◆ Kelly couldn't avoid the accident because the brake couldn't stop the car.

해설 fume [fju:m]   n. (유해·불쾌한) 연기, 김, 독기, 가스

3.
(1) Ⓐ   (2) Ⓑ
(3) Ⓑ   (4) Ⓐ

해설 field [fi:ld]   n. (활동) 범위, 현장
recession [riséʃən]   n. (일시적) 경기 후퇴, 불경기

해설 Brown 박사님은 오늘 우리 수업의 초청 연사이시다. 우리는 박사님께서 언제 강의를 하실지는 알았지만, 무엇에 대해 말씀하실지는 모른다. 아마도, 박사님이 계신 분야에 어떤 종류의 직업들이 있는지 말씀해주실 것이다. 졸업이 다가오자 나는 내가 어떤 곳에서 일을 하게 될지 걱정이 된다. 가끔은 너무 근심스러워서 밤에 잠을 자기 힘들기도 하다. 좋은 직업들은 소수이기 때문에 어떤 분야에 좋은 직업들이 있는지 찾아보는 것은 도움이 될 것이다. 나는 기업들이 많은 사람을 고용하지 않는다고 들었다. 불경기이기 때문에 고용이 저하되었다. 그러나 아무도 나에게 주정부가 무슨 일을 하고 있는지 알려주지 않았다. 나는 정부관련직이 유망하다고 들었다. 비록 경쟁은 치열하겠지만, 정부관련직은 멋질 것이다. Brown 박사님의 말씀을 들어보자!

Grammar Up *p.265*

1. (C) 2. (B) 3. (D) 4. (D) 5. (C) 6. (D)
7. (A) 8. (D) 9. (B) 10. (A) 11. (C) 12. (A)
13. (C) 14. (A) 15. (B) 16. (A) 17. (A) 18. (B)

해설
11. in detail   상세히, 세부에 걸쳐
13. due [dju:] *adj.* 정해진 날이 된, (언제) ~하기로 되어 있는

CHAPTER 17
형용사절 / Adjective clauses

17-1 관계대명사절의 형태와 역할

Check Up   *p.270*

1.
(1) ×   ↳ The clothes that <u>are</u> in the locker are mine.
(2) ×   ↳ I know the man who <u>speaks</u> five languages.
(3) ○
(4) ×   ↳ She loves <u>a man</u> who loves her.
(5) ○
(6) ×   ↳ We know the man <u>who/that</u> is a teacher.
(7) ×   ↳ There is someone <u>who(m)/that</u> you actually want to meet.
(8) ×   ↳ Do you remember Jessica <u>about whom</u> I told you?
    Or Do you remember Jessica <u>who(m)/that</u> I told you <u>about</u>?
(9) ○
(10) × ↳ Here comes a bus <u>for which</u> we've been waiting.
    Or Here comes a bus <u>that/which</u> we've been waiting <u>for</u>.
(11) × ↳ The woman <u>who lent</u> me five dollars was kind and very friendly.
(12) × ↳ They decide on the furniture that <u>is</u> set next to the window.
(13) × ↳ The picture sold for one million dollars which <u>was</u> painted by an anonymous artist.

2.
(1) This is Alice who is one of my good friends.
(2) We all like David who wears a blue hat.
(3) She is the best player whom I've played against.
(4) Peter enjoys watching the TV show which is on the air on Friday nights.
(5) We are to visit the university which is located in Texas.
(6) Daniel said something that I couldn't hear clearly.

3.
(1) The keys which you're looking for are under the blanket.
(2) Tom who is only four can play the harmonica.
(3) The school that he attends is the best in Korea.
(4) I saw the movie last Sunday which you recommended to me.
(5) Did a person who was sitting next to you have a dog?
(6) All shoes that are displayed are on sale today.

4.
(1) He received a call from a woman whose name is Michelle.
(2) Mr. Brown shouted at a driver whose truck was blocking the street.
(3) We measured the speed which we were running at.
(4) Do you have someone whom you can talk to freely?
(5) She came from a very small town that I've never heard of.

5.
whom, who, whose, that

해석 내가 어제 말했던 Sam이란 친구에 대해 알고 있니? 쉬지 않고 돌아다니는 Sam과 친해지는 건 힘들단다. 그는 항상 바쁜 사람이거든. 그는 언제나 해야 할 일을 20가지나 가지고 있지. 그는 역사 수업에 제출해야 할 보고서를 써야 하고, 입원중인 Susan에게 병문안을 가야 해. 그리고 나서 그가 빌렸던 CD플레이어를 돌려주기 위해 Bill을 만나야 하지. 그런 다음, 인터넷 사이트에서 그가 필요로 하는 정보를 조사해야 해. 그걸 마치면, 그가 연주자로 있는 밴드와 연습을 해야 해. 그는 정말 쉽지 않아! 도대체 언제 잠을 자는 걸까?

17-2 관계대명사 what

Check Up
p.273

1.
(1) This piano is what I'm always dreaming of.
(2) Olga listened attentively to what he told her.
(3) What I saw chilled me to the bone.
(4) What we're concerned about is whether it will rain tomorrow.

2.
(1) whoever (2) whatever
(3) whenever (4) wherever

3.
(1) 부사 (2) 부사
(3) 명사

17-3 관계부사절

Check Up
p.275

1.
(1) when (2) where
(3) why (4) when
(5) how (6) where

2.
(1) × ↳ The room <u>where</u> she died in 2003 has been preserved.
    Or The room <u>in which</u> she died in 2003 has been preserved.
(2) ○
(3) × ↳ Many people love the smooth <u>way he</u> plays the drums.
(4) × ↳ I cannot remember the reason <u>why</u> Richard wanted us to leave.
    Or I cannot remember the reason <u>for which</u> Richard wanted us to leave.
(5) ○

3.
(1) ⓐ AC   ⓑ NC
(2) ⓐ NC   ⓑ NC
(3) ⓐ AC   ⓑ NC
(4) ⓐ NC   ⓑ AC

4.
(1) 2002 is the year when the World Cup was held in Korea and Japan.
(2) This is the place where a small temple actually stood.

(3) I can't think of any reason why he refused the invitation.
(4) Experience is the best way you can learn something.
(5) Florida where I stayed for two years is famous for its pleasant climate.
(6) The time of year when the weather is the best is August.

17-4 쉼표와 관계사절

Check Up   p.277

1.
(1) 방에 등이 여러 개 있어서 그 위치를 정확히 밝히지 않으면 어떤 등을 가리키는지 다른 대화 참여자가 알 수 없는 상황을 의미한다.
(2) 방에 등이 하나만 있어서 그 위치를 밝히지 않아도 어떤 등을 가리키는지 다른 대화 참여자가 이미 알고 있는 상황을 의미한다.

2.
(1) Only some   (2) All

Grammar Review   p.279

1.
(1) 명사 ↳ The news that Charlie is getting married astonished me.
(2) 형용사 ↳ The watch that I got fixed has just stopped working again.
(3) 명사 ↳ I've not changed my belief that he is the right person to lead us.
(4) 명사 ↳ Which of them do you think would be the best?
(5) 형용사 ↳ There are lots of skyscrapers in Seoul, one of which has more than 60 stories.
(6) 형용사 ↳ It's the day when the press conference is.
(7) 명사 ↳ Do you check when the press conference is?
(8) 부사 ↳ When Tom was a little boy, he hoped to become a movie star.

(9) 명사 ↳ The police officer asked if I was at home, and I said yes.
(10) 부사, 부사 ↳ Whenever I'm in the basement and the phone rings, I don't run to answer it. If the message is important, the person will call back.

해설
(3) vote [vout]   v. 투표하다, 표결하다, (수동형으로) 선출하다
(6) press [pres]   n. 신문, 출판물, 보도 기관, 언론계, 기자단

2.
(1) Ⓐ   (2) Ⓑ
(3) Ⓑ   (4) Ⓐ

해설 security [sikjúəriti]   n. 경비, 안전, 무사
edit [édit]   v. 편집하다, 발행하다, 교정하다
commerce [kámərs]   n. 상업, 통상, 교역

해석 옆집에 막 이사온 부부는 조용한 이웃처럼 보인다. 그들은 우리가 바랄 수 있는 최고의 이웃 같다. 남편은 그가 야간에 경비원으로 일하는 공장에서 돌아온 뒤 낮 동안에 잠을 잔다. 이는 그들이 낮 동안 조용히 해야만 하는 집을 가졌음을 의미한다. 그의 아내도 또한 자택에서 출판사의 편집 업무를 할 수 있는 조용한 장소가 필요하다. 그들은 멀리서 공부하고 있는 딸이 하나 있는데, 그녀는 무역을 공부한다. 그리고 애완동물로 고양이가 한 마리 있는데, 개가 지어대듯 시끄럽게 하지는 않을 거다. 자, 우리 이웃들이 걱정했던 점들이 괜찮아 보인다. 우리가 언제 시끄러운 이웃을 두었었는지 생각나는가?

Grammar Up   p.280

1. (A) 2. (C) 3. (B) 4. (D) 5. (C) 6. (D)
7. (A) 8. (A) 9. (C) 10. (B) 11. (C) 12. (B)
13. (C) 14. (A) 15. (B) 16. (C) 17. (A) 18. (C)

해설 webbed [webd]   adj. 물갈퀴가 달린

Grammar in Context   p.282

1. that

2. which (, that, which)

3.
(1) T   (2) F
(3) T

4.

(1) 선생님이 (있는데), 완전히 바꾸신 (선생님이 있는데), 내 삶을 (완전히 바꾸신 선생님이 있다.)

(2) Stendahl은 썼다 `무엇을?/누구에게?`
사람들에 관해 (썼는데) `어떤 사람들이냐 하면`
그들은 살았다 `언제?`
약동의 시대를 (살았는데) `어떤 시대이냐 하면`
세상이 변했다 `어떻게?`
크게 (세상이 변하는 약동의 시대에 살았던 사람들에 관해 썼다.)

해설 owe [ou]　　 v. 은혜를 입다, 빚지고 있다
dictator [díkteitər]　 v. 독재자, 절대 권력자
tyranny [tírəni]　 n. 전제 정치, 포학, 횡포
warfare [wɔ́ːrfɛ̀ər]　 n. 전쟁, 전투
pessimistic [pèsəmístik]　 adj. 비관적인, 염세적인

해석 내 인생을 바꿔놓은 선생님

　당신의 인생을 바꿔놓은 선생님이 있는가? 내게는 그러한 선생님이 있다. 대학 시절, 프랑스 문학 수업을 듣게 되었을 때 나는 White 박사님을 만났다. 선생님의 강의는, 그 과목을 정말 재미있게 들을 수 있도록 했으며, 프랑스어로 쓴 작가들에게서 배울 수 있는 모든 것들을 짚어 주셨다. 선생님께서 다루셨던 두 작가는 스탕달과 카뮈였다. 선생님께서 지적하신 것 중 하나는 현대의 베스트셀러들이 스탕달의 은혜를 받았다는 것인데, 스탕달은 세계가 크게 변화하는 역동적인 시대에 살았던 사람들에 대해 글을 썼다. 한편, 상당히 독특한 성향을 가졌던 카뮈 또한 스탕달과는 다른 시대를 살면서 작품을 썼다. 스탕달은 19세기를 배경으로 썼고, 히틀러와 스탈린과 같은 독재자가 지배하던 20세기를 배경으로 쓴 카뮈는 그 시대가 만들어낸 전제 정치와 전쟁에 의해 굉장히 흉악하게 변한 세계를 보았다. 이는 단지 내가 White 박사의 강의로부터 배운 것의 일부에 지나지 않지만, 나에게 완전히 새로운 문학관을 심어주었다.

CHAPTER 18
전치사구 / Prepositional Phrases

18-1 전치사와 끊어 읽기, 이어 읽기

🚌 **Check Up**　　　　　　　　　　　p.285

1.

(1) Robbie was happy / ⌜about⌝ his new job.
(2) People ⌜in⌝ this village / are very kind and generous.
(3) Letters written long ago / are important ⌜to⌝ historians.
(4) Try on shoes / to make sure they fit.
(5) The answer ⌜to⌝ a question / depends ⌜on⌝ how / the question is asked.
(6) Make the sauce / ⌜by⌝ boiling the cream and sugar / ⌜for⌝ 15 minutes.
(7) The original story / that the film is based ⌜on⌝ / has a happy ending.
(8) Around the mid-20th century, / technology put machines / ⌜in⌝ charge ⌜of⌝ many jobs / that humans had done before.

해설
(3) On은 전치사가 아니라 부사이다.
(7) 관계사가 전치사의 목적어인 경우

2.

(1) 부사 ↳ I was in the bank / when you called me.
(2) 부사 ↳ My grandmother, / who is 80 years old, / is in good health.
(3) 형용사 ↳ We want young people / of ability, / confidence, / and ambition.
(4) 부사 ↳ In better times, / he would have led / a better life.
(5) 부사 ↳ Please make yourself at home / and help yourself / to the food.
(6) 형용사 ↳ Have you seen the movie / *Woman in Red*?
(7) 부사 ↳ Jessica arrived earlier / by two hours.
(8) 형용사 ↳ The water in the bath / is so hot / that I cannot step into it.

3.

(in business, since 1990, On Monday, through Friday, at 8 a.m., until 10 p.m., from 8 a.m., to 10 p.m., On Sunday,) for lunch (형용사)

해석 이 식당은 1990년부터 영업을 시작했다. 월요일부터 금요일까지는 오전 8시부터 오후 10시까지 개점한다. 매주 토요일은 오전 8시부터 오후 10시까지 개점하고, 일요일은 휴점한다. 점심 식사의 가격은 절대 5달러를 넘지 않는다. 어떤 샌드위치는 2달러 아래이다. 식사와 함께 손님들은 커피를 무료로 마실 수 있다. 여름에는 식당 내부나 야외에 마련된 탁자에서 식사를 할 수 있다. 출입문 위에는 큰 연이 달려 있고, 문 옆에는 낡은 가스 펌프가 있다. 어디에도 이러한 곳은 없을 것이다. 점심 시간에 이곳에 들러 보아라!

18-2 주요 전치사: in, on, at

Check Up p.289

1.
(1) ⓐ (보통의, 일반적인) 아침에
    ⓑ (특정한) 금요일 아침에
(2) ⓐ 병원 안, 입원 중
    ⓑ 병원 안 또는 부근, 진찰 중, 단순한 방문 중 등
(3) ⓐ 성탄절(날)에
    ⓑ 성탄절 휴가에
(4) ⓐ (특정한) 운명적인 밤에
    ⓑ (보통의, 일반적인) 밤에

2.
(1) in ↳ 나는 제일 윗 서랍 안에 우표를 보관한다.
(2) on ↳ 내 남자친구의 집은 해안에 접해 있다.
(3) in ↳ 정원 안의 모든 나무들이 눈으로 덮였다.
(4) at ↳ 어렸을 때 나는 어른들로 가득 찬 식탁에서 유일한 아이로 앉아 있는 것에 익숙하지 않았다.
(5) on, in ↳ 그의 사무실은 맞은편 건물 안 4층에 있다.
(6) at ↳ Brian이 가족과 함께 호주로 이민을 간 것은 11살 때이다.
(7) on ↳ 그들이 떠나기로 예정된 날에 차가 고장이 났다.
(8) In, at ↳ 여섯 살이던 1762년에 Mozart는 아버지와 함께 유럽 전역을 여행했고 왕과 왕비들을 위해 연주를 했다.

3.
(1) The concert / starts at 7.
(2) Weekly meetings begin / at ten o'clock / on Friday.
(3) Trees grow more quickly / in summer / than in winter.
(4) The mini skirt / was all the rage / in the 1960s.
(5) Mark your answer / on your answer sheet.
(6) Charlie lives / in a small village / in the Alps.
(7) Seoul is / on the Han River.
(8) Sue could see him / very well / because he was standing / at the front.

18-3 기타 전치사

Pop Quiz 1 p.292
(1) under ↳ 그는 담요 밑에서 잠옷을 찾았다.
(2) through ↳ 방문객들이 오른쪽에 있는 녹색 문을 통해 입장한다.
(3) to ↳ 식료품을 집까지 배달시킬 수 있습니다.
(4) for ↳ Jim 선장과 그의 선원들은 신대륙을 향해 항해 중이다.
(5) in front ↳ 차가 그 집 앞에 주차되어 있었다.
(6) near, close ↳ 내 책상은 문 옆이었지만, 지금은 Chris의 책상 옆이다.

Pop Quiz 2 p.293
(1) for ↳ 나는 단지 5분 정도(동안) 앉아 있고 싶다.
(2) since ↳ Carol은 12시 (이후)부터 자신이 말할 차례를 기다려 왔다.
(3) During ↳ 차 마시는 휴식 시간 동안 레몬에이드와 쿠키가 제공될 것입니다.
(4) until ↳ 그는 폐점 시간까지 찻집에 앉아 있곤 했다.
(5) from ↳ 고속도로는 4월 5일부터 개통될 것이다.
(6) between ↳ 그 개는 나무와 벤치 사이에 서 있었다.

Check Up p.295

1.
(1) with ↳ 그 식당의 주방장은 붉은 칠리 소스를 곁들인 갈비를 추천했다.
(2) of ↳ 우리 엄마의 친구이신 Brown 부인이 백포도주를 한 병 가져오셨다.
(3) of ↳ 나무와 짚으로 만든 집들은 크고 못된 늑대가 부는 바람에 날아가 버렸다.

(4) on ↳ 그들은 더 나은 근무 환경을 위해 파업 중이다.
(5) between ↳ 그는 미국의 과거와 현재 사이의 연결고리를 제공했다.
(6) for ↳ 그녀의 초기작에는 아동 잡지용의 삽화도 포함되어 있었다.
(7) With ↳ 그는 그렇게 적은 낱말을 가지고 유명한 책, '녹색 달걀과 햄(Green Eggs and Ham)'을 썼다.
(8) by ↳ 다수의 사람들에 의해 두 개의 서로 다른 언어가 말하여지는 곳에서는 어떤 조정이 일어나게 된다.

2.
(1) along   (2) across
(3) through   (4) toward

해석 Harristown에서 저희 사무실에 오시려면, 5번 도로를 따라 남쪽으로 운전하세요. Stanville의 State가에서 좌회전을 하세요. 샛강을 가로지르는 다리 너머의 State가에서 동쪽으로 운전하시다가 쇼핑센터를 지나 North Hill 아래의 터널을 지나오시면 됩니다. 그러면 정지 신호등이 있는 교차로 근처에 도착하게 될 겁니다. 교차로 옆의 표지판을 찾으세요. 표지판의 화살표가 저희 사무실을 향해 가리키고 있어요. 우회전을 하고 전방에 분수가 있는 건물을 찾으세요. 저희 사무실은 그 건물 안에 있습니다. 건물 뒤에 주차를 하고 왼쪽에 있는 문을 통해 들어오시기 바랍니다.

3.
(1) for   (2) on
(3) between

4.
(1) John has lived in London since 2003.
(2) John has lived in London for three years.
(3) John had lived in London from 2003 to 2005.
(4) She's watching shooting stars through the window.
(5) There is ABC bank across the street.
(6) All roads lead to Rome.
(7) We'll leave for Chicago next Wednesday.
(8) They chose a person suitable for the job yesterday.

18-4 주의해야 할 전치사 표현

Check Up   p.298
1.
(1) at   (2) of
(3) in   (4) to
(5) of   (6) for
(7) ×   (8) ×

2.
(1) 전치사   (2) 접속사
(3) 부사

Grammar Review   p.299
1.
(1) × ↳ Late at night, two men and a woman meet at an all-night coffee shop.
(2) ○
(3) × ↳ Another essayist, Joan Didion, wrote about her time in New York City.
(4) × ↳ Despite a careful search, no trace of the lost car has been found.
(5) ○
(6) × ↳ She became famous by making serious art out of ordinary things like cans of soup.
(7) × ↳ Cartoons, a single drawing in the newspaper, often were comments on events of the day.
(8) × ↳ Ken has been studying Russian for three years, but he still doesn't understand it very well.

해설 starvation [stɑːrvéiʃən] n. 기아, 아사, 궁핍
ranch [ræntʃ] n. 대목장, 농장, 농원

2. (1) Ⓑ   (2) Ⓐ
   (3) Ⓑ   (4) Ⓐ

해설 pack [pæk] v. (보통 수동형으로) 가득 채우다, 싸다, 포장하다
expand [ikspǽnd] v. 넓히다, 확장하다
monument [mɑ́njumənt] v. 기념비, 기념물, 유적

해석 당신은 우리 마을 손님이십니까? (우리 마을에 오셨나요?) 환영합니다. 우리 마을은 식당부터 서점에 이르기까지 모두를 위한

것들이 있습니다. 우리 마을은 또한 역사적 명소로 가득합니다. Main Street을 따라 내려가면서 주위를 살펴 보십시오. Main Street의 주변 광경은 1850년 이후 크게 변하지 않았습니다. 우리 마을은 다른 마을과 달리 전쟁이나 화재, 홍수에도 불구하고 오랜 건축물들은 보존해 왔습니다. Main Street을 따라 걷는 동안 당신은 시간을 거슬러 올라 걷고 있는 느낌을 받을 것입니다. 시청을 향해 천천히 거닐어 보십시오. 시청은 1880년대에 지어져 제1차 세계대전 이후 확장 공사를 거쳤습니다. 시청 안은 지역 역사 박물관입니다. 시청 건물 바깥쪽에는 초대 시장의 기념비가 있습니다. 그는 1776년 역사적 Wilson Creek 너머에 있는 다리 부근 농장에서 태어났습니다. 우리 마을의 방문을 즐기십시오! (즐거운 방문이 되십시오!) 당신은 수 세기의 역사(의 현장)를 보실 수 있을 것입니다.

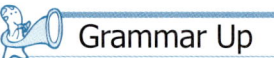

Grammar Up   p.300

1. (A) 2. (C) 3. (B) 4. (B) 5. (C) 6. (D)
7. (D) 8. (A) 9. (D) 10. (C)

CHAPTER 19
구와 절 / Phrases and Clauses

19-1 구와 절 형태 종합

📖 Check Up   p.303

1.
(1) 명사 ↳ It needs / dusting.
(2) 명사 ↳ The beans / want picking.
(3) 형용사 ↳ I saw him / looking at me.
(4) 명사 ↳ I miss you, / but I believe / that we'll be / together soon.
(5) 명사 ↳ There was no hope / that she would recover / her health.
(6) 명사 ↳ Christine forgot / returning / the video tape.
(7) 명사, 부사, 부사, 부사 ↳ Ted forgot / to return the book / to the library / before he went / on vacation / to Puerto Rico.
(8) 부사 ↳ You are silly / to miss / such a good opportunity / as that.
(9) 부사, 형용사 ↳ Brian stopped / to ask directions / to the Hyatt Regency Hotel.
(10) 부사, 부사 ↳ We had to work / throughout the night / to get the shipment ready.
(11) 부사 ↳ I deliberately / didn't read / the book / before going / to see the film.
(12) 형용사 ↳ Julia is the person / responsible for graphics.
(13) 부사, 형용사 ↳ He's been successful / in spite of all the difficulties / that he's encountered / in the business world.

해설

(1),(2) need, want 뒤에 동명사가 오면 수동의 의미를 나타낸다.
(3) 5형식 문장에서 목적어 뒤에 나오는 준동사의 의미상 주어는 목적어이다. (목적어=목적격 보어) / 한편, 4형식 문장에서 목적어 뒤에 나오는 준동사구의 의미상 주어는 문장의 주어이다. (간접목적어≠직접목적어)
　　ex. I promised your parents to look after you.
(8) 조건 및 이유 (~하는 걸 보니)

2.
(1) The house (that) she lives in / has a fine view / over the sea.
(2) We followed the instructions / which were given / at the top / of the page.
(3) When you catch a cold, / you had better rest at home / rather than play outside.
(4) The huge tree / which stands outside the window / throws lovely shadows / on the wall / in the afternoon.

19-2 절의 축약 (1): 생략

Check Up   p.305

1.
(1) Since (she is) a new student, / Carla feels shy / and insecure.
(2) After (he was) bitten / by the parrot, / Robbie's finger / was sore / for a week.
(3) Though (she was) mournful / over her dog's death, / Susan held back / the tears.
(4) When (she was) a teenager, / Rita collected / pictures of / her favorite rock stars.
(5) Raul lives / in the small city / (which is) located / near Seoul.
(6) Olga is writing / a picture book / (which is) on American language / and culture.
(7) Do you know the girl / with dark brown hair / (who is) walking / along the street?
(8) Would you believe it / if I told you / there was a turtle / (which is) faster / than a rabbit?

2.
(1) Mercury, the only liquid metal, has the symbol Hg.
(2) Have you ever visited the Cheongwadae, the home of the President?
(3) Sinclair Lewis, a famous novelist, won a Nobel Prize.

19-3 절의 축약 (2): 분사구

Check Up   p.307

1.
(1) We live / in the house / overlooking the park.
(2) The fence / surrounding our house / is made / of wood.
(3) Anyone wanting / to learn English with us / is welcome.
(4) Our solar system is / in a galaxy / called the Milky Way.
(5) Two out of three people / injured in crashes / survived.

2.
(1) While (being) chopping potatoes, / Kate cut her finger.
(Being) Chopping potatoes, / Kate cut her finger.
(2) As having no one / to go to the concert with, / I went alone.
Having no one / to go to the concert with, / I went alone.
(3) Before writing novels, / plays, / or any other things, / the writer / always collects / enough material.
Writing novels, / plays, / or any other things, / the writer / always collects / enough material.
(4) If having learned French, / she would not have difficulty / reading the book.
Having learned French, / she would not have difficulty / reading the book.
(5) Though (being) injured / in a car accident, / he's not reluctant / to ride / in a car / at all.
(Being) Injured / in a car accident, / he's not reluctant / to ride / in a car / at all.
(6) When having eaten / their fill, / they looked for somewhere / to sleep.
Having eaten / their fill, / they looked for somewhere / to sleep.

3.
(1) A fly / keeping on buzzing / in my ear, / I couldn't concentrate / on my work.

(2) The waiter / coming to our table, / we ordered / spaghetti / and pizza.
(3) The road / (being) frozen hard, / he hurriedly set off / toward the village.
(4) Sam / (being) reading a book / last night, / the light / was turned off / all of a sudden.

4.
(1) 솔직히 말해서, 그는 성미가 까다로운 사람이다.
(2) 일반적으로 말해서, 여자들이 남자들보다 문자메시지를 더 자주 사용한다.
(3) 그 조사에 의하면, 독신 부모의 비율이 계속해서 증가할 것이다.
(4) 엄격히 말해서, 그 문장은 문법적이지 않다.

5.
(1) She not (being) / in New York, / Robin missed her.
(2) Not (being) interested, / I didn't apply / for the job.
(3) Not feeling / like being with them, / I stayed out / for while.
(4) Not (being) / as healthy as before, / my grandfather could run / ten kilometers / without stopping.

19-4 절의 축약 (3): 전치사구와 부정사구

Check Up   p.311
1.
(1) × ↳ It is ture that children tend to act <u>as</u> their parents do.
(2) × ↳ The situation has improved <u>because of</u> their hidden efforts.
(3) × ↳ Bill was late again <u>though/although</u> she warned him to be on time.
(4) × ↳ <u>On taking off</u>, the plane would gain altitude and fly high above the sea.
(5) × ↳ He has bright blue eyes <u>like</u> his grandmother who passed away last year.
(6) ○

2.
(1) On/Upon arriving home, he discovered a letter waiting for him.
(2) We plan to stay at grandmother's in Canada during the Christmas holidays.
(3) Peter was the brother of a painter and went to study art like his brother in New York.

3.
(1) She couldn't make up her mind what to wear on an interview.
(2) Worrying where to start your research, you will find this book helpful.
(3) Neither Harry nor I decided how many people to invite to the Halloween party.

4.
(1) It is important to rest well enough after hard work.
(2) Could you tell me where to register?
(3) I was pleased to receive the box with a lot of toys.

Grammar Review   p.313
1.
(1) 형용사 ↳ The town <u>that the college is in</u> is very small.
(2) 형용사 ↳ The MVP award will be given to the player <u>who performed best</u>.
(3) 부사 ↳ He sat nervously in the dental clinic <u>while he was waiting to have his wisdom tooth pulled</u>.
(4) 명사 ↳ Do you know the fact <u>that a typical house cat may weigh from 3 to 6 kilograms?</u>

해설 (3) wisdom tooth 사랑니
(4) 동격으로 사용되는 that절은 명사의 역할을 한다.

2.
(1) × ↳ <u>(Being) Tired</u>, she went to bed early.
(2) × ↳ When <u>not</u> producing art of his own, he was busy weeding and planting.
(3) × ↳ <u>Washing</u> that wool sweater, you should have looked at the label.

(4) ○

해설 (2) weed [wi:d] v. 잡초를 뽑다, 치우다, 제거하다

3.
(1) Ⓑ (2) Ⓐ
(3) Ⓐ (4) Ⓑ

해설 commuter [kəmjú:tər] adj. 통근(자)의, 통근(자)를 위한

해설 우리는 도심에 살면서, 시청 옆 통근기차 역 근처에 살고 있다. 우리가 매일 기차역을 바라볼 때면, 기차를 타기 위해 기다리는 수많은 사람을 보게 된다. 차를 타고 빨리 이동할 수도 있지만, 그곳에서 통근기차를 기다리는 사람들은 시간마다 매시간 출발하는 그 통근기차를 좋아한다. 어떤 면에서 통근기차는 구식이지만, 여전히 통근기차를 좋아하는 사람들이 많이 있다. 통근기차의 승객들은 기차의 낡은 모습과 소리들은 좋아한다. (당신이) 통근기차를 타면, 도너츠와 커피를 즐길 수 있다. 이것은 자동차를 탈 때에는 할 수 없는 일이다. 다음 여행을 계획할 때에는 기차여행을 계획해 보는 것이 어떨까?

Grammar Up   p.314

1. (B) 2. (A) 3. (C) 4. (D) 5. (C) 6. (A)
7. (D) 8. (B) 9. (A) 10. (B) 11. (A) 12. (C)
13. (D) 14. (A) 15. (C) 16. (D) 17. (C) 18. (A)

Grammar in Context   p.316

1. Ⓑ

2. (Though) Not (being) serious

3. Ⓒ

4.
(1) 통근기차 서비스를 (지연시켰는데), 오늘 아침에 (통근기차 서비스를 지연시켰다.)
(2) 철도 회사는 보냈다 누구를?/무엇을?
  승무원을 (보냈는데) 어떻게?/왜?
  즉시 (승무원을 보냈는데) 왜?
  제거하기 위해 무엇을?
  나뭇가지를 (제거하기 위해) 어디에서?
  철로에서 (나뭇가지를 제거하기 위해 즉시 승무원을 보냈다.)

해설 slight [slait] adj. 약간의, 적은, 대단치 않은
limb [lim] n. 큰 가지, 돌출부, 팔다리
accompany [əkʌ́mpəni] v. 동반하다, 함께 가다, ~을 수반하다

해설 통근기차 사고
오늘 아침 가벼운 사고로 인해 통근기차 서비스가 지연되었다. 5개의 차량과 엔진으로 구성된 통근기차가 도시에 접근하던 중 사고가 발생했다. 열차는 강풍을 동반한 태풍으로 인해 쓰러진 나뭇가지들과 충돌했다. 홍보관계자는 "기차가 빠른 속도로 움직이고 있었기 때문에 나뭇가지들과 부딪혀 큰 소음이 발생했지만, 기차에 타고 있던 사람들 중 위험에 처한 사람은 아무도 없었다."라고 전했다. 비록 사고가 심각한 것은 아니었지만, 이후의 운행에 또 다시 나뭇가지와 충돌하는 것을 막기 위해 열차를 지연시킬 수 밖에 없었던 것이다. 이 사고로 인해 오늘 아침 기차 서비스가 약간 지연된 것이다. 항상 안전을 염두에 두고 있기 때문에, 철도 회사 측은 승객들로 하여금 운행에 위험이 없다는 사실을 보장해 줄 수 있기를 원했다. 그리고 철도 회사 측은 승무원을 파견해 즉각 나뭇가지를 철로로부터 제거하도록 했다.

CHAPTER 20
일치, 삽입, 생략, 강조 / Agreement, Parenthesis, Ellipsis, and Emphasis

20-1 일치

Check Up p.320

1.
(1) is　　　　　　(2) are
(3) are, are　　　(4) are
(5) is　　　　　　(6) have
(7) are　　　　　 (8) are
(9) was　　　　　(10) is
(11) means　　　 (12) is, has, was

2.
(1) ⓑ　　　　　　(2) ⓐ
(3) ⓑ　　　　　　(4) ⓐ

3.
(1) its　　　　　　(2) his
(3) they　　　　　(4) them
(5) its　　　　　　(6) those
(7) those　　　　 (8) that, that

4.
(1) Either you or I am wrong.
(2) Not only you but also she is wrong.
(3) Most of the shops were shut because it is Sunday.
(4) There were a number of people at the party.

20-2 삽입

Check Up p.322

1.
(1) This country, so to speak, needs better gun control laws.
(2) We set a record that I think is pretty good in this season.
(3) She is a girl who I know speaks five languages.
(4) After a few months in Spain, he hoped to become bilingual (speaking two languages).
(5) The West's traditional industries – mining, ranching, and logging – are clear losers in the new order.

20-3 생략

Check Up p.324

1.
(1) Who's a taxi driver? – I am (a taxi driver).
(2) Ms. Kate will come and see you when she can (come and see you).
(3) Let's go for a walk along the bank. – I'd love to (go for a walk along the bank).
(4) Charlie was supposed to clean the room before children arrive, but he hasn't (clean the room).
(5) If we continue to pollute the environment as we have (polluted the environment) in the past, we may live to regret it.

2.
(1) am I　　　　　(2) So does
(3) So is　　　　 (4) have I
(5) Neither can

3.
(1) ⓒ　　　　　　(2) ⓐ
(3) ⓑ

20-4 강조

Check Up p.326

1.
(1) ⓓ　　　　　　(2) ⓐ
(3) ⓑ　　　　　　(4) ⓒ

2.

(1) ⓐ It is Mr. Carry that / who keeps fresh herbs in the kitchen.
ⓑ It is fresh herbs that / which Mr. Carry keeps in the kitchen.
ⓒ It is in the kitchen that / where Mr. Carry keeps fresh herbs.

(3) ⓐ What I took before going to bed was a warm bath.
ⓑ What I did before going to bed was (to) take a warm bath.
ⓒ What happened before going to bed was (that) I took a warm bath.

(4) What Thomas gave me was his phone number.
(5) What I did after I got home was (to) call Thomas immediately.
(6) What happened after I got home was (that) I called Thomas immediately.

5.
(1) Ⓐ   (2) Ⓐ
(3) Ⓑ   (4) Ⓐ

해설 hazy [héizi] *adj.* 흐린, 안개 낀, 멍한, 몽롱한
apparently [əpǽrəntli] *adv.* 분명히, 명백히 (실제는 어떻든) 보기에, 외관상으로는
wreckage [rékidʒ] *n.* 난파 잔해물, 잔해, 파면

해설 1902년 11월 21일 북미에 위치한 슈피리어 호에서 이상한 일이 발생했다. Bannonkburn이라는 배 한 척이 사라진 것이다! 20명이 실종되었고 아무도 살아남지 못했다. 당시 태풍이 지나갔던 것일까? 그렇지 않다. 날씨는 약간 안개가 낀 상태였지만 나쁘지 않았다. 게다가, 이 배는 Algonquin이라는 또 다른 배 한 척이 그 옆을 지나가자마자 사라졌다. Algonquin 호의 선장은 Bannonkburn호가 매우 빠르게 시야에서 사라졌다고 밝혔다. 어떤 이상한 조짐이라도 보였나? 그렇지 않았다. 한 순간 Bannonkburn호가 그곳에 있었고 그리고 나서 사라졌다! 우리는 그 현상을 설명하려고 노력했지만 어떠한 설명도 불가능했다. 이후에 슈피리어 호에서 난파선이 한 척 발견되었지만, 그것은 Bannonkburn호로 생각되지 않는 다른 배였다. Bannonkburn호가 폭발했던 것일까? 우리는 그렇다고 생각하지 않는다. Algonquin호에 있던 사람들 누구도 폭발음을 듣지 못했기 때문이다. 결국 이 일은 풀 수 없는 미스터리로 남았다. 그러나 사람들은 아직도 이 현상을 밝혀내는 시도를 계속하고 있다!

Grammar Review
p.327

1.
(1) ✗ ↳ The cheese <u>has</u> less fat than the ordinary one.
(2) ✗ ↳ The health resort which is for the old people <u>is</u> across the road.
(3) ✗ ↳ A number of books <u>were</u> missing from the shelf.
(4) ✗ ↳ The number of books <u>was</u> indeed large.
(5) ○
(6) ✗ ↳ What I did first, more than anything, was <u>(to) call</u> the police.
(7) ○
(8) ✗ ↳ Tomatoes are not fruit, and <u>neither</u> are pumpkins.

2.
(1) ⓑ   (2) ⓓ
(3) ⓐ   (4) ⓒ

3.
(1) (B)   (2) (A)
(3) (A)   (4) (C)
(5) (A)

4.
(1) It is she that / who wrote this book in 2005.
(2) It is this book that / which she wrote in 2005.
(3) It is in 2005 that / when she wrote this book.

Grammar Up
p.329

1. (C) 2. (B) 3. (A) 4. (D) 5. (C) 6. (A)
7. (D) 8. (A) 9. (C) 10. (B) 11. (C) 12. (A)
13. (B) 14. (D) 15. (C) 16. (B) 17. (C) 18. (A)

해설
5. gospel [gáspəl] *n.* 복음, 복음서, 진리, 진실
8. portrait [pɔ́ːrtrit] *n.* 초상(화), 생생한 묘사
17. chew [tʃuː] *v.* 씹다, 부수다, 곰곰 생각하다
18. hummingbird [hʌ́miŋbəːrd] *n.* 벌새

TOEFL® iBT books from LinguaForum (2008년 4월 현재)

링구아포럼의 6단계별 토플 교재 (eBasic-e-b-m-i-훅톤)

TOEFL® iBT eBasic 시리즈 : Beginner's Level
  TOEFL® iBT eBasic-Reading / eBasic-Listening

TOEFL® iBT e,b 시리즈 : High Beginner's ~ Low Intermediate Level
  TOEFL® iBT e-Reading / e-Listening / e-Grammar
  TOEFL® iBT BASIC VOCA
  TOEFL® iBT b-Writing / b-Reading / b-Listening / b-Grammar

TOEFL® iBT m,i 시리즈 : Intermediate ~ High Intermediate Level
  TOEFL® iBT m-Reading / m-Listening / m-Grammar / m-Writing / m-Speaking
  TOEFL® iBT Core Topic Guide [영문판, 총 4권] / INTRO VOCA [한글판, 영문판]
  TOEFL® iBT i-Speaking / i-Writing / i-Reading / i-Listening

TOEFL® iBT 훅톤 시리즈 : Advanced Level
  HOOKed On TOEFL (훅톤토플)
    Speaking / Writing / Listening (Crash Course) / Listening (Cram Course) /
    Reading (Crash Course) / Reading (Cram Course) / Reading (Crash & Cram)
  빈출 1순위 TOEFL VOCA / Frequency#1 TOEFL VOCA [영문판] / 빈출 1순위 TOEFL VOCA Workbook
  TOEFL® iBT INSIDER-The Super Guide [영문판] / TOEFL® iBT Test Book 1 [영문판]
  VOCA 2004 / 185 Essay Topics / TOEFL Writing 쉽게 연습하기 / Structure Review

영어의 재정립이 필요한 대학생 및 일반 학습자에게는 〈b-m-훅톤〉 또는 〈m-i-훅톤〉의 3단계 학습을 추천합니다.

CBT와 달리 iBT에서는 TOEFL®과 관련된 배경지식의 학습이 고득점의 핵심 전략이다!

TOEFL® iBT
Core Topic Guide

- Vol. 1 History and the Arts
- Vol. 2 Social Sciences
- Vol. 3 Biology, Archeology, & Anthropology
- Vol. 4 Empirical Sciences

"세계가 신뢰하는 Worldwide on-line iBT Test"
www.linguaforum.com

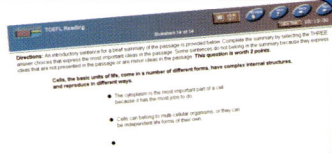

LinguaForum™

우110-846, 서울시 종로구 평창동 66-38 / 교재주문 (02) 395-0249, 대표전화 (02) 395-1468

- www.linguaforum.com   • www.ibttoefl.co.kr   • comments@linguaforum.com
  회사 소개, 도서 구매, 온라인토플테스트   도서 문의 및 상담

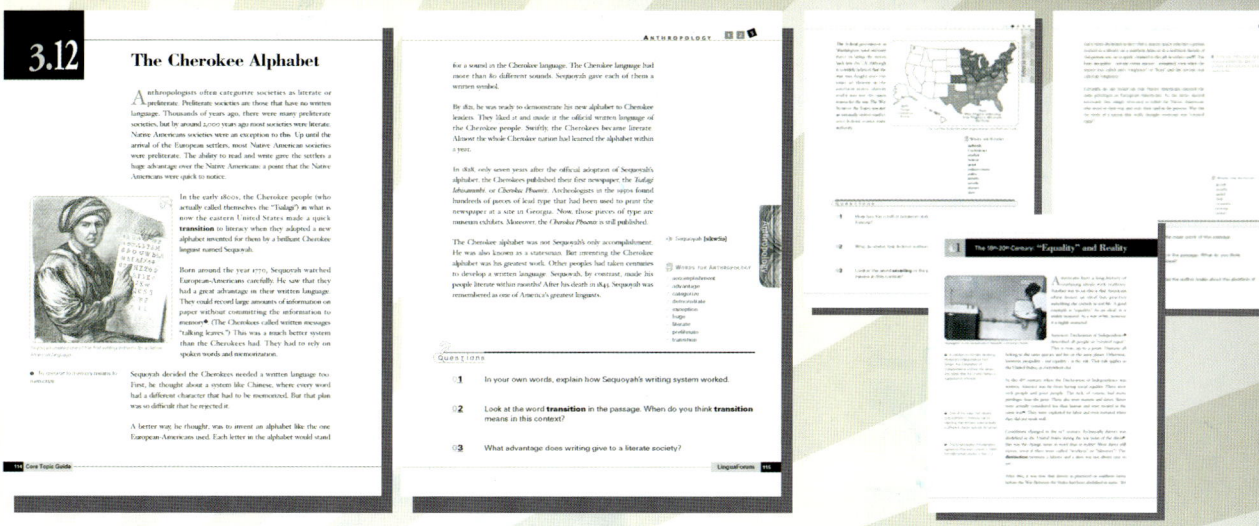

vol.1 History & the Arts
159 pages / 9,000원

North American History	미국 역사와 관련된 14개 토픽
North American Literature	미국 문학과 관련된 20개 토픽
North American Art	미국 예술과 관련된 16개 토픽
World History	세계 역사와 관련된 10개 토픽

vol.2 Social Sciences
162 pages / 9,000원

Basic Economics	미국 경제와 관련된 9개 토픽
Political Science	미국 정치와 관련된 11개 토픽
Psychology	심리학과 관련된 13개 토픽
Sociology	사회학과 관련된 17개 토픽
Communications	커뮤니케이션과 관련된 10개 토픽

vol.3 Biology, Archeology, & Anthropology
158 pages / 9,000원

Biology	생물학과 관련된 20개 토픽
Archeology	고고학과 관련된 20개 토픽
Anthropology	인류학과 관련된 20개 토픽

vol.4 Empirical Sciences
158 pages / 9,000원

Anatomy & Medicine	해부학과 의학에 관련된 12개 토픽
Astronomy	천문학과 관련된 12개 토픽
Chemistry	화학과 관련된 12개 토픽
Physics	물리학과 관련된 12개 토픽
Technology	과학기술과 관련된 12개 토픽

- **특 징**
  - → 미국인의 정서와 시각으로 쓴 미국의 과거와 현재, 미래. 가장 '미국적인' 미국의 이야기
  - → 토플에 항상 등장하는 주제로 구성, 시험 대비 필수적인 배경지식
  - → 익숙하지 않은 인물이나 사건등에는 주석으로 설명
  - → 각 지문마다 주제별, 분야별 어휘 정리, 학습
  - → 어휘 index 제공으로 각 분야의 토플 빈출 어휘를 context 속에서 확인
  - → 주관식 질문과 Answer Key 제공 : 토플 iBT에 새롭게 등장하는 문장 재구성, 정보 분류, 지문 요약 문제 유형 대비. 또한 토플 iBT의 영역 통합형 문제 대비
  - → 400 ~ 500 단어 이상의 긴 지문으로 구성. 기본적인 독해력 증강

- **구 성** → 영문판 전 4권, 각 권 60개 지문. 미국 교과서식 주제별 분류